Perhaps the most effective way to counter populism, and its assault on popular sovereignty is to produce scholarship that determinedly reverses its sleights of hand—its reduction of complex social fields to the brute opposition of 'the people' versus 'the elite' or empathy versus objectification; or that puts back the histories of the present that populism systemically erases. But this sparkling collection—one of the most imaginative engagements with the topic to date—does more: it undertakes the painstaking task of rethinking the political itself, of envisioning forms of inclusive participation that can foster relationality, open contestation and even transformation.

— **Jean Comaroff**, Alfred North Whitehead Professor of African and African American Studies and of Anthropology, Oppenheimer Fellow in African Studies, Harvard University

As 'populism' has turned into a debased token in our everyday political discourse, so has theorizing about it often descended into platitude or polemic. This probing, multi-faceted and sophisticated collection succeeds in revitalizing the question of populism as a problem for thought and practice. Impressively ranging across political philosophy, cultural theory and psychoanalysis, *Populism and Its Limits* excavates hitherto neglected facets of the antagonistic and affective politics of the people while critically displacing a debate that has often been limited by its exclusive reference to the Western hemisphere.

— **Alberto Toscano,** Co-Director, Centre for Philosophy and Critical Thought and Reader in Critical Theory, Goldsmiths, University of London

This volume fills a gap in the literature on populism by bringing in the Indian perspective—without confining the analysis to India-centric case studies. On the contrary, this is a comprehensive study of this -ism from a theoretical, comparative and empirical point of view. A very timely and systematic must-read that shows that populism and authoritarianism have clear affinities!

— **Christophe Jaffrelot**, Professor, King's India Institute and CNRS Senior Research Fellow, SciencesPo, Centre de Recherches Internationales (CERI)

In recent years, there has been a great deal of superficial discussion of populism but not so much deep thinking. Happily, this book offers serious and original intellectual engagement. Its questions are of the utmost importance for both politics and political theory. Its focus is on India but not as a special case. It integrates what is happening in and to the world's largest democracy into a more global discussion of this 'populist moment'.

— **Craig Calhoun**, Former Director and Centennial Professor of Sociology, London School of Economics; University Professor of Social Sciences, Arizona State University; Senior Advisor, Berggruen Institute; Professorial Chair, College d'Etudes Moniales, Paris

POPULISM AND ITS LIMITS

POPULISM AND ITS LIMITS

After Articulation

Edited by

Prasanta Chakravarty

B L O O M S B U R Y

NEW DELHI • LONDON • OXFORD • NEW YORK • SYDNEY

BLOOMSBURY INDIA
Bloomsbury Publishing India Pvt. Ltd
Second Floor, LSC Building No. 4, DDA Complex, Pocket C – 6 & 7,
Vasant Kunj, New Delhi 110070

BLOOMSBURY, BLOOMSBURY ACADEMIC INDIA and the Diana logo are trademarks of Bloomsbury Publishing Plc

First published in India 2021
This edition published 2021

Bloomsbury Academic
An imprint of Bloomsbury Publishing Plc

ISBN: HB: 978-93-89449-53-2; eBook: 978-93-89449-55-6

2 4 6 8 10 9 7 5 3 1

Typeset in Minion Pro by Manipal Technologies Limited
Printed and bound in India by Replika Press Pvt. Ltd.

The weapon of the republic is the Terror, the strength of the republic is virtue—virtue because without it terror is corruptible, and terror because without it virtue is powerless.

Georg Buchner, *Danton's Death*

The crowd really is a spectacle of nature—if one may apply this term to social conditions. A street, a conflagration, or a traffic accident assembles people who are not defined along class lines. They present themselves as concrete gatherings, but socially they remain abstract. Their models are the customers who, each acting in his private interest, gather at the market around their 'common cause.'

Walter Benjamin, *The Paris of the Second Empire in Baudelaire*

There are two great obstacles to developing a knowledge of affairs—shame, which throws a smoke over the understanding, and fear, which, once danger has been sighted, dissuades from going through with an exploit. Folly, with a grand gesture, frees us from both. Never to feel shame, to dare anything—few mortals know to what further blessings these will carry us!

Desiderius Erasmus, *The Praise of Folly*

CONTENTS

BRANCHINGS

INTRODUCTION: AFTER ARTICULATION

Prasanta Chakravarty

> *One can neither understand who is talking nor what he is talking about. Everything expands and contracts like a diseased serpent that falls apart as it vainly essays to make its coils. All is entangled in inextricable verbal knots, and one has to agree with Plautus: "Here no one can understand anything except the Sybil." What's the point of this verbal witchcraft?*[1]
>
> — St. Jerome, *Adversus Jovinianum I*

Populism is its own measure. It suggests that all communication—political and otherwise—hinges upon the *existential confrontation* between 'the people' and the 'elite' or the 'pluralist' or the 'powerful'. There are people and then there are anti-people. As such, populism appears to be the very condition that constitutes the crisis of parliamentary/discursive democracy and its modes of functioning. Seen from the other side, by means of championing petulance and noise, populism seems to be fomenting a crisis for the very possibilities of advanced and nuanced cultural and discursive exchange among human beings as such. What does this unmediated assertion of the 'sovereignty' of the people imply? How and when do fugitives turn into hunters? What does a constant heightening of non-ideological but antagonistic polarization in the socius mean for human lives and relationships, as well as for a political and cultural imagination? If populism is the unleashing of the *general will*, who claims to speak in the name of the people and to what aim? What does populism have to offer to the *constituency of people* once it accomplishes the task of upending its antagonists?

After the reinstatement of the Bharatiya Janata Party (BJP) government to the Indian parliament in May 2019, political scientist Ajay Gudavarthy spoke to Asiaville News.[2] It was a characteristically dispassionate and clinical take on the consolidation of majoritarian democracy at the global level, India being one such location. Among other things, he made a distinction: "thinking *like* the poor and the subaltern and thinking *about* them." To Gudavarthy, *thinking like* the people means taking into account the "human basis in capturing the social psychology of the people" (Gudavarthy, 2019). This is in sync with the larger argument that he provides in some of his recent works.[3] We shall not go into the justifiability of Gudavarthy's claim, especially since a large number of people tend to argue that the ascendency of the BJP is not merely about thinking like the people but has a strong ideological mooring and decades of painstaking work at the grassroots level.[4] Our concern is more to do with the distinction that he marks: between *thinking about* and *thinking like.* What does Gudavarthy imply? At the bedrock level, he is stressing for a *politics of recognition*. People *articulate* their needs and grievances and legislators and executives ought to first recognize and then help fulfill the desires behind such articulations. Therefore, to begin with, he is saying that the governing class must have an everyday, human basis. That ought to be the basis of communication; communication being the foremost value in winning or losing traction in political economics and politics in general. This leads to the procedural aspect of cultivating such a human face: *thinking like the people.* The opposite of this approach is thinking *about* the people, which is apparently speaking arrogantly and in a detached way—from the top, howsoever well-intentioned the basis maybe. What purpose does such a sharp distinction accomplish? First, it iterates the form of a particular idea of human interaction—either you speak from the top or conform to follow and replicate what others do and be one of them. Such a polarized view is the cornerstone over which all populism stands. The confraternity formed out of such loyal identity shall have to sacrifice both individual liberty and substantive equality in the political sphere. The idea of a fraternity has come before liberty and equality. Second, the idea of being humane is the most ameliorating and naïve form of conceiving social and political interactions. Most human interactions are many things at once which surely include compassion and understanding but may not be exclusively centred on clemency and benevolence. We are all fully aware about the underside of civilization, especially the way it works at the behavioural level. Consequently, this short-circuiting to a behavioural moral world not only sidesteps the interplay of power and negotiation in interactions but also gives a short shrift to questions of social ownership and issues of production and circulation of labour.

Finally, and this is not just a rhetorical question: Beyond the opposition between *thinking about* and *thinking like* can there be a possibility of saying *thinking along* or *thinking with the people*? Using *with* has a dual advantage. One, you need not consider others from some pedestal nor do you need to genuflect in front of the general will of the people. Second, since *thinking along with someone* is not only democratic and equitable without being identitarian, it does not foreclose the nature of that relationship as bound within certain structures of the fraternal. *Thinking with* keeps the argumentative possibilities open with others without being emotionless and manipulative. Further, such an idea of exchange does not work at the level of communication and speech-acts but is much more combative and textured. Since *thinking with* others opens up a more textured and open-ended dialogue, engagements are stronger, deeper and the effects are likely to be durable and long-lasting. *Thinking like* the people means we are merely giving heed to the general will of the people and being part of a common articulation which may take any direction. It begins as spontaneous outbursts in the social realm and then gradually conforms to confraternal forms of living with scant possibilities of disagreement, diversions and scepticism. In fact, confraternity ossifies and forecloses all politics. It homogenizes and thereby ossifies conflict. It also essentially leads to the demise of thinking itself, which is always an arduous and demanding task and not necessarily dabbling in abstraction, as many apologists for populism seem to imply. On the other hand, in itself articulation turns self-perpetuating, a reason unto itself, as if we are foredoomed to live forever in a vortex of statements and shareables. If we see articulation as the basis and end of all politics, we are actually going with the idea of what is known as the post-ideological in common parlance that in turn means we lose all sense of discrimination in exercising power. When nothing works, articulation may be an initial point of departure in politics. But it cannot be an end in itself. In order to have a broader view of the social and the natural, one must give shape and direction to all articulations. Therefore: *after articulation.*

The term *articulation,* of course, has been made popular by Ernesto Laclau. For him, it meant linkages of diverse elements within what he called an amorphously political situation. Various classes need to articulate their demands and grievances from time to time rather than be reduced to fixed social positions based on their role in the process of production. For Laclau, populism is always a coming together of heterogeneous elements for an antagonistic synthesis with no fixed class position. Consequently, the demands are always contingent and not with much substantive content. The form of articulation interests Laclau. He evolves the idea further in his later works by making articulation part of a chain of differences against other antagonistic frontiers. Popular articulation then will have three elements within it. It will be hegemonic. It will be heterogeneous. And its demands will be open to revisions. Building upon such ideas like Gramsci's *national-popular*, Althusser's *articulation* and Lacan's *political desire*, he argues that popular hegemony translates the particular into the ethical-political moment of the universal. It is a discursive account of the social. Later writings of Laclau make excoriating criticisms of Hardt and Negri's concept of the 'multitude' and what he calls Slavoj Žižek's 'Martian politics'. Laclau feels that all politics is finally populist and that populist formations of articulation are lateral chains of affective brotherhood/sisterhood.[5]

A chain leading to hegemonic brotherhood/sisterhood in order to articulate grievances leading to certain demands is the thinnest form of expectation that may run a democratic set-up. To begin with, democracies are surely based on the people's participation, but their effectiveness is not contingent on a merely demand-supply process. Second, since from the demand side the primary mode is about articulation—which means seeking redress or revenge or participation or a fusion of all these—it is always a short-term agenda without any ideological or visionary mooring. Populism of this nature will, therefore, by definition have a tendency to exploit and blackmail the processual chinks in the existing regime and maintain a climate of intimidation. The idea of brotherhood/sisterhood also ensures contingent forms of communal and sectarian partnerships on the part of those who are articulating demands, without deepening any form of systemic-democratic or even communitarian set up. There is no question of addressing the issues of class or labour on the left or patriotism, order or tradition on the right in such demands since articulation does not care about deepening progressive or conservative ideologies. On the supply side, giving in or fanning such articulations of the 'people' will mean ways of maintaining power by playing the cards of inclusion (providing a sort of psychological placebo) rather than by inspiring participants in and through some concerted vision of politics and culture. It also means that measures will be stop-gap rather than truly structural, procedural or spiritually uplifting.

The Main Currents

This point about the eruption and circulation of populism alongside democracy and the concomitant concern that whether populist demands and measures weaken or deepen democratic scaffoldings have led to a significant exchange of thoughts circulating within studies about populism. There has been a liberal/social democratic critique of authoritarian populism which stresses that kowtowing to populism will essentially lead to the imperilment of democratic norms, procedural justice and liberal democratic constitutionalism. In this context, Jean Cohen has recently argued that we must take cognizance of the condition of *electoral authoritarianism* (instead of calling such situations as *illiberal democracy*) where one notes the interest of "democratically elected populist executives" in constitutional "reform" and their efforts to undermine judicial independence and constitutional courts (Cohen, 2019). As justification, these executives claim to embody the constituent and sovereign power of the people, purportedly demonstrating the superior democratic legitimacy of "illiberal democracies" over liberal democratic constitutionalism: "They weaken not only liberal and inclusive republican constitutionalist principles—the rule of law, equal basic rights, the separation of powers, the independence of courts, and the media—but also basic democratic norms of political equality, plurality, alternation, legitimacy of the opposition, compromise, and inclusion" (Cohen, 2019).[6] Cohen comes from the supply side of populism and feels that populism from the top means disproportional "expansion of executive prerogative power free of legal limits coupled with assertions of the competence to determine its own competences" which take over all constitutional controls while ordinary spheres of life go on unchanged. Form of authoritarianism imbued within populist regimes undermines democratic politics even as they use democratic means like elections to gain power and use legal means to undercut the rule of law and institutional norms. Cohen makes it clear that there are a couple of 'master norms' for a democratic society and infringing those means the system would gradually but surely veer towards some form of populist authoritarianism. On the demand side, the absolute cornerstone in this regard is 'mutual toleration' that makes parties accept the legitimacy of the oppositional viewpoints. On the supply side, the important factor for the executives, legislatives and the juridical officers is to maintain, what he calls 'institutional forbearance'—that is to say, a certain ethical inclination on the part of the institutions to show sufficient restraint while deploying institutional prerogatives and not come down hard on the people through edicts, statutes, promulgations and executive orders.

Similarly, elaborating on as to why a populist regime from the right or the left does threaten liberal democratic principles, William Galston has offered three reasons. First, since populist gestures thrive by dividing people from a certain 'charmed circle of elites', it is by definition non-inclusive. It shuns the very idea of equal citizenship. Second, a populist definition of people is counter-factual and comes to *judge* 'the rest' in terms of homogenous principles based on a collective notion of *political will*. Hence, with respect to diverse social issues, one often gets to hear the term 'zero tolerance' coming from the identitarians and the nationalists alike, directly challenging that central doxa of classical liberalism: tolerance. Populism does not tolerate divergent interests and values in the civic sphere that goes by the name of pluralism. Third, it is equally counterfactual to suggest that people are 'uniformly virtuous' and the 'charmed circle' is corrupt and decadent. Nothing of that sort happens in real life. The moral base on which populism stands is an idea of seeking and hunting down the 'enemies of the people'. Apart from being political, such a sharp friend-enemy distinction is deeply puritanical and moral at its core. That is the reason as to why populist warfare often leads to political, cultural and personal dead ends, a predicament that Galston has termed: 'moralized zero sum conflicts' (Galston, 2018).[7]

Jean Comaroff has defined populism in terms of a linguistic metaphor: shifter, that is to say, "its deployment being more about marking difference than denoting content, and its meaning being largely relative to the standpoint from which it is deployed" (Comaroff, 2011). The concept is an artifice since people, if invoked as a general term, slides over any idea of the toiling, suffering actual human beings. It becomes a fetish with two faces, one progressive but the other virulently reactionary, for the general will of the people will often manifest itself in practical terms as the lumpen volk/horde. And like Cohen, Comaroff too believes that all these can happen through democratically elected means; there is no need for any overt dictatorial centrality to directly give orders but it just needs mediation and manipulation of volatile opinions into polarized, violent action in the socius. Comaroff is particularly astute on the associating of the progressives with the liberals with theology on one hand and identity politics on another and sometimes a combination of the two through fideistic bridging.[8]

The socialist response to populism is tethered to the more fundamental question of the relation between struggles for attaining socialism and the question of democratic rights. Bourgeois liberal democracy jutting into the socialist spectrum has always been suspected by anarcho-syndicalists just as libertarian forms of anarchism has been suspect for every collective and utopian idea of working-class socialism. The issue gets complicated since a certain kind of socialist thinking also wishes to extol radical democratic methods as legitimate forms of struggle. This is the juncture where we teeter very close to populism.

In his critique of Hegel's *Philosophy of the Right* and his analysis of the Paris commune, Marx, for instance, insisted that true democracy requires a new social content that is imbued with socialism.[9] The tension between concrete social aims and imaginatively carrying forward such a vision is at loggerheads with forms of libertarian anarchism (not truly collective), resurgent humanist liberal ways and communitarian ossification right from the inception of socialism. If current trends show a dangerous entente among those three other options so that capital can run amuck, socialists ought to be worried. Indeed, some are worried and yet have balked from going back to the core principles of left ideology. Does one not recall how Marx had cautioned against giving in to "ecstasy in the everyday spirit" which though "sparkling brilliant" and having "dramatic effects", "after attaining their zenith" actually foster "long crapulent depression in society" (Marx, 1979)?[10] There is a necessity to remember that socialism has little to do with radical/reactionary democracy or with liberal humanism (liberties and institutions of such kind) yet it has everything to do with socialist forms of democracy. To be in solidarity with the working class and extending the class movement has little to do with a certain highly affective social reorganization or putting power in the hands of the masses. The core issue with the chain of equivalence in radical democratic mobilizations (brought together with nationalism or theology on the right and identity on the left) is three-fold: One, that these are often based on hollow rhetoric about liberty without having charted out the ways and processes through which such liberty could be acquired and maintained. Second, often radical democratic forms do not have any imaginative social vision in mind since the solutions they seek are immediate and as such are mere patchworks and travesty of any visionary notion of social collectivity. Third, real democratic-socialist struggles are always spelled out in terms of concrete issues, not by sensationalizing demands and fomenting a divisive climate of intimidation.

Antonio Gramsci has highlighted the division of labour between fascism and democracy.[11] And the critique against the entente between fascism and democratic liberalism has been a staple of more radical forms of communist thoughts and movements. Henceforth, the words subaltern or marginal came to be associated with people in general, often without rigorous specifications.

In his remarkable book titled *Class,* Andrea Cavalletti has taken head-on the issue of the relationship between the crowd and revolution in order to take us back to a rigorous and dynamic notion of class and class consciousness. He reminds us how from Lukacs to Benjamin, Marxist thinkers have always distinguished the revolutionary class from the crowd so that reactionary politics does not overtake the former. For a Marxist, mass is never equivalent to an epiphanic crowd. It is never a mere sum of individuals: 'mass as such'. The word mass can "touch on two different and diametrically opposed meanings: it can compress itself and become the dangerous compact petty-bourgeois crowd or dilate into a revolutionary class" (Cavalletti, 2019).[12] Solidarity is never an auretic submission for the revolutionary. Cavalletti has particularly cautioned us against 'the dark and fathomless domain of internal sensation' of the exclusively individual experience "of the life without words that vacillates with its strange non-facts between corporeal intimacy and 'what is purely psychological'" (Cavalletti, 2019).[13] It is a clarion call to stand up against 'psychic anarchy' and its external manifestation: behaviouralist havoc, created in the name of *affect* among the petty-bourgeois, passing off as revolutionary solidarity.[14]

Other imaginings of human associations have also much to say about populist measures. In the classical republican tradition, for instance, beginning from Aristotle and passing through Machiavelli, Harrington and Montesquieu reaching Hannah Arendt the category of 'people', especially if it begins to congeal into an excess, is at once a problem and a possibility.

If we go back a little to the historical conjuncture that was the mid-1960s through the mid-1970s, we shall see Stuart Hall was a real pioneer in reading the Thatcherite wave in terms of how popular consent can become a historical block seeking to assert hegemony. The explanatory domain of hegemony (hegemony: which Jon Beasley Murray had called the master trope of 'culture studies') is much like it is in Laclau (He was a great reader of Gramsci too. Hence, he emphasized how the balance of forces was shifting in Britain at the time.) but his conclusions are different from the former. Hall foregrounds the political-ideological dimension of Thatcherism instead of celebrating forms of spontaneous and loose chain of 'pink' equivalences. Hall had astutely noticed how Thatcherite populism shuttled between coercion and consent and gradually moved towards the authoritarian pole. He was especially trying to understand how the populist dicta from above received legitimacy from the ground level and came to the conclusion that much of the shift at the top was pioneered by, harnessed to, and to some extent validated by the populist grounds well below.

> The *form* of this populist enlistment—we suggested—in the 1960s and 1970s often took the shape of a sequence of "moral panics", around such apparently non-political issues as race, law-and-order, permissiveness and social anarchy. These served to win for the authoritarian closure the gloss of populist consent. (Hall, 1985)

The term Authoritarian Populism, as Hall explained later, emerged in 1978, after he got inspired by the Nicos Poulantzas's *State, Power and Socialism*, where Poulantzas attempted to characterize a new 'moment' in the conjuncture of the class democracies, formed by "intensive state control over every sphere of socio-economic life, combined with radical decline of the institutions of political democracy and with draconian and multiform curtailment of so-called 'formal' liberties, whose reality is being discovered now that they are going overboard" (Hall, 1985). From Poulantzas, Hall especially gathered the insight as to how much the official left is scornful of civil liberties until those very liberties get hijacked by the authoritarians and the society turns into a closed one.[15]

By the end of the 1970s, Gino Germani, who was hounded out of Italy and found himself embroiled first in Argentinian politics and then in the USA, was also trying to relate authoritarian modes of populism with nationalism, reading the phenomenon as a reaction to the processes of modernization and secularism.[16] Borrowing the idea of the crowd from Gustav Le Bon and Gabriel Tarde, Germani particularly looked closely at the distortions and deviations that populism may foster on democracy. It is the dream of an alternative society with the possibility of quick social mobilization that galvanizes populism. Quite early on, Germani also tried to make a distinction between right and left populism: right-wing populism means middle classes promoted a top-down control of the marginal by a combination of projecting economic mobility, social uplifting and traditional mooring. In the context of the Peronist national-populism that he studied, it seemed that the populist social block made up of the Latin American middle class integrated with the subaltern classes. This theory of the integration of the *gauchiste* and now pop-identitarian middle-class aspirations with actual democratic transformation is far from reality though. In this book, we shall keep the possibilities open and try to investigate how far the democratic nature of such mobilizations from both right and the left are factually true and durable once the articulation of grievances is made and the populist demands are put forth. How prudent it is to be swayed by issues that make us attack our political opponents, sometimes even fellow beings who turn into adversaries at flashpoints and retreat into silence strategically even as we aspire to change the status quo? Are we being able to actually wrest the initiative and move towards a freer and equitable society if we work within close networks of alliances and segmented congregations (ingroups-outgroups, us-them) rather than being able to get into some sort of a dialogue/negotiation/exchange of affective experience with the divergent and diverse pressure groups and orientations that characterize a social set-up at any given point of time?

More importantly, are such alliances able to convert emotional excesses into thoughtful ventures and not see thoughtfulness itself as an elite preoccupation? When and how does *popular sovereignty* slide into rigid and ruthless authoritarian, loyalist and sectarian communities?

Recently Pippa Norris and Ronald Inglehart have extended Hall's and Germani's formulations into the worlds of Donald Trump and Brexit and have once again put the blame of populist upsurge on cultural backlash.[17] They have mostly looked again at the Atlantic world. The argument is that there is a perception among the political and cultural conservatives that since the late 1960s there has been an unprecedented rise of secularism, cosmopolitanism and diversity in the Western world—that is to say, the rise of social liberal values. Consequently, there is a backlash and resurgence of moral and family values, ethnicity, racial purity, faith, nationalism and sexual streamlining in the polity. This is more of a cultural backlash thesis as opposed to the economic backlash thesis (distributive injustice and economic predation) propounded in the 1950s by Lipset and Daniel Bell as they tried to explain Weimer Germany, Poujadism in France and McCarthyism in the USA.

On the other hand, Richard Hofstadter has given a psychological, nay a recurrent pathological, dimension to authoritarian-populism by tracing it to a style that he calls *paranoid* (first published as an essay in Harper's magazine in 1964). So, Hofstadter says, "The paranoid spokesman sees the fate of conspiracy in apocalyptic terms—he traffics in the birth and death of whole worlds, whole political orders, whole systems of human values. He is always manning the barricades of civilization. He constantly lives at a turning point" (Hofstadter, 1964).[18] The operative word here is 'whole'. It is either 'whole' or nothing for the paranoid and apocalyptic populist persona. This persona works within and is governed by a certain *gestalt.* The political options of dialogue and negotiation are unacceptable to him. Hence, Hofstadter reads the issue of cultural backlash through the lens of status anxiety and resentment for certain groups and consequently seeks a psychological explanation of populist overtures. Hofstadter's thesis further argues about a certain schizophrenia embedded within populism: that the question of status based populist solidarity among the cultural traditionalists and retrogressive communitarians is actually hypocritical since the protagonists of such paranoia quite calculatedly embrace market economy and other benefits of modern lifestyle.[19] Hofstadter did connect demagoguery, scapegoating, conspiracy theories, anti-intellectualism and anti-modernism with such a paranoid style of operation. Recently, Arlie Hochschild (2016) has called this phenomenon 'honour squeeze' but, unlike Hofstadter, has come to positive conclusions about such irrational demands.[20] He argues that with globalization and multiculturalism, there has been a perception of undermining of the local and embedded idea of self-respect among the working class and business class in the middle. Hochschild classifies these honour codes as having: (a) pride in hard manly work, (b) pride in region or state, (c) pride in the locality, (d) pride associated with strong family values as an honour code requiring self-control and sacrifice; (e) and pride in religious moral integrity. The interesting part is that if these codes are transferred to the subcontinent, we shall see that most certainly the first three codes tally with the moderate and extreme identitarian politics on the left, and possibly a hidden pride too with the last two codes; certainly strong moral code always binds populism from every side of the political spectrum. Be it what may, it is clear that such an explanation does highlight a thin millennial, pop-spiritualist, segmented and Manichean politics of resentment of the sects seeking status from the so-called elites and/or pluralists.

Looking at the phenomenon from the other side and trying to understand the phenomenon of left-wing populism, Bruno Bettelheim locates a certain kind of psychograph of youth rebellion in adolescent forms of a radical populist mindset, the one that is produced by a simultaneously over-permissive and over-protective childhood in middle-class households.[21] Here is perhaps an early mapping of the notion of the progressive-populist who moves from issue to issue instead of having any clear and thought out picture of transformative politics and produces rancour and self-destructive impotence instead. Bettelheim, in fact, found radical psycho-political rebellion to be an inverted form of authoritarianism: "Power motivation, narcissism, self-assertive psychosocial orientation, lack of affiliative motivation and perceptions of protest and militancy" (Bettelheim, 1969) as sources of populist power was the conclusion after his theories were tested on American college students in 1970–1971. We are seeing the rise of a similar puritan, entitled, resentful, narcissistic and authoritarian strains in forms of populist radical politics around the world, including in certain virulent metropolitan forms of corrosive activism in the subcontinent, primarily exported from the USA. But such a form of populism has a very limited circulation, primarily operating in social media. Engagements are limited and so is the reach of such personalized rancour. The eruptive nature of such a politics of *ressentiment* is even starker than right-wing mobilizations in the current times. This internalization of the political moment and subjective ally formations are the crucial differences of the identitarian radicalizations of the current times, sharply differentiating such formations from those of the 1960s–1970s. In following Hofstadter's and Bettelheim's line of argument too closely, however, one runs the risk of "personalization of historical developments", to use Moishe Postone's words (Postone, 2012).[22] However, history especially gets deeply fractured and personalized in times of populist brouhaha. One of the questions the book hopes to respond to is precisely this aspect: *the personalization of the political.*

In this context, Craig Calhoun has distinguished between what he calls *systems world* and *life world.*[23] Calhoun feels that in order to appreciate the rise to populism one has to understand the key movement in the separation of these worlds: that people experience a growing separation between the logic of what appear to be abstract, removed, calculating, objective institutions of control, and the logic of the organic, personal and locally relevant life-world. Once again such an approach takes segmented *cultural experientiality* (rather than cultural interaction or negotiation) as a key category through which humans make sense of their world and as such is an apology for alienation/precarity as a legitimate reason for indulging in polarized populist methods and tactics.

Recently, Jan Werner Muller has concentrated on the moralist and anti-pluralist aspects of populism.[24] Muller's conclusions seem surprisingly close to Edward Shils' 1956 pronouncement: "Populism identifies the will of the people with justice and morality" (Shils, 1956). Margaret Canovan traces the notion of sovereignty in the polysemous notion of populism. By invoking Ludwig Wittgenstein's theory of family resemblance, she offers a third possibility where "populism is no longer a closed concept, rather a family of concepts or, even better, an open concept, similar to democracy and ideology" (Canovan, 1981).[25] It is unmediated and it tries to delegitimize what it sees as an authority. It also arises out of action from *community-people*, through a network of interdependencies (what Cas Mudde calls 'networks of networks' in *Populism, a Short Introduction*). The essential point is that how tenable are these networks of mutual orientation and how successful and long-lasting their capacity to truly overturn ossified authority and construct newer social and cultural possibilities in their wake. Chantal Mouffe has been consistently supporting the populist strains among the new new left and other spontaneous uprisings that bring communitarian articulation into the forefront of political negotiation. Her latest work tries an almost impossible conjoining (contra Muller): that between populist measures and agonist/pluralist politics. In this regard, she significantly departs from the radical antagonistic tendencies of her own earlier works with Ernesto Laclau.

Idiom, Style and Mobilization

One way to fathom and read populist mobilizations has been to understand the extending of a certain discursive and communicative style. Such frameworks either see form and rhetoric as the key components in all populist mobilizations or try to assess the nature of the political and discursive idiom within the more substantive aspects of the populist demands, culture and governance. Ernesto Laclau had already delineated the role of linguistic capacity to articulate grievances and generate a certain kind of political subjectivity that works through sharp Manichean polarities.

One way to address the subject of mediatization of populism is through styling, that is to say, eliciting of affective response through careful and tactical playing with behavioural and rhetorical vulnerability in and through public manipulation of immediate issues and grievances (by taking the victim-oppressor rhetoric to its retributive extreme, for instance) is to study the difference of gradient between tactics and pure formal rhetorical manipulation. The concern can be put somewhat like this: Is playing up a certain garish and hysterical rhetoric part of a tactical plan on the part of the populist sect in order to get the grievances heard and addressed and for the demagogue/populist leader to plan ruling effectively or is it that whole thing is purely opportunistic, formal and ephemeral with little substantive base underneath?

Benjamin Moffitt and Simon Tormey argue that although at the inception, the use of a 'political communicative style' is important for those who work within a populist regime, gradually through the use of such idioms forms of collective organization may get more concretized. The effectivity and impact of such styles are significant for those operating within the structure of a populist alliance.[26] Paris Asalandis has put forth the idea that the communicative aspect of populism can be studied in terms of frame analysis and rhetorical perspective.[27] Framing suggests that we often filter our perceptions of the multidimensional world by making certain aspects of 'reality' more significant than others and giving certain information more salience. In *Rhetorical Criticism: Perspectives in Action* Jim A. Kuypers provides the basis for exactly what Asalandis hints at—the relation between rhetoric and framing of our known world into neat silos, an essential trait of all populist politics:

> Framing is a process whereby communicators, consciously or unconsciously, act to construct a point of view that encourages the facts of a given situation to be interpreted by others in a particular manner. Frames operate in four key ways: they define problems, diagnose causes, make moral judgments, and suggest remedies. Frames are often found within a narrative account of an issue or event, and are generally the central organizing idea. (Kuypers, 2016)

In current situations populist moments ignite when the projected frames by certain actors (demagogues, mass leaders, cultural activists) begin to align with the ones participants 'believe in' and a resonance is effected between the two poles. Frame alignment is essential for populist movements. Such eruptions may keep burning as embers for a while, may get modified into more orthodox tyrannies or may dissipate quietly until a new moment arrives. A populist moment can lead to an amorphous movement and then transition to an allied one. Similar cycles with cognate frames may operate in a certain historical conjuncture for a time. Since the idea of framing itself is based on the idea of partial reality, the success and durability of such rhetorical framing depend on the relationship of the proposed frame with the larger belief system. The more the given populist frame is connected with a deeper belief system/ideology (nationalism, religion, revolutionary socialism), the greater is its chances of staying relevant.

The other pole through which one can calibrate and understand political styling and discourse is of course to read the populist leader: his/her body language, dressing, modes of speech-act, styles and genres of writing, interaction with media and the people. In order to build up a new political consensus, the new populist leader at every level will have to distance with the older protagonists of the nationalist and left politics. Every populist leader must vouch to be changing with the expectations of the time (and dovetail his with the latest 'generational frame' and community expectations) and yet he/she will also have to set the agenda with his/her very styling and visual appeal.

The obverse of highlighting the perceptual and formal aspects of rhetoric is to expand on the strategic notion of populist politics. The argument is that the personalistic leader wishes to strategically channelize and use governmental power by means of receiving unmitigated support from the hitherto largely unorganized followers. At the level of political movement, populism relies on a strategic partnership/alliance as a pragmatic way to keep pushing for the demands. To look at the phenomenon of populism in this manner would mean not to relate it with a movement or a regime but what

Robert Jansen has called 'flexible way of animating political support.'[28] In such readings, populism becomes a dynamic model of configuring power and mobilizing consensus. Populism becomes a mode of *political practice.*[29]

In her works, Nadia Urbinati also tries to look carefully at the use of rhetoric and public opinion in developing populist politics that she designates as *disfigured democracy*. Paradoxically, such disfigurement happens by creating new possibilities for representative democracy. She astutely sees populism as an elitist governing strategy masquerading as outbursts of direct democracy and/or as grievance redressing platforms. She, therefore, tries to understand populism through an oxymoron that she calls *direct representation*. In situations of direct representation "populist leaders wish to speak directly to the people and for the people, without needing intermediaries (especially parties and independent media)."[30] Her work enables us to be more attentive to the ways and methods of populists when they actually try to govern within representative democratic structures. Her work also allows us to avoid the mistake of sharply distinguishing liberal democratic set-ups from the working and stratagems of populist techniques.

In this context, Paul D. Kenny's work on populist mobilization as practice in India is a particularly illuminating example.[31] Kenny looks at the mobilization and organizational strategies of populist leaders who seek power "based on direct, unmediated, and uninstitutionalized support from large numbers of mostly unorganized followers" (Kenny, 2017) in a cultural space like India where patronage is the predominant form of party-voter linkage. In order to bypass the entrenched patronage system, demagogues would develop direct linkage with voters through personalization of policy measures, win over subnational brokers, threaten the privileges of the national aristocracy, alter internal dynamics of the party system, build up a war chest with illicit electoral funds, privilege private right to property over social directives of welfare, personalize judiciary and bureaucracy and mobilize the media. Kenny concludes that "patronage-based parties become vulnerable to outflanking by populist campaigners when subnational brokers gain autonomy and control over resources, and patronage parties thus become more internally fragmented" (Kenny, 2017). Besides, such populist strategies are fundamentally based on moral goodness and badness rather than sound structures of governance.

Those highlighting on populist style, idioms and strategy as parts of a process of *political practice* try to look at resources, opportunity, organizational capacity and strength of affective rhetoric in order to mobilize/foment a populist wave. Such an approach resonates far more with scholars sympathetic to understanding the phenomenon after the 1990s—sometimes called *neopopulism*.[32] Read through such a lens, populism is no more a *thing* to be hunted down, but a *means* of achieving certain political and moral goals. Mobilization through certain idioms means an enactment of a *project*. It publicly visibilizes certain demands, that is to say, we revert to articulation once again. But the question of means, animation and articulation cannot stop at those points. To what purpose and aim is such a styling and mobilization? What are the gains and what might be the pitfalls? How distant are such stylings from those participating in mass democratic politics? Are such overtly rhetorical and framing projects finally *clientelist* in nature? Looked from the other side, if we agree about the argument of the means, the question to follow would be to ask whether populist strategies, awareness-raising/problem solving or rhetorical excesses and projects enough motivated to give them the power and doggedness that is required of genuine anarchist or guerilla warfare?

There is no gainsaying that the idiomatic, affective and formal aspects are crucial to understanding and distinguishing the phenomenon of populism from both procedural politics and genuine mass mobilization (not 'constructing people'). One can perhaps also appreciate better the inherent contradiction in temporary and affect-based mobilizations that lead to and stratify status-alliances rather than ideologically work with and within mass solidarities. The contradiction is quite clear in Ernesto Laclau's notions of the chain of equivalences itself which requires a double injunction in order to be successful: that, on one hand, the populist moment has to be endlessly prolonged through such means of gung-ho rhetoric and by playing the victimhood card to its limit so that the social remains guarded, while on the other hand, the very idea of temporary articulation is based on the idea of contingency, a kind of groundless ground so that the social will forever remain open and slippery. One cannot guarantee the other. Besides, once the genuine populist moment should pass, it would be only through such *formal means* that *members of the alliance* would try to capture that moment time and again in future mobilizations, a kind of spectral search for traces that might revivify and ignite what might seem like situations with fresh populist possibilities. And this ever deferred radical moment shall then simultaneously create and nurture a kind of deepening of the sense of victimhood and belligerence among the participants in populist mobilizations, leading to a kind of impasse in all social and political progress in the public sphere. This constant effort to rearticulate and reactivate the sedimented forms of the social is the tragic condition of populism.[33] Therefore, it is germane to seek a modicum of the horizon for future work. What are the consequences of a politics of pure style and moral signaling? What lies after such a metaphorization of politics which must lead to a series of decisionist gestures and articulations that foment political and cultural impasse among various contending social actors and groups? How can one get back to sustained, slow, differentiated and constructive teamwork that relies on a common political language instead of prolonging a raging fervour into nothingness? Perhaps, that would once again require the act of mutual listening and a gradual, painstaking process of constructing from scratch.

Genealogies/Trajectories

As we think further about the discriminating conceptual possibilities about populism, it would also be necessary to have a sense of the main historical trajectories through which it has passed, in order to reach us in its present incarnations. Pierre Rosanvallon has rightly pointed out that populism has an enduring history right from the sycophants of ancient Greece through Jean-Paul Marat and his cohorts in the French revolution, within the South American patriotic leagues and in the nineteenth century populist movements in America and Russia. Therefore, a historical and cultural sense of the subject is necessary.[34] In two senses: One, in order to have a recognition of the conditions that have spawned populist regimes or movements. At the least, such a cartography shall offer us a genealogy of the populist eruptions of the long twentieth-century and we shall be in a better position to take stock of the claims of the newness of the populist overtures in current conditions. Second, having a historical sense of populism shall make us aware that there could be various kinds and shades of populism that may have emerged in different parts of the world at various times. While we have a fairly well-charted history of populism about Europe and Latin America, it is less evident what has happened/is happening in other parts of the world, although it is quite clear from our access to news items and other informational sources that populist movements, regimes and figures have been a more common phenomenon than we think of in many parts of the world, including in the Indian subcontinent.

Dwayne Woods has identified three modern waves of populisms: the agrarian populism in Russia and Eastern Europe beginning in the late nineteenth century, the Latin American populism in the 1940s and

1950s and then the third wave of European populism in the 1990s and after.[35] Federico Finchelstein, the foremost proponent of giving context to populism, has made his own transatlantic junctures and phases (as opposed to charismatic, functionalist or regionalist variations). To the first phase, he gives the name of classical populism. That would imply "Argentine Peronism was at the forefront, but this term also encompasses the second stage of Varguismo in Brazil (1951–54), Gaitanismo in Colombia (late 1940s), and the José María Velasco Ibarra era in Ecuador (1930s to the 1970s), as well as postwar populist experiences in countries like Venezuela, Peru, and Bolivia." This is followed by neoliberal populism: "Carlos Menem in Argentina (1989–99), Fernando Collor de Melo in Brazil (1990–92), Abdalá Bucaram in Ecuador (1996–97), Alberto Fujimori in Peru (1990–2000), and Silvio Berlusconi in Italy (1994–95, 2001–6, 2008–11)." The next is what he calls neoclassical populism of the left, which includes "The Kirchner administrations in Argentina (2003–15), Hugo Chávez (1999–2013) and Nicolás Maduro (2013–) in Venezuela, Rafael Correa in Ecuador (2007–17), and Evo Morales in Bolivia (2006–), as well as the leftist neoclassical populist parties in Europe, such as Podemos in Spain and Syriza in Greece." Finally, neoclassical populism of the right and extreme right. Here he goes back again to the "Peronist neofascism of the 1970s, to the predominance of current right-wing movements and leaders that are generally in the European opposition but can also be in power in countries like the United States, the Philippines and Guatemala, as well as in power coalitions like those in Austria, Italy and Finland." These forms of neoclassical populism also include the regimes of Recep Tayyip Erdogan in Turkey and Viktor Orbán in Hungary. Opposition forms of neoclassical populisms of the right and extreme right include "UKIP in England, the National Front in France, Golden Dawn in Greece and the movements led by the xenophobe Pauline Hanson in Australia and Avigdor Lieberman in Israel, among many others" (Finchelstein, 2017).[36]

Enzo Traverso has traced a genealogy of populism and fascism/neo-fascism and called our times post-fascist: a moment which lacks the cult of the state in the classical sense of the term but is a compromise and submission of the antidemocratic forces to the financial sector that often fails to deliver but keeps the system on a limbo. To his alarm, Traverso detects a trend of anti-anti-fascism among certain sections of the populace in our times. There is also caution in Traverso against identitarian forms of populism that has increasingly turned oblivious to any left vision of emancipation. Universalistic and emancipatory claims of the internationalist left and considered classical republican ways are being gobbled up by narrow, shrill and breakaway populist demands.[37]

Among those who have tried to delineate a specific history of populism in India, Christophe Jaffrelot and Louise Tillin's essay stands out.[38] They begin from the 1960s and

> identify a category of political leadership in India characterized by direct, personalized appeals to "the people" by leaders who deploy particular cultural registers to secure and maintain political power by circumventing intermediaries and neutralizing institutions. In doing so, we recognize that populism consists both of a distinctive form of political strategy and a politics conducted within a political cultural register grounded in a "plebeian grammar". (Jaffrelot and Tillin, 2017)

They suggest that when the populists try to highlight words like *lok*, *janta* or *jan*, they identify the will of the people around a moral claim to the purity and authenticity of the masses in contrast to the corrupt elite. For instance,

> For agrarian populists, the image of the "kisan" (peasant farmer) elided rural inequalities particularly between large and small farmers, and landless labor; for Hindu nationalists, the assertion of a primary Hindu identity glosses over caste differences; and for regional populists of southern India, cultural identity has been used as a capacious umbrella to relate to the "authentic" people. (Jaffrelot and Tillin, 2017)

Chapter 3 of Partha Chatterjee's recent work *I am the People* too gives us a wonderful account of the various trajectories of populism played out in post-independent India. Besides giving us a sense of the different dimensions and variations of populisms, ranging from the national-hegemonic to the regional variants, the particular chapter also reminds us about the cultural dimension of Indian populism, especially as manifested in the reception and circulation of cinema in the Indian subcontinent. The chapter also makes a pitch to distinguish most lucidly one of the central differentials of the book: the modal difference between 'tactically extended state'/passive revolution and populist mobilizations and a different set of tactics and the risks involved in opting for the latter option—both by the right and the left.

Such diagnostic genealogies have often tried to relate the question of the nation with a strong demagogue at the helm (sometimes with regional variations) with that of the movement or a populist regime. On rare occasions, such histories have delved into the contemporary conditions by looking more closely at the amalgamation of the market forces, people's adherence to social and religious hierarchies and the rise of the fascist-popular. Apropos of Partha Chatterjee's compact and sharp pronouncements on popular sovereignty, its cogent thesis apart, the central *aporia* is the following: while the analysis clearly warns us about the limitations of populist adventurism—a sense of mere survival by and of the masses as a tactic of democratic politics without any clear counter-hegemonic strategy or any pedagogical project, the work stops short of taking head-on the full implications of such romanticized and strident use of emotion and rhetoric as the authentic mode for *doing democracy* in itself. This happens owing to a simple reason: while Chatterjee rightly identifies the notion of the 'sleeping sovereign'—the people and the possibility of its rising from slumber—he loathes accepting forms of subjectivity (individual or collective) that mobilize populism in the first place. The assessment, therefore, manages to deflect our attention from the real springwell of populism: *playing out of the deepest forms of the irrational, rank partiality and encouraging a politics of ally-ship, crookedness of intent, pleasure-seeking, opinion mongering, alienation converted into performative energy converted into cunning and gulling, free play of envy and other violent sediments, nursing of grievance, silently fomenting and gestating in our many relationalities—intangibles that help provoke social impasse in the first place until they turn combustible and burst forth.* In other words, "the dirt in the eye/the thorn in the feet/and the suspicion in the mind" (Prabhu, 2019) as the twelfth-century saint-poet Allama Prabhu hath phrased in a different context: What do we do with these? [39] It is perhaps not a question of 'more of Mill and less of Rousseau' but the roles that both Mill and Rousseau may play in their different ways in effecting various styles of populisms. The dangers of mobilizing a whole people in the name of organized religion or ossified tradition are obvious. But we shall do well to remember the cautionary pronouncement of Charles Peguy: "It will never be known what acts of cowardice have been committed for fear of not looking sufficiently progressive" (Peguy, 1905/2017).[40] It is precisely this point that has been raised by Federico Finchelstein in the context of Latin America as he takes on Mouffe:

> Are the latest adventures of Latin American populists from corruption, to repression and even to the Chavista remnants of the Maduro dictatorship inconvenient truths? Why can't these authoritarian pasts be addressed? Why does Mouffe not include their latest experiences in a critical, and self-critical, theory of a populism of the left? Overall, Mouffe insists, the populist leader would bypass institutional channels and effectively create a more direct form of democracy. But in the current context, is this new left populism going to have an infallible leader, who in impersonating and ventriloquizing the voice of the

> people also caters to nationalism and the current ethnic intolerance of diversity? (Finchelstein, 2019)[41]

Indeed, repression and reaction work in many directions. How do we convert our social-emotional impasse into lasting and visionary solidarity rather than resort to being part of crowd-corpuscles of identity and micro-revulsion? In other words, how do we change the very modes of ossified and skewed relationalities that populism loves to sustain? In fact, the issue gets compounded since Chatterjee is acutely aware of the real failing of the counter-hegemonic forces: "An important lesson of the populist moment, however, is that rational critique of mistaken and harmful policies is not sufficient for mobilization of democratic opinion. What is necessary is an alternative narrative with the emotional power to draw people into collective political action" (Chatterjee, 152).[42] We eagerly await that very pedagogic project to unfold.

The aforementioned trajectories do not include questions of exclusions and participations in populist mobilizations and especially the story of the micro-history of 'little' populisms and the deeply relational nature of their tentacles are left unaccounted for. In fact, here Ajay Gudavarthy seems to speak from a better vantage though his method is more diagnostic and accepting of the current conditions. We must acknowledge the underside of enlightenment: that populist tendencies do not come from afar but are entrenched within *us*—the people, before making quick value judgements. The very fluidity of transition that marks certain movements from the right to the left and *vice versa* characterizes current mutants of populisms across the globe, including those in the Indian subcontinent: in questions of economy, sentimentalized victimhood masquerading as precarity, disdain for rule of law and due process, rank opinion mongering, threatening of independent media, affective blackmailing as intimidation and in the immediacy of violent reactions followed by silent retractions there is often a remarkable mirroring of equal and opposite tendencies though their expressions and agendas might be different. The sacralized nature of its operations at the level of political form is evident to those who are beholden to a critical and examined life.

The chapters that follow hope to address what lies at the very inception of the populist compulsion—primal moments of anger that give rise to *arche* forms of rifts, the insatiable penchant for gratification and accessible pleasure, certain sub-lunar reciprocity between love and hatred, hypertrophic pride, morbid anxiety, stupefying panic and deep reveling in scapegoating, perennial hopes to morally cleanse the society of every evil, craving for quick remedy and mitigation from social and personal animosities and, at the same time, turning collectively and gleefully violent in achieving our desired goals.[43] This is the zone of incongruous and frenzied ecstasy where time gets *caught up*. The contributors have tried to listen with care to the voice of the people, including its baroque loneliness, when they indulge in such activities—in actual practice and thought. But none have tried to follow the pack in *thinking like* the people. One of the central problems with populism has been pointedly underlined by Stephen Mergenthaler: "Rather than seeing political mobilization as a process aimed at convincing a skeptical public of difficult but important policy choices, the acceptance by the political mainstream of an agenda set by populist interpretations of policy challenges contributes to the pathologies of the political process" (Mergenthaler, 2015).[44] Therefore, we mark the limits of populism in this volume even as we try to understand its deepest moorings and many tentacles. Mere articulation of our grievances is a trap that is ultimately self-consuming. Articulation hardly gives any real closure or allows any horizon for genuine hope for the aggrieved. Besides, articulation itself may not lead to widespread *inclusiveness* within the system in the sense that the right to participation for people is not automatically ensured if a free and fair system of *contestation* is stifled in the process.[45] Genuine forms of inclusive participation must imagine a visionary, open-ended and yet-to-arrive futurity and rework afresh the processes that accompany such a future. That would require time-taking and painstaking investment in reinventing the very relational spheres of the political. Therefore, Paul Kenny cautions us that "Without the rule of law, political conflict cannot be institutionalized, with the result that the implementation of public policy is particularistic, haphazard, and ephemeral" (Kenny, 2017).[46] Rule of law is hardly about affirming positivism. It essentially means imagining and settling processes of human interaction and disputes in capacious and imaginative terms. Politics of articulation instead ends up perpetuating the divide between *thinking about* and *thinking like* the people.

After Articulation welcomes *thinking along* and *thinking with* the people.

Notes

1 See the introductory essay in Umberto Eco, *On the Shoulders of Giants* (London: Harvill Secker, 2019).

2 Ajay Gudavarthy on *Asiaville News*, May 2019. Available at https://www.asiavillenews.com/article/questions-left-unanswered-after-the-2019-ls-results-6414 (last accessed 24 April 2020).

3 See Ajay Gudavarthy, *India After Modi: Populism and the Right* (Delhi: Bloomsbury India, 2019); and his chapter "Theorizing Populism in India," in *Minorities and Populism: Critical Perspectives from South Asia and Europe*, eds. Volker Kaul and Ananya Vajpeyi (Cham: Springer, 2020). See also his article "How BJP Appropriated the Idea of Equality to Create a Divided India." *Economic and Political Weekly* 53, no. 17 (28 April 2018). Available at: https://www.epw.in/engage/ article/BJP-appropriated-Idea-Equality-Divisive-India (last accessed 24 April 2020).

4 See Partha Chatterjee, "Populism Plus." *The India Forum*, 3 June 2019. Available at: https://www.theindiaforum.in/article/populism-plus? (last accessed 24 April 2020). Also, see his *I am the People, Reflections on Popular Sovereignty Today* (Delhi: Permanent Black, 2019). Ranabir Samaddar supports certain forms of the antagonistic-popular but makes a clear distinction and opposition between the impulses of the nationalist-corporate complex and populist politics. This was articulated quite succinctly in a lecture titled "On Left-Wing Populism," delivered on 7 June 2019 in Kolkata at CRG. This lecture was part of the Calcutta Research Group's ongoing research project on Populism and Populist Politics in South Asia.

5 See Ernesto Laclau, *On Populist Reason* (London: Verso Books, 2005); and Ernesto Laclau and Chantal Mouffe, *Hegemony and Socialist Strategy*. (London: Verso Books, 1985). Also, the section called "Towards a Theory of Populism," in *Politics and Ideology in Marxist Theory* (London: Verso, 1997); and "Populism: What's in a Name?" in *Populism and the Mirror of Democracy*, ed. Francisco Panizza (London and New York: Verso, 2005). For a comprehensive discussion of this point see also, Samir Gandesha, "Understanding Right and Left Populism," in *Critical Theory and Authoritarian Populism*, ed. Jeremiah Morelock (London: University of Westminster Press, 2018). For the particulars about Laclau, see the chapter by Samir Gandesha in this volume and his other works.

6 For an early intimation of this line of argument, see Seymour Martin Lipset, *Political Man* (Nevada: Avebury, 1983); and William Kornhauser, *Politics of Mass Society* (London and New York: Routledge, 2008). Many of Lipset's arguments have been updated in the light of recent global developments by Jean L. Cohen, "Populism and the Politics of Resentment." *Jus Cogens* (2019). https://doi.org/10.1007/s42439-019-00009-7 28 May 2019. In this context, also see Edward Shils, "Populism and the Rule of Law." *University of Chicago Law School Conference on Jurisprudence and Politics*, Conference Series No. 15, April 1954, 99–107.

7 See William A. Galston, "The Populist Challenge to Liberal Democracy," *Journal of Democracy* 29, no. 2 (April 2018): 5–19.

8 See Jean Comaroff, "Populism and Late Liberalism: A Special Affinity?" *The Annals of the American Academy of Political and Social Science* 637, no. 1 (September 2011): 99–111.

9 See Karl Marx, "Introduction to A Contribution to the Critique of Hegel's Philosophy of Right," in *Karl Marx and Friedrich Engels, Collected Works*. Vol. 3, *Marx and Engels, 1843–1844* (London: Lawrence and Wishart,

1979). See also his commentaries on the *Paris Commune and The Civil War in France* in the *Collected Works*, Volumes 6 and 7.

10 Karl Marx, "The Eighteenth Brumaire of Louis Bonaparte," in *Karl Marx and Friedrich Engels, Collected Works*, Vol. 11, *Marx and Engels, 1851–1853* (London: Lawrence and Wishart, 1979), 106.

11 See Antonio Gramsci's 1924 essay "Democracy and Fascism" collated in *Selections from Political Writings (1921–1926)*, trans. and ed. Quentin Hoare (London: Lawrence and Wishart, 1978). For an elaboration on the same subject see his "Notes on Politics" from his *Selections from Political Writings*.

12 Andrea Cavalletti, *Class*, trans. Elisa Fiaccadori, ed. Alberto Toscano (Calcutta: Seagull Books, 2019), 36.

13 Ibid., 18. Cavalletti takes recourse to Charles Blondel's work *The Troubled Conscience and the Insane Mind* in order to elucidate this particular point.

14 On a related note, there is a curious circling back in Bhaskar Sunkara's opening piece in Jacobin magazine's dedicated issue on the question of populism ("From Socialism to Populism and Back", *Jacobin Magazine*, no. 35, 25 November 2019). Sunkara cautions at the liberal usage of populism as a catchword in order to discredit socialism itself and stresses how populism has often accompanied socialism in practice. He extols the tactical nature of populism. And yet, he would not compromise with the universal project of socialism which is hardly populist in scale, scope and nature. The issue itself addresses the question from diverse points of view.

15 See Stuart Hall, *The Hard Road to Renewal: Thatcherism and the Crisis of the Left*. (London: Verso, 1988) Also see his "Authoritarian Populism, A Reply," *New Left Review* 151 (May–June 1985); and *Policing the Crisis: Mugging, the State and Law and Order* (United Kingdom: Red Global Press, [1978]2013). See also, Daniel Bell, *The End of Ideology: On the Exhaustion of Political Ideas in the Fifties* (Cambridge: Harvard University Press, [1960]1988); and "Democracy and Working-Class Authoritarianism," *American Sociological Review* 24 (August 1959): 482–501.

16 See Gino Germani, *Authoritarianism, Fascism, and National Populism* (New Brunswick: Transaction Publishers, 1978). B. Celarent, "Authoritarianism, Fascism, and National Populism by Gino Germani," *American Journal of Sociology* 119, no. 2 (2013): 590–596.

17 Pippa Norris and Ronald Inglehart, *Cultural Backlash: Trump, Brexit and Authoritarian Populism* (Cambridge: Cambridge University Press, 2019).

18 Richard Hofstadter, *The Paranoid Style in American Politics and Other Essays* (Cambridge, Mass.: Harvard University Press, 1964); and J. Gest, *The New Minority: White Working Class Politics in an Age of Immigration and Inequality* (Oxford: Oxford University Press, 2016). Interestingly, Partha Chatterjee has recently cautioned against paranoid reactions to extreme nationalism as arising out of exaggerated feelings of persecution. "Modi 2.0 and the State of National Paranoia." Available at: https://thewire.in/politics/bjp-citizenship-telangana-encounter-paranoia (last accessed 20 March 2020).

19 Jean Cohen has explained Hofstadter's points lucidly in "Populism and the Politics of Resentment."

20 Arlie Hochschild, *Strangers in their Own Land: Anger and Mourning on the American Right* (New York: The New Press, 2016).

21 Bruno Bettelheim, *The Children of the Dream* (London and New York: Macmillan, 1969); and his essay "Obsolete Youth: Towards a Psychograph of Adolescent Rebellion," *Encounter* 32 (September 1969): 29–42. Also see S. Robert Lichter and Stanley Rothman, "The Radical Personality: Social Psychological Correlates of New Left Ideology," *Political Behavior* 4, no. 3 (September 1982): 207–223. See also Bettelheim's articles about this subject, along with those of Robert Nisbet, Edward Shils and Seymour Lipset, in the journal *Encounter* from 1967 through 1972. Also, Paul Jacobs and Saul Landau, *The New Radicals* (Harmondsworth: Penguin, 1967).

22 Moishe Postone, "Thinking the Global Crisis." *South Atlantic Quarterly* 111, no. 2 (2012): 1–23.

23 Craig Calhoun, *The Roots of Radicalism: Tradition, the Public Sphere and Early Nineteenth Century Social Movements* (Chicago: University of Chicago Press, 2012).

24 Jan Werner Muller, *What is Populism?* (London: Penguin, 2017).

25 Margaret Canovan, *Populism* (New York: Hartcourt Brace Janovich, 1981). See also, Paul Taggart, *Populism* (Buckingham: Open University Press, 2000); and Manuel Anselmi, *Populism: An Introduction* (London and New York: Routledge, 2018).

26 Benjamin Moffitt, *The Global Rise of Populism: Performance, Political Style, and Representation* (Palo Alto: Stanford University Press, 2017). See also, Carlos de la Torre (ed.), *The Promise and Perils of Populism: Global Perspectives* (Lexington: The University Press of Kentucky, 2014).

27 See Paris Asalandis, "Is Populism an Ideology? A Refutation and a New Perspective," *Political Studies* 64, no. 1 (2015): 1–7. The root of Asalandis' argument can be detected in Erving Goffman, *Frame Analysis: An Essay on the Organization of Experience* (Boston: Northeastern University Press, 1974); and George Lakoff, *Don't Think of an Elephant!: Know Your Values and Frame the Debate* (Chelsea: Chelsea Green Publishing Co., 1990). See also, Jim A. Kuypers, *Rhetorical Criticism: Perspectives in Action* (Lanham: Lexington Books, 2009); and David A. Snow and Robert D. Benford, "Ideology, Frame Resonance, and Participant Mobilization," in *From Structure to Action: Social Movement Participation Across Cultures*, eds. Bert Klandermans, Hanspeter Kriesi and Sidney Tarrow (Greenwich, Conn.: JAI Press, 1988), 197–217.

28 Robert S. Jansen, "Populist Mobilization: A New Theoretical Approach to Populism," *Sociological Theory* 29, no. 2 (June 2011): 75–76.

29 See Kurt Weyland, "Clarifying a Contested Concept," *Comparative Politics* 34, no. 1 (2001): 1–22. Also, D. Woods and B. Wejnert, *The Many Faces of Populism* (Bingley, UK: Emerald Group, 2014).

30 See the Introduction and Chapter 4 in Nadia Urbinati's *Me the People: How Populism Transforms Democracy* (Cambridge, MA: Harvard University

Press, 2019). See also, her earlier work *Democracy Disfigured: Opinion, Truth and the People* (Cambridge, MA: Harvard University Press, 2014).

31 Paul D. Kenny, *Populism and Patronage: Why Populists Win Elections in India, Asia and Beyond* (Oxford: Oxford University Press, 2017).

32 The locus classicus that analyzes threadbare the nuances of political mobilization is Charles Tilly's *From Mobilization to Revolution* (New York: McGraw-Hill, 1978). For contemporary evaluations, see Rogers Brubaker, *Ethnicity Without Groups* (Cambridge, MA: Harvard University Press, 2004); Christopher K. Ansell, *Schism and Solidarity in Social Movements: The Politics of Labor in the French Third Republic* (Cambridge, UK: Cambridge University Press, 2001); and Marc Traugott, *Repertoires and Cycles of Collective Action* (Durham, NC: Duke University Press, 1995). See also, "Populism and Mobilization," (Chapter 3) in *Populism, A Very Short Introduction*, eds. Cas Mudde and Cristobal Rovira Kaltwasser (New York: Oxford University Press, 2017).

33 See Peter Baker, "(Post) Hegemony and the Promise of Populism: Reflections on the Politics of our Times," *Politica Comun* 10 (2016). See also, Jon Beasley-Murray, *Posthegemony: Political Theory and Latin America* (Minneapolis; London: University of Minnesota Press, 2010); and Reiner Schürmann, *Broken Hegemonies*, trans. Reginald Lilly (Bloomington: Indiana University Press, 2003).

34 Pierre Rosanvallon, *La Contrademocracia. La política en la era de la Desconfianza* (Buenos Aires: Manantial, 2007), 260–261.

35 Dwayne Woods and Barbara Wejnert, *The Many Faces of Populism: Current Perspectives* (Bingley, UK: Emerald Publishing Ltd., 2014).

36 See Federico Finchelstein, *From Fascism to Populism* (Oakland, California: University of California Press, 2017). For a remarkable idealist–populist history of the *Narodniki* drawing on a Slavophile heritage and glorifying natural Russian rural institutions, such as *Obshchina* in nineteenth-century Russia, see Franco Venturi, *Roots of Revolution: A History of the Populist and Socialist Movements in Nineteenth Century Russia* (London: Weidenfeld and Nicolson, 1960).

37 Enzo Traverso, *The New Faces of Fascism: Populism and the Far Right* (New York: Verso, 2019). See also, Cas Mudde and Cristobal Rovira Kaltwasser, *Populism: A Very Short Introduction* (Oxford: Oxford University Press, 2017). For a genealogy leading up to the current conditions of digital populism, see Jamie Bartlett, Jonathan Birdwell and Mark Littler, "The New Face of Digital Populism," *Demos* (2011). Available at https://www.issuelab.org/resources/12404/12404.pdf (last accessed 20 March 2020). To appreciate the complex interlocking between globalization, violence and ethnic strife, see Arjun Appadurai, *Fear of Small Numbers, An Essay on the Geography of Anger* (Durham: Duke University Press, 2006).

38 Christophe Jaffrelot and Louise Tillin, "Populism in India," in *The Oxford Handbook of Populism*, eds. Cristobal Rovira Kaltwasser, Paul Taggart, Paulina Ochoa Espejo and Pierre Ostiguy (Oxford: Oxford University Press, 2017). For the question of image and populist success

in the Indian cultural context, the best work is M.S.S. Pandian, *The Image Trap: M.G. Ramachandran in Film and Politics* (New Delhi: SAGE Publications, 1992).

39 Allama Prabhu, *God is Dead, There is no God: The Vachanas of Allama Prabhu,* trans. Manu V. Devadevan (New Delhi: Speaking Tiger, 2019).

40 Charles Peguy, *Notre Patrie* (California: Createspace Independent Pub., [1905]2017). For an important and detailed intervention that clearly brings to light the tactical limits of left populism in the recent European context and its hijacking by demagogic adventurers and cynics, see Anton Jager, "We Bet the House on Left Populism and Lost," *Jacobin Magazine* (25 November 2019).

41 Federico Finchelstein, "Populism of the Left?" Available at http://blogs.law.columbia.edu/praxis1313/federico-finchelstein-populism-of-the-left/ (last accessed 20 March 2020). See also his *From Fascism to Populism in History* (Oakland: University of California Press, 2017).

42 Partha Chatterjee, *I am the People* (Ranikhet: Permanent Black, 2019).

43 For an elaboration, see Gabriel Tarde, *The Public and the Crowd* (Paris, PUF, 1989/1901).

44 Stephan Mergenthaler, "Countering Populist Mobilization," School of Public Policy at Central European University, Budapest, February 2015. Available at https://spp.ceu.edu/sites/spp.ceu.hu/files/attachment/article/995/counteringpopulistmobilization.pdf (last accessed 20 March 2020).

45 See Robert Alan Dahl's well-known rendering of polyarchy/democracy into two dimensions of contestation and inclusiveness in *Polyarchy: Participation and Opposition* (New Haven: Yale University Press, 1971).

46 Paul D. Kenny, *Populism and Patronage: Why Populists Win Elections in India, Asia and Beyond* (Oxford: Oxford University Press, 2017).

Bibliography

Bettelheim, Bruno. *The Children of the Dream*. London & New York: Macmillan, 1969.

Canovan, Margaret. *Populism*. New York: Hartcourt Brace Janovich, 1981.

Cavalletti, Andrea. *Class*. Translated by Elisa Fiaccadori and edited by Alberto Toscano. Calcutta: Seagull Books, 2019.

Cohen, Jean L. "Populism and the Politics of Resentment." *Jus Cogens*, 2019. https://doi.org/10.1007/s42439-019-00009-7, 28 May 2019. Springer International Publishing. Online ISSN 2524-3985.

Comaroff, Jean. "Populism and Late Liberalism: A Special Affinity?" *The Annals of the American Academy of Political and Social Science* 637, no. 1 (September 2011): 99–111.

Finchelstein, Federico. *From Fascism to Populism*. Oakland, California: University of California Press, 2017.

Galston, William A. "The Populist Challenge to Liberal Democracy." *Journal of Democracy* 29, no. 2 (April 2018): 5–19.

Gudavarthy, Ajay. *Asiaville News*, May 2019.

Hall, Stuart. "Authoritarian Populism, A Reply." *New Left Review* 151 (May–June 1985).

Hochschild, Arlie. *Strangers in their Own Land: Anger and Mourning on the American Right.* New York: The New Press, 2016.

Hofstadter, Richard. *The Paranoid Style in American Politics and Other Essays.* Cambridge, Massachusetts: Harvard University Press, 1964.

Jaffrelot, Christophe, and Louise Tillin. "Populism in India." In *The Oxford Handbook of Populism*, edited by Cristobal Rovira Kaltwasser, Paul Taggart, Paulina Ochoa Espejo and Pierre Ostiguy, 232–249. Oxford: Oxford University Press, 2017.

Kenny, Paul D. *Populism and Patronage: Why Populists Win Elections in India, Asia and Beyond.* Oxford: Oxford University Press, 2017.

Kuypers. *Rhetorical Criticism: Perspectives in Action.* Lanham, Maryland: Rowman and Littlefield, 2016.

Marx, Karl. "The Eighteenth Brumaire of Louis Bonaparte," in *Karl Marx and Friedrich Engels, Collected Works*, Vol. 11, *Marx and Engels, 1851–1853*, 106. London: Lawrence and Wishart, 1979.

Mergenthaler, Stephan. "Countering Populist Mobilization." *School of Public Policy at Central European University*, Budapest, February 2015. Available at https://spp.ceu.edu/sites/spp.ceu.hu/files/attachment/article/995/counteringpopulistmobilization.pdf (last accessed 20 March 2020).

Postone, Moishe. "Thinking the Global Crisis." *South Atlantic Quarterly* 111, no. 2 (2012): 1–23.

Shils, Edward. *The Torment of Secrecy. The Background and the Consequences of American Security Policy.* Glencoe: The Free Press, 1956.

FIRST PRINCIPLES

1

THE RIFT

Milind Wakankar

The Ruin

It is all in ruin. The openness to another's experience, a culture's openness to the historical experience underlying the expressions of another culture and the very possibility of mutual understanding (dialogue and recognition) between the West and the East. These pulpits of the past are now strangely deserted. Academic 'post-colonialism' is now merely an aspect of one's job profile. Anti-colonialism is in abject disarray in the era of nations. And yet, there remains firmly in place the need for a new vigilance. This chapter argues that the mutual exposure of West and East has already taken place in the past, indeed in the past that precedes the historical past. We each inhabit the flood-tide of antiquity, not its ebbing path into oblivion. We are each marked by the memory of antiquity in us. Its recognition as a sign is a matter of an introverted archeological process of discovery.

But this process does not yield a self. What we discover are the conceptual resources to be gleaned from an original insight into the rift between God and the good. Just as psychoanalysis strives to translate the inner remnants of trauma into a language of conceptuality, in a similar fashion we are in the unique situation where, beyond mere theorizing or polemic, in the ingathered realm of a new humanism, we can now attend to the rift at the beginning. Is it not true that historically we exist no longer in the realm of original breaks and consequent leaps? This was the era of 'origins' understood as a mode of originating events in incalculable ways, ushering in newness beyond plan or programme. Instead, we have been ushered into the silence of the vigil, attending to an earlier mark of division, an earlier difference, prior to cultural dissension, far older than Occident and Orient.

The newness of this time is shot through with the shadows closing over the original rift between God and the good. This is the epoch of beginning (*Anfang*): it is a time of harbouring, preserving, holding close in safe-keeping the 'I' that is yet to emerge. And, therefore, we are projected into a time prior to the empowerment of the 'I'. The political freight of this emergence resides in the fecundity of a promise that was always in place before our time; it is prior to the promise of nationalism, empire or perhaps even the opposition to nation or empire. It is always already prior to populism. I am gesturing towards a philosophical disposition not of melancholy or despair but to a sharp and rigorous retrenchment of concepts precisely in the inner domain of the 'I' that is yet to appear. This moment of reflexivity before subjectivity or subjecthood is replete with conceptual possibilities but only as long as we take seriously the learning that comes with an insight into the rift—which is to say, into difference, negativity—a living death. This chapter is in some ways about the antiquity of this insight.

A phrase used by a philosopher of unmatched nobility of purpose is relevant here—I am thinking of Gotthold Ephraim Lessing, but in a way that detracts from his own Christological or theological emphasis.[1] The phrase that I have in mind is "the education of the human race," an expression of Lessing's that Hegel was especially fond of. Now it is not a matter of saying: How can Christianity or how can Hinduism educate the human race? The point is to say that in antiquity, prior to the advent of the cultures of primary narcissism that devastated ethics (so many crises in religion, as I will suggest further), centuries before the primitive nihilism that Nietzsche detected at the very heart of modernity, there was a glimpse into a hint of the primordial severance between God and the good. We are already exposed to this break; we are *in the exposure to* this break. And this will have happened at the tectonic level where concepts take root and produce a trace-filigree with millennial implications. Millennial, not in the sense of a promise (a messiah, a saviour) that is to come but in the sense of the memory of the rift that addressed itself to us in antiquity.

Indeed in the posture of this "seeking to remain open", there may yet be the chance of memory, of recall, a massive *anamnesis* of the rift. Not a trace of the good but the memory of the rift between God and the good. And so we are no longer locked into the contest of religions, Christianity versus Judaism, Islam or Hinduism. We inhabit a time prior to religion and theology where there is no God but only a glimpse of the good across from the rift. Beyond the difference between the phenomenal and the intelligible, there's a rift before the very possibility of perception. The signal disclosure of the rift was in Plato. I refer to the allegory of the cave in Book Seven of the *Republic*. There is the instance of those shackled cave-dwellers who can only gaze at the shadows of moving shapes in front of them in the dim candlelight of the cave. And there is that one dweller among them who dares to step out and look in the direction of the sun. But since the light of the sun is too harsh, he turns to its reflection in the puddle. And here for all antiquity is the after-image of the good that is also at the same time the final instance of the receding tie between God and the good. For, at that point, the world in which things are manifest (the *eidos* of the *idea*) falls away to the lot of the perceiver already inured to questions of truth, the correctness of perception and pedagogy. He cannot look unmediated at the sun which is the good (*touagathou*) that grants perception to perception. What he can do is to grow accustomed to the harshness of the sun by dint of its reflection in things perceivable, that is to say by entering into the difference between things hidden and unhidden, the process by which truth reveals itself as contestable, giving rise to a pedagogy (*paideia*) that involves "bringing out from the hidden to the unhidden" and, therefore, into the openness of truth.

Implicit in my account here is Heidegger's reading of the 'allegory of the cave' in his essay on "The Doctrine of Truth" in Plato.[2] His account is often faulted for having ignored the analogy of the line in the previous book of the *Republic* where Plato makes his explicit reference to the good by severing it from the domain of truth and knowledge altogether. There he says that knowledge and truth are indeed 'good-like' (*agathoeide*) but that neither of them can take the place of the good itself. And from here Plato's language acquires a hyperbolic tenor where the good is "yet more prized". Not only is the good not the same as being but it also surpasses being (*epikeinatesousias*), exceeding it in rank and power. The criticism is: Heidegger could not but have known how important the *topos* of the "good beyond being" was for such commentators as Plotinus (he seems to have acknowledged this in the lectures on Neoplatonism at the start of his career). What then accounts for the privilege he later accords to the "allegory of the cave" as the scene of the emergence of truth from untruth, 'un-hiddenness' from hiddenness? As I will underscore in the next section, Heidegger is pre-eminently the thinker of the rift. And even if this meant for him the historical oblivion of the insight into the difference between thinking being and thinking beings, still the rift could also (it seems to me) point to the absolute division between the idea of the good and the world of truth and manifestation, which is to say, the oblivion of being (the rift in Heidegger's sense) presupposes the oblivion of the tie to the good. As I will explain below in greater detail, we could well argue that the rift between being and beings (the oblivion of God, as in Heidegger) is already informed by the rift between God and the good. This trace (*ichnos*) of the good prior to the difference between being and beings is what lends to Neoplatonism both its pathos and its energy. It surprises me that the extraordinary community of intellectuals working on Plotinus and the other Neoplatonic commentators do not make this point. It would restore Plotinus to the heart of the present ruin of ethics. On the other end, those who seek either to tie Heidegger to Plato or sever their link would again seem to have neglected the inward tracing of the rift in Heidegger. His understanding of the emergence of truth as 'un-hidden' (*a-letheia*) is by no means a turn away from the pre-eminence of the good. It seems to me that the very movement of 'unhiding', wherein the cave-dweller frees himself from the shadows of the cave and then returns to educate those still inside, is marked by the absolute exteriority of the good. If we are agreed on this then we would see how the severance of the tie between God and the god in Plato, the careful and loving attention to the trace of this rift in Plotinus and Heidegger's focus on the rift inherent in the process of truth's unhiddenness—are actually three commensurable modes of thinking the prior evanescence of the good.

There was a time when thinking was able to approach the good. Thinking could push itself to such a point that, thinking beyond itself, it could catch a glimpse of the good. Not the good itself, for its glare may perhaps be too harsh for the naked eye, but at the very least the image of the good. That tie has now been severed. One indication of this is that marks of erasure around 'God' are almost always implied in our current usage. This is not because the divine is ineffable, or because 'God is dead'. It is because the word now marks the absent tie with the good. It once seemed that religion could help preserve the tie. Sadly, the hard fortune of God in the world has given us not religion as solace but the history of religions. At the other pole, we see the everyday struggles of men and women in the world prostrate before God. But this struggle is more about these men and women in their relation with themselves and the world than with God, to whom sceptical questions are directed. It would appear thus to be further removed from God, whom we may think has a link with the good. If not God in the world (religions), if not man in the world abject before God (anxiety), where would one look for the archaic tie between God and the good? For this tie—if its traces can be discovered—comes before the three great events whereby God came into relation to man, that is to say, the advent of the three Abrahamic theologies, to whom I turn later in this chapter with the help of Freud. The relation between God and man in these theologies is part of the inward catastrophe I will describe shortly as primary narcissism. But the good is prior to the narcissistic undoing of the religions that (for better or for worse) transformed the world and announced each time anew the coming of God to man.

God, man and world are realities we cannot know but which we can perceive. They regulate from outside our experience and our approach towards the good. In the implicit triangle above (with two axes, "God and the world" and "man and world"), the third axis "God and man" is theologically compelling no doubt. But it restricts us to a language of revelation, God coming to man. I am seeking here something older than theology which is God attuned to the good. Like Nietzsche, I too detect in our inherited modernity the primitive nihilism of Christianity. I could be an ancient Gnostic since I seek a dramatic separation between the Christian ecumene whose primitive nihilism we inhabit without acknowledging it, and antiquity that continues to offer hope. Hope: but not in the form of a monument to be claimed for national pride. Are Indians Hindu? Are Germans Greek? These are the passions of national self-searching, the disturbing implications of which are evident in recent modern history. Instead, I speak of antiquity as an instance of the primordial, always in the neighbourhood of death, but also within reach of the good. Death and the good are realities that compel us to think outside the theological triangle of God, man and world.

The search for the link between God and the good may perhaps lie in the efforts of ancient thought. As an ideal of thought, antiquity does not make a distinction between Greek and Asian, Athens and Jerusalem. The ideal is prior to such distinctions. It resides in antiquity that is near us, right next to me, because it contains within itself a pull towards the good. I seek this trace of the good in antiquity, but it eludes me. You can imagine what it is like. I walk across town to meet a friend who is visiting. I arrive only to discover that he has left. This is the mark of antiquity in us. The friend has left, but in me he has left behind a new sensation, that he has always already arrived.

By the same token, one of the gifts of antiquity is the idea that God has a kind of double belonging. As the very possibility of thought, God has a relation to "thinking thinking itself," to use a phrase of Aristotle's that was much favoured among Platonists. The latter considered this to be the highest aspiration for a mortal man. Man is able to think because God, as the absolute, has some role to play in thought's ability to return to its own earliest impulses. The thought is able to come full circle precisely because it emulates the movement whereby God can make thought possible (his outward being) and can withdraw from thought into himself (his inward being). Man emulates this movement and thereby acquires in his own thinking the recursive, self-thinking nature of the absolute. The youthful Hegel captured the shape of this movement in this account of 'reflection': "Reflection in isolation is the positing of opposites, and this would be a suspension of the Absolute, reflection being the faculty of being and limitation. But reflection as Reason has a connection with the Absolute, and it is Reason only because of this connection. In this respect, reflection nullifies itself and all being and everything limited, because it connects them with the Absolute. But at the same time, the limited gains standing precisely on account of its connection with the Absolute."[3] Thinking (as reflection) is precisely this movement between the Absolute that must ennoble the limited on the one hand, and the Absolute that too must undergo the test of being brought so perilously close to the limited in a moment of universal dissolution, on the other.

The late-ancient Puranas responded to the challenge of Buddhism in a similarly recursive way, as I have shown elsewhere in an analysis of the narrative of Prahlada. This is why one can speak of antiquity in a general way, across latter-day cultural divides. My point is not that the findings of antiquity are 'axially' comparable, as was once proposed by Karl Jaspers. In any case, the idea of the good in Plato is quite patently unique to the Greek understanding of being and the world since the Pre-Socratics.

Admittedly again, substantial culturally specific conceptual entities are indeed untranslatable across cultures. But it is a central claim of this chapter that they can be juxtaposed *from the vantage point of difference*. This is why I have insisted on the idea of antiquity as the glimpse into the rift between God and the good, or into the primordial ruin of ethical coordinates. It is from within the terms of the rift that antiquity is indeed 'universal' (*katholou*). The rift is prior to difference as such and by the same token prior to cultural difference. In the expansive and yet inward testimony of the concept to itself, we can detect the universal reach of the rift.

In the opening decades of the nineteenth century, Hegel wrote two different masterworks to capture the thread of these compulsions in thought. He wrote a history of consciousness which sought to show the different positions of the object as it appeared gradually to thought (the *Phenomenology*). This work ended with the fullest insight of thinking into itself, at the end of the journey towards a point of closeness to the absolute. Here was the point of departure for his second major work (the *Logic*) that undertook a history of 'the concept'. What the concept implied here was thought to expose itself to the mark of God. That is to say, this was a history of "thinking thinking itself" that, in laying out the emerging forms of the concept (forms such as being, reflection and essence) attempted to come closer to the ways in which God retained a tie to the good by occupying the place of the absolute. But to the extent that God's tie to the good was unattainable by "thinking thinking itself", we might say that "the concept" as the highest achievement of philosophy presupposed a break from the good and this is why the concept for Hegel is always the thought of an absence, a lack. In seeking itself in itself (the concept is best understood as the "self-concept") thought could only ever think "negativity".

The Rift

Let us linger for a moment with Plotinus, who in the third century of the Common Era read and thought deeply about Plato. Staying with him is important for my larger premise here, for I want to remind us of how the keen sense of the nearness of the good is also characteristic of poets in pre-modern India. These poets sang gloriously of the stature and beauty of their specific deities. In doing so they established the semantic fund of India's vernacular languages. They spoke about God in their mother tongue. But this posture would be unthinkable without their relation to antiquity. At every moment, antiquity was for them the memory of the good. This could be accessed here and now because it was always already there, in the sense that I have spoken earlier. Antiquity was nearby: this means that the link between God and the good was at hand to be recalled.

There is a tendency among born-again Hindus to commemorate antiquity as an indication in advance of a Hindu nation not yet in place. Elsewhere, I have tried to detect in pre-modern poets a different kind of relation to antiquity. It was not a question of renewing ancient tradition, even if in ways it was critical of some of its aspects, especially those relating to social iniquity. There can be no doubt that the poets take the ancient tradition for granted. But that is saying it too quickly. What does "taking for granted" mean? A word that figures in the Krishna traditions is useful here. The devotee seeks at every point to recall the divinity of the divine. The word in Sanskrit is *smarana*, which is not a commemoration of something put in place and set up; it is a kind of bringing back to mind. One wishes we could use the word "re-memorate" here, but that would be awkward. This is a moment of *de ja,* the sense one has of having experienced something before. The present is like a pivot. It swings back momentarily. But it turns to something that, precisely because it is primal, is not really available as such. The pre-modern devotee conjures antiquity in this moment as primal. More strictly, one might define "primal" in the following way: it is a moment when the avenue to the past (the tie between God and the good in antiquity) is blocked, but it is "also" a moment when the ruse of language is opened up. How one moment can contain both instances, something pushed away that returns in another form constitutes the millennial interruption of all populisms, old and new. In poetry that is so fecund, that embraces the lived world in all its physical force, depth and tenderness, one might speculate that the cumulative effect of this curiously double-faced moment is to suddenly body forth antiquity as "near". The renewal is that of a primal connection between God and the good. God has arrived. In this nearness, the devotee cannot stop singing song upon song of praise. Not just the poet. Entire communities dedicate themselves to verse. This is the prodigious epoch known as Bhakti in the subcontinent.

Similarly, those who looked to Plato in the centuries after him tried to cling to his glimpse of the "good beyond being." This meant that thought bore the mark of this glimpse, at the very least. In the third century CE, Plotinus perceived that the movement of thought contained a paradox. For the "being of intellect…is activity" (the being of *nous*is *energeia*) but this is an activity "directed to itself" (*heauto*).[4] The ambivalence lay in Intellect's being at once other-directed and self-directed; the internal activity did not nullify the external activity, nor did the external activity find its own self-sufficiency to be under threat. Since the Intellect itself is an emanation of the One (that is to say, the good) we might say the Intellect returns to that aspect of itself that has the One as its source. And for this reason, although the Intellect's self-sufficiency is unimpeachable, it is nonetheless derivative of the One (*En*). Imagine the pattern of a thought that is gloriously recursive, recessive in nature. Typically, it moved from the body to the soul, from the soul to the Intellect and from the Intellect to the One or the good. In each case, each entity answered to (was accountable to) the trace of the grounding "hypostasis". So the soul answered to the trace (*ichnos*) of the intellect in itself, the Intellect to the One and so on. Why is the good the ground of this regressive synthesis of the "I"? This is because it is the principle (*arche*) of individuation itself, the final home of the singular, the unique, the irreplaceable, all that thinking seeks to think through. The good *looks out* for thinking (in the latter's search for the essence of the singular). So the good must emerge from itself. It "needs" to do so. But this need is not premised on lack. Its basis is love. What drives the good is something "simple" if not paradoxical: it reaches out to give but it yearns to return to itself.

In all of antiquity and the period of the passage through Arabic and Syriac of the works of Aristotle, the tradition thought of Plato as a sage.

The "sage" was practiced in "recalling" the good; he could perceive the arc of this return of the good into itself. But this is always a good that is self-sufficient. It keeps to itself, and as such need not have anything to do with thinking. Here Plotinus disagreed with Aristotle, for whom "thinking thinking itself" was the final horizon for thought. For the latter, this meant that while thinking too needed to withdraw itself (it could be inactively secure in keeping to itself) it nonetheless needed to extend itself outward. It needed to think "another thing". The being of thinking was dual *(ta duo einai)*. Plotinus had this to say in response: but the good does not need to think in a dual way. It need not think at all! It would be, said Plotinus, "absurd" if the good did not "know" itself; for it "has nothing" in itself to "learn about". It is after all the good; it is "one". Nonetheless, the good is nothing if not generous: the good makes itself available to thinking, so that thinking can "lay hold" of it (Plotinus, 1984, V.6).

If we compare the lure of antiquity for the Platonist and the premodern Indian poet, we can see how the good lay within reach. It was simply there, in peace with itself, sufficient unto itself. Antiquity meant in each instance at once the nearness and the rift with the good. The proximity of the good made the thought, speech, prayer possible. But since the good was nothing if not fugitive we can say that *antiquity preserved an original insight into the devastation of ethics*. This is not tantamount to negative theology, the tradition that brackets and avoids naming or citing the existence of the God. Though we can see how negative theologies under a Christian aegis would use this idea, from Pseudo-Dionysus to Cusa. Let us recall here one of the key formulations of Cusa on the negative instance of God. "As not-other God is not other than not-other." Like a leap unto death (*saltomortale*), we are invited to undertake a headlong descent into the maelstrom of God's infinite distance from "not-being", but only after having traversed the infinite proximity to it. Something different is at work in Plato and we can perceive the difference very quickly in his phrase, "the good beyond being". This already implies that we are no longer in the realm of being, not-being or not not-being. We no longer inhabit the realm of human thinking and acting where being is conventionally spoken of and addressed.[5] The "beyond" implied in the phrase is the mark of a rift, a rift that is, if anything, hidden since the very image of the rift is an after-image. Rather than think of the beyond as something out there, mysterious and inscrutable, we can imagine that the beyond "informs" being. There is, concealed at the very heart of the ways in which being is spoken of, an insight into the rift. Between the good and God, there is a rift that is no longer about ethics. Emmanuel Levinas's work in the aftermath of the Second World War uniquely exposed this rift to the possibility of thinking, in its enormity, the claim of the other human being upon me. But here I am trying to imagine the antiquity of a link between the good and God whose loss precedes the great themes Levinas explores those of God, death and time. I try to think of antiquity as having just arrived with tidings of the good, but in an unsettling, disturbing mode of evanescence leaving time itself in disarray. And yet despite this disruption of time, this event has something of a relation not to eternity but the eternality of another experience. Eternality in this sense applies to the perduring relation between the vanishing of the good and the idea of its proximity.

The most rigorous formulation of the duality of the rift is in Heidegger's late work, and it has greatly informed my own understanding of how the rift frames and designs our notion of being. In the quiet but unrelenting tones of his essay on the relation between thinking and being in Hegel's *Logic*, "The Onto-theo-logical Constitution of Metaphysics", Heidegger is at pains to show that despite the ability on the part of thinking to incorporate what lies outside it, to bring within its purview as "identical" what remains "different" from it, we have yet to think difference itself, outside its implication in identity.[6] To think the difference in itself is to think the rift. As opposed to this, he discerns in Hegel a dedication to push thinking to its own final unravelling in the realm of negativity. To wit, Heidegger wants to uncover Hegel's stake in ground. First, Hegel appears to understand negativity as the undoing of the endless regress inherent in reflection, where beings are thought *as such* differentially from each other. Second, he thinks of negativity as the point when thinking rediscovers itself at its moment of absolute externalization when it is enabled to think of being *as a whole*. Heidegger believes Hegel, for this reason, remains bound to think about the difference between being and beings "as such" (ontology) and "as a whole" (theology). But this is the very figure of the "onto-theo-logical" ground of thinking. Hegel seems to be unaware that what he has uncovered is a nexus between God and being, grounded in negativity. In contrast, by insisting on the rift not as the ground but as the site for a "perduring" glimpse of difference, one that reaches out and reaches in from within the possibilities of language, Heidegger tries to deflate Hegel's over-insistence on thinking as the ground for the difference. He wants to insist on difference *as* the ground of thinking, suggesting that difference is one god no man will want to prostrate himself before. Persuasive as Heidegger's critique of Hegel is, there remains the problem of what I want to emphasize as the original rift prior to the rift of difference. I see this as a kind of difference before difference which is the vanishing tie to the good. In Hegel, there is the nobility and the height of thought pushing itself to its own outside. In Heidegger, there is the vision of a rift that precedes the rift between thinking and being, prior to the negative. Here I understand the beginning (*Anfang*) differently too. It seems to me that the "good beyond being" institutes a millennial primordiality that is prior to the epoch of a mode of thinking grounded in God (Hegel) as well as in the epoch of the 'perduring' difference between being and beings (Heidegger). The good remains in place in a subterranean fashion but not as an orgiastic or mystical myth haunting reason, as it does for Jan Patoçka.[7]

Curiously, it is Heidegger himself who turns to the idea of this primordial in his late work on the "appropriative" dimension of the event. But here again, though he has very illuminating things to say about the relation between beginning (*Anfang*) and the event (*Ereignis*), he tends to lean more enthusiastically on the side of an exegesis of the "event." Nonetheless, his bringing together of beginning and event provides a clue towards the origin of primary narcissism (as the dark emergence of the 'I' on the cusp) that has some affinities with what I am attempting to do here. At every point in his exposition of *Ereignis,* we see closely guarded, as though in secret, the shadow of the "*Eigen*" which is not the "I" but the mere hint of an original reflexivity. Heidegger insists that the event (*Er*-eignis) throws this "I" out from itself (it is ex-propriated, so to speak). But in this, we see paradoxically the fullest possibility of this emergence from the very cusp of annihilation which is to say that the perpetual nearness of the negative (*Nihil*) and not the negative itself. The most crucial link for my purposes is the family resemblance between the *eternality* of the good and the *perduring* relation that Heidegger discerns between the two aspects of the rift, its receding inwards and its opening outwards. Indeed, perdurance (*Austrag*) is precisely the peculiar coincidence of this double modus of the rift. Eternality and perdurance are ways of saying: We should attend patiently to the instance of the "I" that slowly but surely emerges and yet recedes from out of the rift.[8]

Primary Narcissism

Freud's late work gives us an important clue into the relation between the rift on the one hand and primary narcissism on the other. Tellingly, the problem of the tie between God and the good returned in the aftermath of the Holocaust as the "face", understood now from within the theme of radical otherness. There was a sense after this unprecedented horror that received notions of morality would need to be questioned. Rather than linger in the calculable domains of decision, deliberation and the effort to ensure that one's moral maxims are universal, the critique of ethics moved to the realm of the incalculable. The attempt was to elaborate a new understanding of ethics beyond morality. The other human being became not simply the locus of my moral compass. Even as he was simply other in relation to me, there was an effort to think of his otherness as "wholly other" which is to say outside the ken of the subject. The question was whether morality could attune itself to the "call" of the other. And whether the violence experienced by the other could make a demand on me that was (not reciprocally but immeasurably) "violent". In the work of Levinas, for instance, there is an explicit reference to the "good beyond being". The face was understood as the fragile borderline where God comes into relation with man.[9] One might say that the uniqueness of God lay in lacerating the face so that 'man' is the space of an invasion, a persecution, a relentless "being held accountable for (the other)". Ethics implied experiencing this excessive accountability as plenitude. Despite the harsh vigil this implied for man, one can see that the tie between God and the good is presupposed here, even if it is stretched to its uttermost limit. But from our perspective, we can see how, in the years before the Second World War, his last years, Freud had already undone in advance the very possibility of this tie. In this period Freud composed his most recalcitrant but perhaps also his most notorious text. He was accused of defaming Judaism, a charge that after the Holocaust took on additional valence. *Moses and Monotheism* was published in 1939.[10] In psychoanalytical circles, it is the peculiar textual history of the book that has attracted the most attention, it's almost episodic in structure, its iterations and the fact that part of it was written in flight from the Nazis.

Freud argued that Jewish monotheism was derivative of an earlier heresy in ancient Egypt. This was the Aton religion of sun worship established by a pharaoh who began to call himself Ikhnaton. Attempting an absolute break with the past, this religion shunned black magic, the worship of images and denied the afterlife. However, the heresy was swiftly overthrown and the Egyptians returned to older forms of worship. Moses, an Egyptian priest (not a Hebrew) sought to salvage Aton monotheism by imposing his beliefs on a Semitic tribe that craved relief from Egyptian oppression. He helped to bring this tribe out of Egypt and introduced the notion of circumcision. His followers rebelled and murdered him and the memory of this crime was repressed. The Israelites adopted as their own a volcanic deity of the Midianites known as Yahweh which they subsequently merged with the god of Moses. The prestige of a second Moses, a Midianite priest, led to the reemergence of the old faith. The repressed memory of the murder, however, appeared in changed form in the traditions of Christianity.

What seems at first glance to be a curious fiction turns out on a second look to have disturbing implications. Freud's historical account of the origins of monotheism is scandalous because it undermines the very basis of the face. We should recall that the face is the metaphysical limit for infinite exposure before an implacable form of alterity. With his argument, Freud exposes exposure itself, revealing violence before violence. To the great paradoxes of Judaic generosity (love but laceration, plenitude but persecution) so imaginatively brought out by the great Jewish philosophers among his contemporaries (such as Rosenzweig and Buber and further by Levinas in the 1950s)—to these paradoxes that would greatly inform Jewish thought after the decades after the Second World War, Freud opposed in advance with premonition, if not foresight, the primary violence of narcissism.

It seems to me that Freud's critique at this point is no longer about Judaism or anti-semitism. To my mind, Yerushalmi (the historian of Jewish memory) rushes in too quickly to defend Judaism, for the real scandal lies in Freud's insistence that generosity is grounded in narcissism.[11] At first glance, this may strike us as commonsensical since we often assume that gifts are derived from an interested generosity. But to say that generosity is narcissistic is to say something much more unsettling. What takes place here in Freud is as follows: prior to "productive" violence, so to speak, wherein the loving glance of God to man opens his inner life outwards, directing it to the other, narcissism hollows out his inner life; it does not expose in a kind of transcendental nudity; it does not open an aperture toward the transcendental alterity of the human being next to me; it undoes in advance the impossible relation wherein "every other is (wholly) other". Instead of making the self infinitely answerable to the other, it inwardly turns against the very possibility of inwardness. At one stroke this reduces the warmth of God as caress (Rosenzweig) and the idea that what first responds to God is the ego (Levinas). In the latter case, the ego can no longer reach inward in order to reach out (Heidegger).[12] Freud seems to imply that the ego is itself hollowed out from within by its disassociation from a unique God *and* by its use as a place to hide a secret which is the killing of Moses, the original violent reaction (itself the subject of repression) to monotheism. The scene of this secret is one of utter devastation. Because it is reactive, the response to this devastation brings into being the ethical apparatus, installed after the fact and after the caress (of

God). And its new habit of keeping jealously to itself implicates the ego in primary narcissism. From there it is a short step to the ego-ideal set up as internal censor, with the end result that all ethics are rendered narcissistic. Freud unequivocally repudiated the tie between God and the good which was the basis of ethics after Auschwitz.

In sum, rather than give generously and in excess, religion (in its most radical possibility as the face) keeps jealously to itself. It keeps to itself secretly; it keeps the secret. Almost by way of a cruel joke, Freud reverses the very idea of the uniqueness of God which is self-avowedly the basis of Judaic monotheism. It was the violence of the original monotheistic moment that was in a sense rehearsed in the killing by the Jews of Moses. In this original monotheistic rebellion again the religion of Egypt there appears already as though in a template the key features of Judaic religion:

> We would not, however be doing justice to [Ikhnaton] if we regarded him merely as an adherent or promoter of an Aton religion already in existence before his time. His activity was a far more energetic intervention. He introduced something new, which for the first time converted the doctrine of a universal god into monotheism—the factor of exclusiveness (260).

Its "negative" side, as Freud points out, was equally of the moment: "Throughout the kingdom temples were closed, divine service forbidden, temple property confiscated. Indeed the king's zeal went so far that he had the ancient monuments examined in order to have the word "god" obliterated in them where it occurred in the plural" (261). What, by accepted tradition, appeared to be the unique and original feature of Judaism turns out after historical inquiry to have been derivative, at the very least. But the elements of the earlier monotheistic turn in Egypt, once interpolated into the scene of Israel give rise to certain secondary processes. One cannot know if similar secondary processes came about in ancient Egypt. But if they did or did not (one would have to turn here to Assmann)[13]—they could clearly not have served as the basis of a civilizational claim; a claim, that is to say, such as that of the originality of "Judeo-Christian" civilization. Both the claim of uniqueness as well as the disdain for everything hitherto held sacred, beginning notably with the scourge against idol-worship, puts in place the negative elements necessary for the onset of primary narcissism. The original monotheistic violence against what is all of a sudden perceived as "polytheistic" originates from a cataclysmic event in Ancient Egypt, whose memory was expunged quickly from the historical record of Egypt soon after. Moses repeats Ikhnaton, and this secondary monotheism provides the locus of the retroactive elaborations that go into the making of narcissism proper.

By moving back the origin of monotheism from Moses to the era of Ikhnaton, Freud analytically separated the advent of monotheism on one hand, and the monotheistic-narcissistic complex on the other. From his argument we gather that the idea that God is One was historically not vouchsafed to the Abrahamic religions alone; at a particular point in Egyptian history, a similar concept held sway, however briefly. What is uniquely an aspect of the Abrahamic religions is their belief in the "uniqueness" of their God. But behind this claim lies at work something deeper, which is the peculiar legacy of their monotheistic-narcissistic complex. This legacy implies the devastation of ethics. How emptying this inner turmoil seems to have escaped all the commentators. One kind of critic looks back to this original moment and tries to argue for an internal hollowing out that, in fact, opens monotheism to its historical counter-theses (Derrida and Assmann in different ways); another kind tries to defend Judaism against Freud (Yerushalmi) or Freud against the charge of anti-semitism (Bernstein contra Yerushalmi).

The force of ethical thought after the Holocaust had thoroughly compromised any idea of morality that did not expose morality itself to its limits. Hence, the notion of the face that thoroughly and ruthlessly exposed morality to the demand of the other. Now if one were to say that Freud had in a prescient way undone the idea of the face four decades in advance, one is clearly not in a position to fall back on an unreconstructed notion of morality not undone by the experience of the Holocaust: one is not in a position to retreat from the searing heat of the face to the relatively cooler realm of moral judgement and agonized decision. More crucially, the crisis of the face (as one understands it after Freud's account of Moses) is a crisis afflicting not just an ethics emanating from the Judeo-Christian frame of reference; the crisis of the face is a universal crisis bordering on nihilism. For in narcissism, envy or jealousy rankles, but self-destructively in that envy gnaws at itself.[14] All values are undone if the face itself is compromised. The loving gaze of God provides no succour.

The question is: What is the precise nature of this universal crisis? Rather than argue that it concerns Judaism alone, let us say it is a crisis that draws attention to the relation between the universal and the particular. Another way of saying this is that the crisis draws attention to the self-working on itself, generating the subject in its moment of singularity. That is to say, that the self-reflection of the self uncovers negativity, not a self wholly restored or salvaged. Negativity is not nothingness but draws attention to all that is fundamentally fragile and singular about the subject. Narcissism feeds on itself, leaving behind the pattern of a gnawing, a rankling. Ethics or philosophy are brought down from their lofty purpose and reduced to this minimal instance of reflection. This is the flesh-and-blood human being who inhabits the scene where the face gives no solace.

So the universal here is not a matter of mere extrapolation or extension into a kind of bad infinity. It pertains to the way in which all that is abject and vulnerable in "being human" is folded into narcissism as the absolutely minimal notion of the singular. Narcissism is itself the retroactive response to an original crisis. And so the singular is in a sense "what remains" amid the ruin of ethics. By this token, the idea of caste in Hinduism is not a "Judeo-Christian" misconception. (The latter argument has its own peculiarities because it demands restitution and recognition from those who perpetrated the misrepresentation in the first place; but the defenders of Hinduism do not at any point question the historical basis of Western representation itself or its Judeo-Christian basis, as does Freud.) We know today from the historical research of Michael Witzel that the ethical edifice of Hinduism is in its entirety a retroactive and secondary elaboration of the institution of caste.[15] The fallacy among apologists is to argue in the reverse direction: that Hinduism has as its basis universal love and understanding and that this can extend to the anomalous instance of caste (such is the premise of Hindu nationalism and was in a different sense also Gandhi's position). From the perspective of Freud's "fiction" of narcissism, one might say that caste is exactly not that: it is by no means an anomaly. Caste is in every instance what Hinduism does not want to talk about. More strictly 'Brahmanism' is the elaborate ethico-philosophical justification for the original institution of caste as a secret that must be disavowed. In short, one might say: Brahmanism is structurally constituted by disavowal. This goes beyond the argument that caste is an "ideological" construct of Hinduism, for this would mean that Hinduism is a Brahmin conspiracy to exercise domination over low-castes. Quite the contrary, Hinduism presupposes the disavowal of caste; and this is why Hinduism "is" Brahmanism, a point that the anti-Brahmin philosopher Sharad Patil made forcefully in the opening pages of his masterwork on primitive slavery, to which I turn later in this chapter.

In disavowal and projection, in an inwardness that hollows itself out, in this vast and cataclysmic emptying out, all that remains is the singular being who is the subject of disavowal. And so we might say what is lacking here is precisely the absence of attestation by the other. Not only is there no God, there is, in addition, no face. A little differently from Agamben for whom "bare life" is similarly prostrate before the abyss where God has died and the face has receded, I wish to linger at the point at which self-reflexivity or the inner life is left without recourse, except to consume itself. A similar predicament can be read into the historical mandate of Sufism as it was understood by one of its exponents, Haydar Amuli in the fourteenth century. Certainly, this is a very different Sufism from what is popularly understood as Sufism today (which Islamophobes tolerate as a kind of soft Islam of love and song). At stake is the adumbration of an "inner Islam." Here is Patrick Laude discussing the work of Henry Corbin (1903–1978), the scholar of Islam whose work borrowed many of its gestures from Heidegger.[16] Laude notes that "Corbin follows Haydar Amuli in stating that Shi'ite imamology is the very foundation of Sufism, and that the latter proceeds from the former as its development and perfection." And yet

> It would be inaccurate—however tempting it may be when reading some of Corbin's texts—to consider that Shiʿa Islam is the esoteric dimension of the Islamic tradition, the exoteric side of which would be found in Sunnism. Haydar Amuli's views do buttress the vision of an esoteric Shiʿism, but they go in fact further, in a direction that identifies Shīʿa Islam as the totality of the tradition, by contrast with the incompleteness of Sunni Islam, confined to the province of the Law. However, this principle does not go without a paradoxical complement: While Shīʿism can be "exotericized" by those, within the Shiʿa, who do not perceive, or even deny, the esoteric essence of their tradition, Sunni Islam, for its part, can be practiced as a de facto esotericism, or to use Corbin's term, as an "incognito representative" of Shiʿism within Sunnism. This situation allows the Shiʿite theosopher to enunciate a statement that Corbin will make part and parcel of his own gnostic philosophy. According to this view, an authentic gnosis must integrate both the exoteric and the esoteric sides of the religion. It therefore involves a middle ground between two opposite excesses. The first excess, curiously attributed to some of the Sunni Sufis, consists in severing the esoteric from the exoteric by claiming that inner Islam (or the truth of Islam, its *haqiqah*) exempts its faithful from the legal prescriptions of the shariʿah. The second excess is characteristic of "metaphorical Shi'ites," that is, those who within the Shīʿa do not recognize that inner Islam (*batin*) is the true meaning of outer Islam (*zahir*). However, what may not appear as clearly from Corbin's introduction and commentary as in his translation of Amuli's text itself, is the fact that "the table has been turned," in the sense that it is now, in Haydar Amuli's words, the Shiʿite side that is associated with the exoteric side of the tradition, that is, "the literal religion such as it

> is practiced by Imamite Shi'ites among the various branches of Islam," whereas it is the Sunni side—in the person of the Sufis—that represents esoteric Islam, that is, "the esoteric which is the spiritual truth to which is attached the Sufi group."

In Corbin's reading of Amuli, the crossing lines of inwardness in Sunnism and Shi'ism have the effect of "turning the tables" as in a chiasmus. What was presumed to be the *Sharia*-addiction of the Sunni Sufis turns out in retrospect to be secondary to their esoteric proclivities; whereas what we could have thought would be the inner-directed mystic temperament of Shi'ite Sufis appears to be wedded to rites and forms of exteriorized Shi' practice. One could describe this as a crisis in inner Islam. The crisis places the very idea of interiority under the spell of ambivalence. A rigorous and terrifying form of Sufi *tasawwuf* is envisioned; one that distances itself from rigidly defined notions of inner questing but also from an excessive zeal for outward habits. If in the end, Amuli relocates esoteric practice in the figure of the Sunni Sufi, this is only because the very idea of inwardness would have to be at once embraced and cast aside. The fate of "inner Islam" is to come to terms with an inwardness that must first turn against itself. Here again, the lack of a figure for alterity is sobering. The mystic quest is unable to endorse either an identifiable inner self or an outer law as its surrogate. And what would appear to be in force here is the narcissistic attenuation of the so-called esoteric dimension in Islam, a predicament more troubling than the religion's Abrahamic fixations as they have been uncovered by Fethi Benslama.[17]

Ordinarily, in a Kantian schema moral action benefits when it extracts from itself all manner of cultural, cultic or ritual baggage. This is so as to be able to focus exclusively on the relation between one's actions and the universalizability of the maxims on which they rest. So if Sufism is to redefine itself de-ontologically, so to speak, it ought to derive some mileage from having rid itself of *Sharia* (Sunnism) and the mystic and introverted physiognomy of tradition (Shi'ism). Strangely, neither development helps to reduce the emptying out of the inner life of Islam. Again this is a crisis of self-sovereignty or what Foucault would have called "self-subjectification" discernible *universally*, in the sense I have sought to define previously. A forest fire in the serrated realms of rectitude. Such is the sheer force of this crisis, which appears to have escaped the attention of Talal Asad.[18] For those who follow Asad, it seems easy to say that both Christianity and the religions that it has encountered in its history (such as Islam and Buddhism) are equally marked by traditions of self-conduct outside the pale of doctrine and rite. Indeed, this is Asad's polemical standpoint:

he seeks to universalize the conduct of the self along the genealogical lines broached by Foucault; his point is that such traditions of the "care of the soul" were not vouchsafed to the West alone even as the West's own religious traditions evolved millennially, incrementally rather than precipitously, always in slow, daily shifts in practices of care toward oneself. But we may ask: What if self-subjectification were itself in crisis? And could this not be the crisis of religion but in the sense of dehiscence in its inner life? Would this mean that the State (the inner refuge of the "concept", as I will explain further) experienced narcissistic hypertrophy of the self in the period following the collapse of the Roman empire when as Garth Fowden contends, scribal cultures dramatically relocated religion (Christianity, Judaism and Islam) in the Law?[19]

Its effect in Islam was to generate an internal revolution in the idea of the State that was always an aspect of interior life in its traditions. The relation between this crisis and the fact of actually existing political entities such as the Caliphates then and Arab states now is pertinent here, only if it is read outside the psychomachia between "Islam" and "the West"; my point is to attend to the crisis of sovereignty in the interior realm, where the "concept" (as Hegel would understand it) is prior to cultural difference. Indeed it is at the level of the concept, where the self-embraces the idea of the negative that this problem plays itself out. This is the challenge Islamic modernity has addressed to itself in the last millennium. To put it simply, there is no longer an adequate attestation by the inner State of the self. All such attestation is phantasmatic, occurring after and not before the ruin of the inner citadel. Abrahamic reconstitution, the imposition of the law of the father is also, as I have said previously in reference to Benslama, a happening after the fact. The relation between Sufism and the state is therefore more than simply a matter of accord or discord;[20] this relation has always been "political" because the space where the self ought to exercise its sovereignty is also the place where a primary narcissism has been at one with a range of retroactive elaborations. To take an example: the fact that Amir Khusrau wrote poetry in the twelfth century in praise of his preceptor Nizamuddin Auliya *and* penned panegyrics in praise of the Sultan is an important indication of his double loyalties; but more crucial than this is the internal effigy of the Auliya, its disfiguring or refiguring place in his psyche. "An inwardness that must turn against itself," I said earlier. And, indeed, here we can draw an arc between Khusrau and someone like Ghalib in the nineteenth century. Even if the former's vocation was not above partisanship and latter's pathos lay in his distance from the court, their poetry attests both in what it affirms and what it quickly denies, a profound link to the State. The collapse of a connection between universal and particular, self and State is of course most keenly felt at the level of the singular being who inhabits the infinite spaces in which the "I" persecutes itself. This is the realm of the counter-will where the will would, in Nietzsche's words, "rather will nothingness than not will;" the nexus between narcissism and nihilism could not be starker. I wrote earlier that "it is at the level of the concept, where the self-embraces the idea of the negative, that this problem plays itself out." I also made an implicit connection between the concept and the State. It is time to formalize these links by entering more deeply into the inner life of the negative.

Hegel's Unfinished Task

No more compelling account of this inner life exists, to my mind, than the concept (*Begriff*) as it develops between Hegel's *Science of Logic* (1816) and his *Philosophy of Right* (1821). Only recently, and thanks in part to the work of Ferrarin on Hegel's lifelong fascination with Aristotle's *De Anima*,[21] have we begun to understand that the 1821 *Right* was for Hegel the first panel in a diptych which was to include both subjective and objective spirit. Without this image in mind we could easily dismiss the text on *Right* as simply a set of ruminations on the institutional framework of the family, civil society and the state. It could be an instance of a philosopher ranging rather far from his avowed stake in the "science of consciousness" to a realm of inquiry best left to political theorists. But this is to ignore the fact that his early work on "Natural Law" (1802–1803) is already ample evidence of Hegel's need to sustain a kind of caesura between the singularity of tragic experience on the one hand and the notion of ethical life on the other. True, in "Natural Law" he wishes to historicize traditional natural law theory and at the same time ensure that *Right* is not understood in a merely empirical fashion. Nonetheless, his *hesitation* in not immediately assimilating individuality to the state as the pinnacle of ethical life was oddly unnoticed by Hyppolite and Reidel, the great commentators on the

"Natural Law" essay.[22] The essay is to my mind only outwardly about the absolute nature of "ethical life" (*Sittlichkeit*); more crucial is Hegel's insistence on the link between individuation, singularity and the concept in their embrace of the concept in its negativity (the unifying theme of the *Logic* and the text on Right) as can be seen very clearly in this sentence: "But though freedom itself—or infinity—is the negative, it is also the absolute, and the individual being of the subject is absolute singularity elevated to the concept, negatively absolute infinity, or pure freedom" (138). But the drift towards the persistent counterpointing of the state is evident in the arc of his researches as a whole, as it was clear to his early collaborators and students, though this was quickly obscured by the brilliant polemic of the young Marx on the "political economy" of *Right*.

The fact is that, as the "Introduction" to the 1821 text illustrates, Hegel sought in his last decade to firmly bind together the objective potency of the will, of which the three institutions just mentioned were for him phenomenal instances, to the will's subjective potency.[23] Indeed, the tenor of the Nürnberg *Propaedeutic* of 1808-1811, the *Encyclopedia of the Philosophical Sciences* (1817) and the final lectures on the *Philosophy of Subjective Spirit* (1827–28)[24] are proof that this was the philosophical avocation of the mature Hegel and so should be taken seriously despite its apparently unfinished character.

Reconstructed in this way, one could imagine that the basic impetus for Hegel was to be able to read back into the will the capacity for self-determination that in the *Right* was embodied in the actuality of the state. In the state, the will accedes to the concept in that self-consciousness and finds in the state the point of its farthest exteriorization, but this is still its own; i.e., self-consciousness finds itself in itself through the alterity of the state, but it nonetheless finds itself. The will is marked by its commitment to individuality (*Einzelheit*) at every step of the way in trajectory of the *Right*. But this is because it is the unity (*Einheit*) of the particular and the universal, and in a specific way (31): "particularity reflected into itself and so brought back to universality." And in such a way that individuality shares with the concept "the innermost secret of speculation—of infinity as negativity relating itself to itself, this ultimate spring of all activity, life and consciousness"(32). Elsewhere, in the *Encyclopedia Logic* (Para 164), Hegel establishes the nexus between individuality and the concept in this way: "The concept is what is altogether *concrete*, because negative unity with itself as being-determined-in-and-for-itself (which is what singularity is) constitutes its own relation to self or individuality."[25]

Hegel consistently maintained that the travails of the "I" in relation to itself are the domain in which both the concept and individuality come into play. But what we tend to forget is that for Hegel the concept "is" individuality in that it represents an exacerbation of interiority to the point of implosion. Indeed, the concreteness of the concept is attained *in* and *as* this devastation because it is in this moment (in all its visceral violence) that the "I" comes to embrace the negative. Now, the crucial moment in the *Right* is when the monarch becomes the counter-echo as

Individuum of the absolute individuality of the individual (*Einzelheit*). It is the point at which the singularity of the subject finds its greatest concreteness, the point at which the individuality-in-excess-of-itself of the "I" locked in morality finds its highest possibility (higher than the family and civil society) in the body of the monarch. Rather than see this as an inflationary account of monarchical power, we should recognize here Hegel's need to find in the movement of the *Right* a most objective instance of individual will, that is to say the precise node at which the will, the concept and individuality cohere. Since the *Right* is the place in Hegel's oeuvre where the argument for objective spirit is worked out fully, it is fitting that the will finds here its point of greatest exteriorization, which is neither the monarchy nor any existing state, and certainly not the Prussian state. The infamous words from the text linking the real and the actual imply precisely this: the farthest exterior point of the inward experience of negativity, which is the same as the concept pushing itself and experiencing itself as the nearly unbearable point of self-destruction, this point outside its momentous internal trajectory is precisely the state.

Clearly, despite having achieved an insight into the objectivity of the will—and with great rigour and clarity—what remained to be attained was its counterpoint in subjectivity. Would this have been Hegel's own attempt to write a *Critique of Judgement* (which was Kant's own attempt to surpass his own account of morality in the *Critique of Practical Reason*)? Surely his account of ethical life (*Sittlichkeit*, of which the family, civil society and the state are constitutive) had already greatly undermined and surpassed the very Kantian notion of morality that features transiently in *Right.* But in that text morality as individual solipsism and agonizing had had to acquiesce to the demands of ethical life. Morality, precisely because it was a little too much at home in subjective life, had to expose itself to the negativity inherent in the family (always on the verge of collapse), civil society (potentially anomic) and the state (the peculiar location of the monarch as both particular and universal). But here its limit was outside it in the vast garrulity of ethical life. There remained the problem of what would be the internal limit of interiorization, that is to say "an inside" that would remain resistant to the concept's embrace of the negative. The search for this internal limit for the concept was compelled by the problem of the primordial source for the self-motivation of the will. For the text on *Right* had achieved an insight into how the "I" can be taken to its farthest limit in exteriority, in ethical life, and returned to itself. More than ethics, justice or right, and far more than morality, *Right* is an elaboration of the prospect of freedom envisaged from the standpoint of the "I". But an insight into freedom is not yet an insight into the good. To the extent that ethical life's relation to individuality or the ego was external (if objective), there remained the need to find an echo of the "naturalness" of the monarch in the spontaneity of the soul. As early as the *Propaedeutic,* which was a curriculum for high school students in a Nürnberg gymnasium where he was teaching at the time (he wrote the *Logic* at night), Hegel had suggested that rote-learning was an important model for the cultivation of spontaneity. This may seem counter-intuitive to us today; we tend to associate rote-learning with mindlessness, which is to say mechanical, "un-interiorized" memory. So for instance, we assume that those who chant the Vedas without understanding them are simply not exercising their critical abilities; interpretation and explication are what our modern, secular mindset prefers to ideology and thought-control. Hegel's point is exactly the opposite: he was looking for a form of spontaneity where "thinking thinking itself" (to use a phrase from Aristotle dear to him as well as the Neoplatonists) would happen of its own, without the conscious intervention of the will. For the deepest insight into the negative, which is also the point of the greatest internalization of the good, it needed to happen in a moment of auto-regulation. This appears to have been Hegel's desideratum; it was not a way of ushering in Kantian ethics through the back door, ethics he himself had done everything to discredit because of its fixation on the merely internal calibration of morality; this was a way of finding the plumb line with which to gauge the nethermost regions of the State (i.e. the "I" at one with itself in interiority).

Freud and Hegel both uncover, although through different means, the ruin of the good in the realm where the "I" finds itself with itself. The will rendered quiescent must now seek comfort in a range of narcissistic elaborations after the fact. The devastation of the will is also the place where the singular flesh-and-blood individual, the singular "I" whose singularity is posited and named as such, is made prone. (I understand "flesh and blood" here in the sense of Rosenzweig for whom it always signified the figure of the absolutely vulnerable, more abject than abjection itself.) Here there is no longer the counter-echo of the state as the apotheosis of ethical life. "Thinking thinking itself" finds itself without an objective echo in itself. Plotinus's God has stepped aside. In the agency of the Good, this God may well have been the primordial source of the ego's investment in the Good. But since he is also self-sufficient, he can also abscond. Here the ego can no longer derive its inner source of strength from a good before itself and "beyond being." This is the point of contact with the primordial rift between God and the good that Plato first points out. The will in its state of abjection is all that the ego has left. In the sphere of the objective spirit, Hegel had sought in the state the counterpoint of the individuality of the will; here in the narcissistic scenario that the ego finds itself, the counterpoint of its own quiescence is in the farthest auto-destruction of the negative (the negative finding itself). If the echo of the "I" in objective spirit was the state, the counterpoint in subjective spirit is negativity severed permanently from the good. But because this is still an integral aspect of the trajectory of the negative, the ego is able to come to terms with it, not cathartically as in the history of tragedy between Aristotle and Hölderlin (bitter medicine to be purged if it is to heal), but in the position of having no recourse, no place to turn, no refuge. In the end, the minimal gain is the ego's cognizance of its own internal limit, its farthest internal point of negativity. But no matter how minimal this may seem given the utter prostration of the flesh-and-blood individual, the singular being who experiences violence, there is still the chance that a historical transition will have happened at another level. This is because the insight of the ego into itself is the uttermost undoing of individuality, the absolute point of its own self-delimitation, but this is also the point at which the concept finally, at the beginning (which is also its end), comes into its own. The place for the movement into freedom as future is therefore no longer an ethical life but the domain of the concept. And it is here that the work of religion would henceforth have to be attended, before East and West, before ethical life, but at the point at which, in a kind of universal wreck, the concept broaches its own future. Such is the new task of the freedom it—that is to say the concept—will need to think. "Thinking thinking itself" having sought in primary narcissism the point of departure for its own task will finally have brought together the objective and subjective life of the soul.

Freud's seminal essays on mourning and on narcissism, to which his late work on Moses is closely related, point in the same direction. There we detect again the problem of subjective spirit as the loss of ground, the emptying of a will that cannot determine itself on the basis of a genuine relation to singularity. Inwardness appears to have lost its connection with what would have been its counterpoint, which would have been ethics directed at the flesh-and-blood human being who is utterly prone in violence. Abraham and Maria Torok's very helpful analyses of Freud's texts direct us to what subjective spirit sees as its receding point of origin, which is a crypt.[26] We access here something like the poetics of dormancy. We can understand this as the bringing together of individuality and the concept at a point of origin. But that is simply a beginning (*Anfang*), not a point of departure (*Ursprung*).

Again there are sufficient indications in Hegel of this void at the heart of the concept, but a void which is nonetheless conducive of the event.[27] The opening paragraphs of the section on being in Hegel's *Science of Logic* nicely encapsulate the issue at hand: "The truth is neither being nor nothing, but rather being has passed over into nothing and nothing into being—'has passed over,' not passes over [*nicht übergeht, sondern übergegangen ist*]."[28] What this "has passed over" implies is that there is, already at the very beginning, a holding back *of* passing over. What cannot be reduced any further is prior to what can be reduced, determined, nullified; the irreducible is for Hegel prior to history. Elsewhere in the same text, he expatiates at length on the very notion of a beginning prior to the movement between and nothing. In this enigmatic opening excursus on the problem of the "beginning," which itself begins *The Science of Logic*, Hegel writes:

> The beginning is not pure nothing, rather, from which something is to proceed; also being therefore, is already contained in the beginning. Therefore, the beginning contains both, being and nothing; it is the unity of being and nothing, or is non-being which is at the same time being, and being which is at the same time non-being. Further, being and nothing are present in the beginning as *distinguished*: for the beginning points to something other—it is a non-being which refers to an other; that which begins, as yet *is* not; it only reaches out to being. The being contained in the beginning is such, therefore, that it distances itself from non-being or sublates it as something which is opposed to it. But further, that which begins already *is*, but *is* also just as much *not* yet. The opposites, being and non-being, are therefore in immediate union in it; or the beginning is their *undifferentiated unity*. (*The Science of Logic*, 51. Italics Hegel's)

Here in this notion of an "undifferentiated unity," we have a hint toward a new relation between individuality and the concept, another way of defining the problem of "thinking thinking itself."

Schelling's Stuttgart Lectures

And finally, giving us an unprecedented insight into the rift, there is Schelling at Stuttgart.[29] At the time he was in mourning for his beloved wife Caroline, who died in the autumn of the previous year, 1809. Her death was the unlikely bridge between the great "Treatise on Freedom" of 1809, the untimely fragments of the 'Ages of the World' in the middle of the next decade, the Erlangen lectures of 1821 and the series of lectures on the philosophy of mythology and the philosophy of revelation that culminated in the Munich lectures of 1841, with Kierkegaard in attendance. The Stuttgart lectures were written for a private gathering and as such bear within themselves an esoteric and an exoteric aspect. This is demonstrable both in the movement of the lectures, which issues forth from the question of nature through to the question of the spirit, retaining the trace of nature in the movement of spirit, and then in the grand exoteric culmination leads to a stunning reversal of spirit and nature, one in which Schelling goes so far as to imagine the spiritual world after death. The final reflections on death contain an adumbration of the afterlife of interiority, that is to say the final "redemptive" unification of the spirit with God from within the element of a profound sleep. For our purposes here I want to use some of Schelling's insights at Stuttgart to outline what I want to now call the philosophy of the rift, or the *Riß*. One could argue that Schelling's post-1809 thought is almost entirely dedicated to the problem of the beginning or *Anfang*, although his term of choice is *Prius*, not *Anfang* itself. We are now in a position, I hope, to assume that the beginning refers us to a rift, to *the* rift as I have tried to show. And so I will now use *Anfang* somewhat liberally, if only because the German word redirects us to the crucial link between the question of the beginning as such, and the problem of the rift between God and the good.

To summarize what we have premised thus far, the philosophy of the rift departs from the idea of origination as a break or a leap. I would like to imagine that where things begin, at the point of origin of any process, there is also a backward movement into a rift. *Ursprung* understood as an original break or leap into an uncharted future is a favoured technical term of Romanticism, and there is no finer culmination of that particular tradition than Benjamin's luckless dissertation on the "idea of criticism in German Romanticism."[30] Again, instead of the *Ursprung* as origin I wish to postulate here the originating pull of the *Anfang* or beginning. This beginning refers us to an original bifurcation (*Entzweiung*) that presupposes the priority of the Real to the Ideal, that is to say what lies at the limit of the concept both in terms of its future and its past. Its past bears a traumatic relation to the Real, just as its future has been presupposed since Hegel and Schelling as the line that opens up into the future, as ideality or reason.

At the outset, what this means is that we cannot mistake the hyphen for the rift. For the hyphen takes for granted the ideality of the ideal: hyphenation presupposes an original unity, and even though a hyphen is indicative of difference, the horizon of unity cancels the reality of that difference and restores it to ideality. If, for instance, we take up the phrase, "The Indo-Islamic Millennium," the hyphen cannot have the same implication that it has in the stitching together of political identities (African-American, Asian-American and so on). "Indo-Islamic" is much more than the dialectical relation between the universal and particular, as it would be in the work of Laclau.[31] Instead, the hyphen here works as an "in-finitive": it "infinitizes" an original finitude; in other words, it cancels (sublates) the opposition between the Indic and Islamic but also *sustains* the bifurcation. The great paradox that comes to light in Schelling at Stuttgart is that even as the bifurcation recedes into an inwardness (a mystery) that would seem to shun the outward movement of history, it is that very inwardness that makes possible the outward pull toward the ideality of the hyphen. We can choose not to use the Christian Neo Platonic notion of divine love that is at play here in Schelling. But what is crucial is that the bifurcation keeps in reserve the essential priority of the Real before the Ideal. The bifurcation is prior, because Islam at the level of empire is world-transforming; but at the level of the state it is nothing if not inward, messianic, seeking always to devastate any figure of inwardness. Indeed, as I have argued above, the hypertrophy of the interior world is arguably "the" figure of the state in Islam. Another name for this inner catastrophe (*kata-strophe*; permanent parabasis) is Sufism; Islam is the hallowed name for the antiquity of this catastrophe. The Mughal state is sustained by a perennial return to this inward scene of strife, as the recent work of Azfar Moin has reminded us.

And, on the other hand, in the realm of the Indic the exactly opposite process is at work, as I have shown in my recent work on the 17C Marathi saint-poet Bahinabai:[32] here the preeminence of the yogic physiognomy of the soul requires a perpetual push from the "stha" (being-there) that is within oneself toward the deity (Ram, Krishna, Vitthal, etc.) that is out there; it is a matter of restitution of the inward Substanz of this "stha" toward the being-there that is the deity. Here the devastation is in the realm of exteriority: the deity is the locus of an inexorable force which transforms the outer world and brings it in line with the eternality of a Shiva or a Vishnu. When we use the term the "Indo-Islamic" millennium we refer then to the harbouring (*pradnya*) of the bifurcation between the devastation of the interior world (Islam, Sufism) and the devastation of the exterior world (Bhakti). Kabir stands at this crossroad, as Hazariprasad Dwivedi famously pointed out, but the crossroad itself must be seen not as point of convergence: it is a fundamental bifurcation, which makes Kabir's "God without qualities" or *nirguna* (and Nanak's too?) possible.[33]

In retrospect, this insight into the hyphen in the Indo-Islamic opens out into the most ancient rift in all of Indian philosophy, the one rift that sustains all Indic thinking up to the present, the rift that perennially disturbs, motivates, galvanizes, which is the rift between the Vedic and the anti-Vedic (Buddhist and Jaina). The two most eloquent responses to this rift, which are Advaita Vedanta and Kashmir Shaivism, continue to fascinate us precisely because of their proximity to this rift. And if there is a retrospect, there is a prospect too that the rift allows us to perceive: the insight into the Indo-Islamic opens out into the modernity of the colonial project, into the great debates about brahmin-led social reform, into the modernity of a reconstructed Hinduism. Indian or Hindu modernity is this rift between the Christianity of the West and the response to this "Christian" modernity. To use the always productive terms of Schelling, these are not periodizations of the rift along the lines of antique, medieval and modern; nor do they refer us to civilizational entities. These are the potencies (*Potenzen*) of the rift, but the latter must always be understood as the place of the original divide within identity and difference, not outside it. Neither empire nor nation can suture this rift. Suturing is to tie up the seams inwardly. When the scene of an original devastation is inward there can be no suturing, only a form of auto-psychoanalysis. For the potencies of the rift have gone into the making of what we are and who we are. We are reservoirs of these traits.

How so? Schelling enables us to think of the *Anfang* as the place of an original division (Scheidung) in God. The *Anfang* is the "unity of the opposition and the bifurcation (Entzweiung)" between the real and the ideal. The originating position (positing) of the *Scheidung*—this is what is meant by primordial. To be sure, empty talk of primordial runs the risk of turning "the primordial" into a concept. If the primordial is to be the locus of the recessive, of the secret, the involute, if it is to be the threshold for interiority, we must maintain the priority of the Real. Nature is the repository of this trace of the Real, which then makes possible the advent of the spirit as ideality. Here again the thought of the *Ursprung* as institution is not always helpful (although it was the motor for the great Habilitationschrift of Benjamin on German tragic drama). In the Heidegger of the period of the "Contributions" (circa 1937),[34] the *Ursprung* is premised on the strife between earth and world. Earth pulls down all that has been figured and the world "figures" in its worlding. It is true that the strife here is prior and cannot be figured. But the strife is not yet (at least in this phase in Heidegger) located in primordial being (Ur-Wesen). Still the cross-hatching of his "esoteric" writings so to speak, between 1937 and 1941, suggests that the he was at this point breaking from the idea of *Ursprung* into a kind of "leap" (*Sprung*) into the question of the *Anfang*.

Schelling turns us toward the most crucial implication of the *Anfang*: this is nothing less than the priority of the cosmological understanding of change, of death, of finitude, to the anthropological understanding of finitude. He never loses sight of the priority of this primordial being, a priority that can be discerned in philosophical thinking seemingly at a great remove from German Idealism. For instance, from a great essay by F.B.J Kuiper from 1975[35] we get a sense of how the cosmogonic divide between Varuna and Indra (marked by an original postulation in the Indo-Iranian imagining of the Zend-Avesta) is a crucial point of entry into what is arguably the *locus* classicus of this question in the ancient Hindu world, the Rig Veda Mandala 10, Verse 129 (that is, RV, 10. 129).[36] It is a mistake to read the *nasadiya* sutra (or the sutra of non-being, *asat*) anthropologically. Only a cosmological understanding of an original divide, one that is only retrospectively spoken of in the later RV text, enables us to sustain the tension of this primordial "neuralgic point" (113) to use Kuiper's wonderful turn-of-phrase. Indeed, we too must turn toward this *Anfang*, which is cited in Sankhya (and in the Mokshadharma section of the Mahabharata, as the great Erich Frauwallner demonstrated in the 1930s)[37] too: this time we must examine the nature of change, transformation and finitude at the level of the cosmological. The uncommonly insightful Heidegger-Fink seminar of 1966 on Heraclitus reminds us that the "*puros tropai*," the transformations of the elements from fire into air, water and earth:[38] the theme of transformability has to be seen in terms of life and death but in a non-anthropological way. The cosmological enables us to examine the instance of fire as the secret source of change. The tropisms of fire, so to speak, help attenuate the idea of death as privative.

In Heidegger on Trakl earlier in 1953 there is a hint of this aspect of fire.[39] It is at one with "pain" and the "threshold that has turned to stone." The fire guards the original bifurcation. It stands over the event of the *Anfang*. In the intimate heart of the *Anfang* there is a profound sense of the uncanny. "'Flaming' pain tears away." Pain's rending implies the *Fortriß*, or the institution of the *Riß*, the rift. The instituting is experienced as a tearing away (*Reißen*). For "pain's rending, [its] sweeping force consigns the wandering soul into that conjunction [*Fuge*] of storm and hunt which could storm heaven and hunt down God" (180).

And a few passages later, "Spirit is flame" (181). Contrary to Derrida (whose exemplary reading points out that here 'spirit' has been mentioned without quotes, with the deepest implications for Heidegger's idea of spirit and of history)[40] I want to turn here to pain as the *Anfang*. Indeed pain is here the root of fire. And fire is spirit.

The tropism of fire involves then a devastation of spirit. But in this devastation spirit is devastated from within itself. It is opened to itself as its innermost possibility. Spirit is restored to the original division in God, but this time not as the bearer within itself of the trace of the Real: spirit is restored to itself as itself. Spirit is pain; flame is spirit. One might say, following Schelling that spirit is addicted to pain; there is a *Sehensucht* for pain. But in pain, spirit is transformed. And yet the transformation is not simply a sea change from finitude toward infinity. Spirit is not the cancellation or *Aufhebung* of finitude.

In fire, spirit discovers within itself the rift. It stands over the rift. It guards the rift. The rift navigates the divide between identity and difference, between the cosmological and ontological, between men and the gods, between earth and sky. The rift is the original tie to the original bifurcation which is the *Anfang*.

Let us read at this point some lines from the final pages of Schelling's Stuttgart Lectures (Pfau, 242; KFAS 7.483):

> there will be a third period...where all [powers] will be subordinate to the absolute Identity—that is, [a period] where the spirit or the Ideal no longer excludes the physical or the Real, but where both are subordinate to the higher [Being] together and as equals. This redemption, however, remains impossible for as long as the same separation has not yet taken place in nature. Yet there this separation evolves much more slowly, because it possesses a much more profound life-force [*Lebenskraft*]. In this respect, man himself is a sacrifice for nature as, in turn, nature had previously been the sacrifice for man. In his perfect existence, man must await an [equally] perfect state of nature. Finally, a crisis of nature must surely come that will push the long-festering disease to the point of decision. All crisis involves some kind of exclusion. This [afore-said crisis] then is the last one for nature, for which reason we speak of the *final judgement*. All crisis, also in the world of matter, is a judgement [*gericht*] [...] [Now] good and evil are separated, and evil will be expelled altogether from the good...nature will be freed from all false being, that is, from non-being Instead, this nonbeing which previously had arrogated to itself the status of Being in nature is now being subordinated *to nature* as its foundation; this nonbeing, then is placed at the utmost depth *below* nature, and with nature herself being an already tempered variant of the divine egoism, this nonbeing will be consumed by the fire of the latter, i.e., by hell. Following this last catastrophe, then, hell would be the foundation of nature, analogous to nature itself, which is the foundation or basis of heaven, i.e., of the divine presence. At that point, evil no longer exists in relation to God and the universe but only within itself. It will have attained what it had always sought, a total self-enclosure

> [*In-sich-selbst-seyn*]; that is, a separation from the universal, divine world. It is henceforth subject to the tortures of its own egoism and to the hunger of self-addiction.

From what we have said so far, we may be in a position to introduce some shifts in this formulation. For as we have seen, we must think of this solitary being-with itself of evil as the very scene of the inner life, at the farthest point of the inward devastation of ethics, religion and morality. In Schelling's view nature must at once recede into itself and make possible the elevation of spirit. For Schelling, once the priority of the Real to the Ideal has been established the stage is set for the movement of spirit from out of nature and into history. For him, it is enough to think of the ideal as marked indelibly by the Real. In the architectonic of divine love, the movement of self-enclosure (being for itself) and self-alienation (being for another) must resolve itself at the eschatological limit of finitude.

And yet in this Stuttgart formulation itself, we can see a different possibility at work. What it could also be seen to adumbrate is the rift between God and the good. It is no longer a question of evil as apostasy. It is also the institution of a rift that frees evil from ideality. In consuming itself, evil is set free, but no longer as evil. In the fire of its self-enclosure we can detect the birth of a new understanding of nature. Here I take my cue from Whitehead. For the universe must now make way for this egoism in its self-enclosure. But so must egoism itself open itself to how it is judged by the universe. The rift between God and the good implies that God as the principle of ideality has turned away, but the universe must yet judge. Whitehead describes this as a process that takes place between what he calls the "prehension of feelings" and the institution of "eternal objects."[41]

In the final instance the rift between God and the good is genealogically compelling. It removes the self-enclosure of the ego from all valuations of evilness. In a very specific sense, the embrace of the Real (modelled after death) makes possible a new kind of judgement. In the Mahayana Buddhist philosopher Vasubandhu's masterwork (written in Sanskrit) the *Abidharmakosa* (c. CE 400),[42] this judgement is understood as a fulfilment of the perennial and remorseless archiving of action-traces. Actions are guided by a set of conditions, a cause that is also an end, and the sought-after fruit. But the movement of actions (which *is* the world: *karmajamlokavaicitram*, IV, 1) is haunted by the possibility that some form of comeuppance is already at play. This is the retributive freight that all action carries within it. Retribution (*karma-vipaka*) is retroactive and devastating. Indeed, it would seem as though the possibility of this future retribution casts a dark shadow on human action. Yet, the opposite is the case.

Indeed what Vasubandhu broaches is the pathos of action, of history in its proximity to the self-enclosure of the Real. In its rift with the Good and with God, this pathos is the mark of a profound quiescence, but not in the sense of the surrendering of the will. If there is now a rift between God and the good, there is also at the same time a new bond. This is the bond between the self-enclosure of the ego and the retroactive persecution that is implied in karmic retribution.

On Fame

How can there be a bond between the egoism that is born in the rift and the retribution that marks the return of the rift? This bond (which is at once, as Schelling reminds us, the binding itself and the bond, or the belonging together of the bond and the bind)—this bond is the key to the *positivity of fame* (as opposed to the negativity of flame-spirit-pain), and enables us to understand society itself as a medium or *Mittel* in which the bond is forged on the basis of a new generosity of perspective. To think fame as no longer privative, no longer the bravado that is requisite if one is to grip Fama or fortune by the forelock (Machiavelli), but to think fame "as" media. Media as the *Mittel* or medium can no longer be the refuge of evil, as a gnawing or a grasping that tears at one's innards. Media implies neither the education of the prince nor the commoner. We must think fame from outside the great strictures of *ressentiment*, beyond primitive nihilism. If society is saturated with mediation, with *Mittelbarkeit,* but also with evil this is because the last traces of ideality continue to define the will. This is why "media" is suffering: it is ambush, entrapment, deprivation for the sake of a personal trajectory that must bear with injustice because every trajectory must shine. Fame must be thought outside the shine (*Schein*). No doubt, fame is the inverse of the *flame* in which spirit finds itself in its devastation. But as an inverse it is still indebted to regimes of truth and ideality. We must make a break with this provenance of fame in competition, strife, polemic, populism, shaming and so on, because now in its self-consuming self-addiction it cannot but sever its ties to evil. It will be embraced by fame because fame is universal: it is not privative, it donates (Being), it gives futurity because it understands the inevitability of retribution.

Fame is compassionate. In fame there is an absolution that is at a great remove from the vestiges of the spirit in its internal self-recovery from its own devastation. When fame is understood from within the regime of mediation it cannot ever be an endorsement of pain. Pain, fire, spirit—this is how fame has been understood. But if we think fame differently, if we allow fame to enclose itself, to lay claim to its place in the universe, we respect its adumbration of a will, we think with compassion of fame as subject. And from the point of view of retribution or *vipaka* we nonetheless keep in view the priority of the rift between God and the good. The words of the great pre-modern Marathi saint-poet Eknath, electrified in the singing of Bhimsen Joshi, point to the effulgence of fame understood as *khyati*. The deity Vitthala, chants Eknath, has a fame that cannot be extolled enough (*tyacikhyati kai sangu*). In the demesne (*kshetra*) of Vitthala is located my natal home (*majhe maher Pandhari*); there flows the river Chandrabhaga, who is my sister. And so the fame of Vitthala points to the prodigy that "there is" Vitthala, that he has been there for 28 epochs (*yugas*).[43] It seems to me that it is precisely to this primordial being (*Ur-Wesen*) of fame that Schelling too directs us. In this retrospect the subject of fame is rendered objectively; it is judged by the universe. And this judgement is compassionate. A more utopian prospect opens up here. Media shorn of pain, of evil, of ideality can open unto a new vision of nature that is itself removed from its fatal link to ideality (this is what continues to haunt eco-consciousness). If we can imagine here a rift between nature and the anthropocene (or with history, ideality and the spirit) we can then restore nature itself to its proximity with fame. History as *Anfang* is then replete with these transformative possibilities.

Notes

1 See Lessing (1729–1781), "The Education of the Human Race" (written between 1777 and 1780), in *Philosophical and Theological Writings*, ed. H.B. Nisbet (Cambridge: Cambridge University Press, 2005), 217–240.

2 See Heidegger, "Plato's Doctrine of Truth" (1931–1932/1940) in *Pathmarks*, ed. William McNeill (Cambridge: Cambridge University Press, 1998), 155–182.

3 Heidegger recalled this passage perceptively in one of his final seminars (at Le Thor, 1966). See Hegel, *The Difference between Fichte's and Schelling's System of Philosophy*, trans. H.S. Harris and Walter Cerf (Albany: State University of New York Press, [1801] 1977), 94.

4 Plotinus (born ce 205, died 269/70), *Plotinus: Enneads V*, trans. A.H. Armstrong (Cam, Mass: Harvard UP, 1984), 93–95.

5 This is why I cannot agree with Werner Beierwaltes that there is an affinity here between Heidegger and Cusa. See his outstanding 16 February 1977

lecture on Heidegger, Hegel and Cusa, *Identität und Differenz: Zum Prinzip cusanischen Denkens* (Opladen: Westdeutscher Verlag, 1977).

6 In Martin Heidegger, *Identity and Difference*, trans. Joan Stambaugh (Chicago: The University of Chicago Press, 1969), 42–74.

7 See Derrida's discussion of Patoçka's *Heretical Essays*, *The Gift of Death*, trans. David Wills (Chicago: University of Chicago Press, 1995), 1–34.

8 Here it is useful to juxtapose texts that hark back to the unpublished grand conspectus of his own work up until the late 1930s, Heidegger, *Contributions to Philosophy* (1936–1938). First, "The Incipient Saying of Being in the Fragment of Anaximander" (1941), which is Part Two of Heidegger, *Basic Concepts*, trans. Gary E. Aylesworth (Indiana: Indiana University Press, 1993), 81–106. And second, a text from the same year, 1941, *Über den Anfang* (Frankfurt: Vittorio Klostermann, 2005).

9 The key texts are Franz Rosenzweig, *The Star of Redemption*, trans. Barbara E. Galli (Madison: The University of Wisconsin Press, [1920] 2005); Emmanuel Levinas, *Otherwise than Being or Beyond Essence*, trans. Alphonso Lingis (Dodrecht and Boston: Kluwer Academic Publishers, 1978); and Emmanuel Levinas, *Totality and Infinity: An Essay on Exteriority* (Pittsburgh: Duquesne University Press, 1969). The later writings of Jacques Derrida, too numerous to recount here, are all relevant. Richard J. Bernstein's *Freud and the Legacy of Moses* (New York: Cambridge University Press, 1998) is by far the most exhaustive account of the reception-history of the text. The list of responses to this text in the last decade (by Eric Santner among others) is too vast for me to be able to account for every nuance in the archive; in any case, exhaustive documentation is not my purpose here.

10 See Sigmund Freud, "Moses and Monotheism: Three Essays" (1939 [1934–1938]). In *The Penguin Freud Library*, Vol. 13: *The Origins of Religion* (London: Penguin, 1990), 237–385; corresponding to Volume 25 of the Standard Edition by Strachey.

11 Josef Hayim Yerushalmi in his otherwise extremely compelling text, *Freud's Moses: Judaism Terminable and Interminable* (New Haven: Yale University Press, 1991).

12 See Levinas's reading of Heidegger on tools, in *Totality and Infinity*.

13 See Jan Assmann, *Moses the Egyptian: The Memory of Egypt in Western Monotheism* (Cambridge: Harvard University Press, 1997).

14 Friedrich Nietzsche, *On the Genealogy of Morality*, trans. Carol Diethe (Cambridge: Cambridge University Press, 1997); Melanie Klein, "Envy and Gratitude," in *Envy and Gratitude and other Works 1943–1963*, trans. Carol Diethe (New York: Free Press, 1975).

15 Michael Witzel, "Early Sanskritization: Origins and Development of the Kuru State," *Electronic Journal of Vedic Studies* (EJVS) 1, no. 4 (1995): 1–26.

16 See Patrick Laude, *Pathways to an Inner Islam: Massignon, Corbin, Guenon, Schuon* (Albany: New York University Press, 2010), 41.

17 Trans. Robert Bononno, *Psychoanalysis and the Challenge of Islam* (Minneapolis: University of Minnesota Press, 2009).

18 See Asad, *Genealogies of Religion* (Baltimore: Johns Hopkins University Press, 1993).

19 See his *Before and After Muhammad: The First Millennium Refocussed* (Princeton: Princeton University Press, 2015).

20 The term 'political Islam' is unfortunate in its tautological structure, for it dissimulates the primary narcissism of prophetic Israel in antiquity and Christianity under the Roman state, just as it entirely ignores the historical agency of Islam: the latter presented itself as *the* eschatological overcoming of both Judaism and Christianity by persistently relocating the specular itinerancy of the ego in the realm of primary narcissism. The apocalyptic and messianic dimension of Sufism in its attestation of divine love would be unthinkable if it did not occur repeatedly in the ruin of the state which is also the ruin of the self.

21 Alfredo Ferrarin, *Hegel and Aristotle* (Cambridge: Cambridge University Press, 2004).

22 See Manfred Riedel, *Between Tradition and Revolution: The Hegelian Transformation of Political Philosophy*, trans. Walter Wright (Cambridge: Cambridge University Press, 1984); Jean Hyppolite, *Introduction to Hegel's Philosophy of History*, trans. Bond Harris and Jacqueline Bouchard Spurlock (Gainsville: University Press of Florida, 1996 [1948]). I have used H.B. Nisbet's translation of 'On the Scientific Ways of Treating Natural Law, on its Place in Practical Philosophy, and its Relation to the Positive Sciences of Right' (which translation replaces T.M. Knox's flawed earlier effort) in G.W.F. Hegel, *Political Writings*, eds. Laurence Dickey and H.B. Nisbet (Cambridge: Cambridge University Press, 2004), 102–180. For the hesitation I speak of, see also for instance this passage: 'But what we [earlier] put on one side in connection with the external form of the first class [*Stand*] is the real absolute consciousness of ethical life. It is consciousness and, as such, in its negative aspect pure infinity and the highest abstraction of freedom—i.e., the relation of constraint [*Bezwingen*] pushed to the point of its own cancellation [*Aufhebung*], or freely chosen violent death; but in its positive aspect, this consciousness is the singularity and particularity of the individual. But this inherent negativity—namely consciousness in general…is absolutely incorporated [*aufgenommen*] into the positive, while its particularity and infinity or ideality are absolutely incorporated, in a perfect manner, into the universal and real; this oneness [of universal and particular] is the Idea of the absolute life of the ethical' (156).

23 I referred to the following editions: Hegel, *Elements of the Philosophy of Right*, trans. H.B. Nisbet (London: Cambridge University Press, 2003); Stephen's Houlgate's recent revised version of the legendary translation by T.M. Knox of Hegel, *Outlines of the Philosophy of Right* (Oxford: Oxford University Press, 2008). The quote from Para 7 is from the Houlgate-Knox edition.

24 See Hegel, *The Philosophical Propaedeutic,* trans. A.V. Miller (London: Basil Blackwell, 1986); see the very useful Introduction by Robert R.

Williams to his translation of Hegel, *The Lectures on the Philosophy of the Spirit: 1827–8* (New York: Oxford University Press, 2007), 1–56; Hegel's *Philosophy of Subjective Spirit* [Part Three of the Encyclopaedia], trans. M.J. Petry (Dordrecht: D. Reidel, 1978).

25 See *Encyclopaedia Logic: Part 1 of the 'Encyclopaedia of the Philosophical Sciences' with the Zusätze*, trans. T.F. Geraets, W.A. Suchting and H.S. Harris (Indianapolis: Hackett, 1991), 241.

26 *The Wolf Man's Magic Word: A Cryptonymy* (Minneapolis: University of Minnesota Press, 1986).

27 Here Badiou is correct to read Hegel robustly. See Alain Badiou, "Hegel and the Whole," in Badiou, *Theoretical Writings* (London: Continuum, 2008), 227–238; and *Being and Event* (London: Bloomsbury, 2007), 169–178.

28 G.W.F. Hegel, *The Science of Logic* (1812–1813, rev. 1831), trans. George di Giovanni (Cambridge: Cambridge University Press, 2010), 60 (emphasis in original).

29 See "Stuttgart Seminars (1810; based on posthumous manuscripts)," in *Idealism and the Endgame of Theory: Three Essays by F.W.J. Schelling*, trans. and ed. Thomas Pfau (Albany: State University of New York Press, 1994), 195–243. The German original is in K.F.A. Schelling (hereafter 'KFAS') *Sämmtliche WerkeSiebenter Band 1805–1810*, ed. F.W.J. Schelling (Stuttgart: Cotta, 1856–61), 417–486.

30 See Walter Benjamin, "The Concept of Criticism in German Romanticism," in *Selected Writings: Volume One: 1913–1926* (Cambridge, Mass.: Harvard University Press, 2004), 116–200.

31 See Ernesto Laclau, "Universalism, Particularism and the Question of Identity," *October* 61 (Summer, 1992): 83–90.

32 Forthcoming in Vinay Lal, ed. (Proceedings of the) Backwaters Collective in Metaphysics and Politics (III), Kochi (Delhi: Oxford University Press).

33 I extrapolate here from my essay, "History and Allegory: Affinities between the Puranas and Kabir, in *India and Civilizational Futures: Backwaters Collective on Metaphysics and Politics II*, ed. Vinay Lal (New Delhi: Oxford University Press, 2019), 157–181.

34 See trans. Richard Rojcewicz and Daniela Vallega-Neu, *Contributions to Philosophy (of the Event)* (Bloomington and Indiana: Indiana University Press, 1989).

35 "The Basic Concept of Vedic Religion," *History of Religions* 15, no. 2 (November, 1975): 107–120.

36 See Stephanie Jamieson and Joel Brereton trans., *The Rig Veda* (New York: OUP, 2014), 1607–1609.

37 "Frauwallner, *UntersuchungenzumMokshadharma*." *Kleiner Schriften*, eds. Gerhard Oberhammer and Ernst Steinkellner (Wiesbaden: Franz Steiner Verlag, 1982), 55–82.

38 Trans. Charles Siebert, Martin Heidegger and Eugen Fink, *Heraclitus Seminar* (Evanston: Northwestern University Press, 1993), 80–81.

39 Heidegger, "Language in the Poem," in *On the Way to Language* (New York: Harper Collins, 1982), 159–198.

40 Jacques Derrida, *Of Spirit*, trans. Geoff Bennington and Rachel Bowlby (Chicago: University Press, 1989).
41 Alfred North Whitehead, *Process and Reality* (New York: The Free Press, 1978).
42 Vasubandhu, *Abhidharmakosabhasyam*, ed. P. Pradhan, rev. Aruna Haldar (Patna: K.P. Jayaswal Institute, 1975).
43 *Abhanga* no. 424 in *Sri Eknath Gatha*, ed. Nanamaharaja Sakhre (Pune: Varda Books, [1908] 1998), 422.

2

THE PASSAGE OF HATE[1]

Sanil V.

Is Hate a Revolutionary Sentiment?

On the walls of Jawaharlal Nehru University, Delhi, I found a piece of graffiti that was the following quote from Che Guevara written in multicolour alphabets.

> Hatred as (sic) an element of the struggle; a relentless hatred of the enemy, impelling us over and beyond the natural limitations that man is heir to and transforming him into an effective, violent, selective, and cold killing machine. Our soldiers must be thus; a people without hatred cannot vanquish a brutal enemy.[2]

This quote celebrates hate as a revolutionary sentiment. Today, no lover of Che would dare to acknowledge this celebration. However, on the university wall, these words were chosen as part of an anti-left propaganda by the student's wing of a right-wing party. Disgusting caricatures of the political symbols of the left groups were drawn around this calligraphy of hate. Che's statement about hate was quoted as part of a hate campaign by Che haters.

Against the prevailing moral and political correctness, Che affirmed the necessity of hate. He did not limit himself to the usefulness of hate. Hate impels us beyond the natural limitations of being human. The Che lover would place this quote in the context of Guevara's other texts and his martyrdom for the liberation of the oppressed people of the world. For them, his speech in favour of hate is only a rhetorical device to arouse the love needed for revolutionaries to fight together. However, the right-wing campaigner need not go to any length in being critical of Che or his ideology but simply quote his own statement out of context to demean Che as well as left politics. Che's own statement on hate can be quoted against him.

This graffiti speaks to us about the power and logic of hate. It alerts us to the possibility of appreciating the labour of hate in a liberating struggle. It also shows the power of hate in perpetuating itself by quoting and re-signifying a philosophical statement. Perhaps, this is the fate that awaits any philosophical reevaluation of hate.

Hate targets race, religion, gender and caste and unleashes verbal, physical and emotional violence. Lynch mobs and hate speech mark the advent of populism. However, the relationship between hate, enmity and violence is not clear. As Carl Schmitt argued absolute enmity based on the moral condemnation is not political. The real enemy calls for a friend. Hate disrupts the ever-escalating violence of revenge and also the clam procedures of justice (Sanil 2010). Dialectic and dialogue seem to be inadequate to capture the negativity of hate.

No wonder, reason prefers love over hate. However, shouldn't we hate the world that we wish to change or a structural injustice we wish to annihilate? Is there a labour of hate, however, negative and destructive it may be? Is there a wisdom of hate that can clear the passage from hate to love? In the second section of this chapter, we shall consider some instances from the Sanskrit tradition where hatred towards the god is seen as a path to salvation. The third section will explore the resources of language that can resignify hate-speech. How can we be brothers in hate who are proud of our enemies? How do we transform the sadness of hate into a joyful affirmation of life? The final section will pursue these questions with two philosophers of hate—Nietzsche and Spinoza.

Hate and Moksha

kīṭaḥpeśaskṛtāruddhaḥ
kuḍyāyāṁ tam anusmaran
saṁrambha-bhaya-yogena
vindate tat-svarūpatām

(*Srimadbhagavatam* 1982, 7.1.28)

A worm confined to a hole by an attacking bee, through fear and hate, takes the form of the bee. In camouflage, the victim overcomes death by becoming the attacker. This mimetic becoming combines fear and hate and liberates the entrapped worm. Similarly, those who contemplate Krishna whether in devotion or enmity become one with him and attain liberation. A combination of fear and hate is a mode of focusing one's attention on god and working one's way towards him.

In the classical Sanskrit texts like Vishnu Purana and Srimadbhagavatam, hatred is accepted as one of the paths for salvation like those of wisdom, action and devotion (Sheth 1999). One can reach god by hating him. The hate needs to be pure and totally focused on its target. In the apocryphal story of Jay-Vijay (Rosen 2017), Vishnu suggests two options for salvation to his two gatekeepers cursed by the Sanatakumars—being born as Vishnu devotees and attain salvation after seven births or be born as Vishnu haters and attain salvation in three lives. It is fascinating to note here that the tenure for haters seems to be shorter than that of devotees! Jay and Vijay's first two births as Vishnu-haters were as Hiranyakasipu (and Hiranyaksha) and as Ravana (and Kumbhakarna). In neither of these two births was their hatred pure and unwavering. Hiranyakasipu was too preoccupied with his kingly status and hated Vishnu only in so far as his subjects worshiped the latter. Ravana's hatred for Rama was clouded by his desire for Sita. Finally, in Sisupala (and brother Dantavakra) the hatred, accumulated through previous births, was unwaveringly focused on Vishnu in his avatar as Krishna. Sisupala began to blaspheme god before he could properly speak and maintained this enmity till death. Despite such hate speech, his tongue was not affected by white leprosy—svitronajatojihvayam (*Srimadbhagavatham*, 7.1.19). The fire of hate kept the image of Vishnu alive in his mind. The hateful invocation of the name of god becomes indistinguishable from prayer.

Putana, with nipples coated with poison, was sent by Kamsa to kill Krishna when he was a baby. Putana traverses a spectrum of emotions ranging from motherly love to hate. Krishna sucks the life out of Putana, who in turn becomes one with Krishna, the object of her unwavering attention.[3] Krishna sucked her breasts treating her as his mother and killed her by taking on her as an enemy. Krishna sucked her in anger but, as she was dying, he was found playing fearlessly upon her torso (Urvasikridanaakutobhayah). The same object is at once an object of love and hate. In the end, Putana ceases to be an external object—cause of passions—and becomes one with the god.

This does not mean that hate and love/devotion have equal status with regard to salvation. While haters gain deliverance, the path of devotion has definite superiority. The latter is preferred to the former. Not all who hate Vishnu achieves salvation. However, haters in some cases, with their focus, have an advantage over devotees (*Srimadbhagavatham* 7.1.27).

There are various ways to account for this deliverance through hate. The hater may have been a devotee in one of his previous lives. Deliverance might be the result of leaving behind the path of hate and following that of devotion. However, such interpretations come against the fact that the hater's salvation does not depend on his repentance. The hater knows that his enemy is god and will be killed by him. The intensity of hate could overwhelm that of love and quicken salvation. Hatred towards any object does not lead to salvation. Only the god who makes no distinction between hate and love can be the object of liberating hate. Enmity turns the god ferocious and he too fights with anger and hate. A physical encounter with God is necessary for becoming one with God. Those who plead mercy and escape this encounter lose the privilege of being slain by god. How does the destructive hate transform an encounter with god into one of salvation? Can hate speech ever be prayer?

How to Hate with Words?

In the contemporary world, speech harbours the potential to articulate and resignify hate. Judith Butler has pointed out this potential and affirmed it against judicial and statist remedies for hate speech (Butler 1997). Such remedies identify hate speech with the hateful act and determine certain speech acts as punishable offence.

How can speech hurt? A combination of Austin's speech act theory and Althusser's theory of interpellation is often used to account for the violence of speech. The former views all sayings as doings and accounts for the injury caused by speech as an illocutionary effect. The theory of interpellation accounts for the constitution of the subject through language. Once we assume a determinant and necessary relation between speech and act, we may hold the speaker responsible for the act. Here we treat a threat as the act it threatens to do. From this perspective, declaring one's sexual orientation in public is already a sexual act. Speech act causes injury by constituting the subject as subordinated. For example, according to Mackinnon, pornography is hate speech because by showing women in a subordinate position, it addresses women as already subordinated and thereby constituted them as subordinate (Mackinnon 1993).

Judith Butler (1997) has analyzed the limitations of this combination in guiding resistance against hate speech. Activists have used this framework to seek judicial and state intervention to counter hate speech. Such efforts often occlude the gap between speech and conduct and identify the causation of injury with the constitution of the subject. According to Butler, this could lead to the judicial appropriation of the language of feminist resistance which could be used to silence articulations of resistance in other walks of life like the ban on the racially loaded lyrics of Black rap or censorship against sexually explicit artworks. Instead of appealing to state intervention and censorship, Butler explores the possibility of a counter-speech that transforms hate speech into a voice of resistance. Counter speech re-signifies or restages hate speech.

Judith Butler, while acknowledging that speech has a significant performative dimension, refuses to close the gap between speech and act. Speech has an excess that, though no longer pure speech, has not yet exhausted in action. Butler develops this idea of excess by focusing on two aspects of the speech act. First, every speech act, while being conventional is also citational and hence ritualistic. Second, speech is always an address. The speaker of hate speech is not its originator. He quotes from an available vocabulary of insults. The speaker who addresses his victim is already an addressee. Hate speech exposes and exploits a certain vulnerability within us as linguistic beings. Judicial remedies are based on the assumption that hate speech always succeeds. For Butler, this is not true. The potential failure of speech has its source in our vulnerability to language and hence harbours the potential for resignification.

Since language forms us as speakers, we are not 'sovereign subjects' and our speech could fail. In this failure, Butler gleans the possibility of resistance and counter-speech. Hate speech, though it repeats the stock of addresses, fails to address. Since it fails to address it does not fully constitute the addressee as a subject. It succeeds in injuring in so far as it fails to be an address.

Attempts to counter hate speech through judicial means demanding state intervention could come into conflict with freedom of expression. Judith Butler has shown that judicial intervention could itself become an occasion for the perpetuation of violence. Judicial moves against hate speech often presuppose a determinate and necessary relation between speech and act. In hate speech, speech causes injury. Speech act theory accounts for injurious consequences of speech as the illocutionary effect. A judicial system that protects speech, judges the injurious character of a speech act in so far as speech is not only pure speech but also an act. Speech is injurious by constituting the addressee as a subject.

Judith Butler, while acknowledging that speech has a significant performative dimension, refuses to close the gap between speech and act. The US army has made a declaration that homosexuality is a condemnable act. However, Butler argues that declaration is not the same as being sexual or performing sexuality. The law treats the speech act as causative and constitutive.

Hate speech exposes our prior vulnerability to language. It addresses those who are already constituted by such addresses—those who are dependent on such addresses to be. When called a hurtful name, one is demeaned but also called into the language to respond.

Thus, the injurious address may appear to fix or paralyze the one it hails, but it may also produce an unexpected and enabling response. If to be addressed is to be interpellated, then the offensive call runs the risk of inaugurating a subject in speech who comes to use language to counter the offensive call (Butler 1997, 2).

Where does this resignifying potential of addressing lie? Ramachandra Gandhi, a prominent twentieth-century Indian philosopher explored addressing as the presupposition of human communication (Gandhi 1974). Drawing upon Whitehead's philosophy and the idea of non-dualism available in the life-world, Gandhi read Austin against the grain (Sanil 2013). He affirmed the primacy of communication over the transport of information or meaning. Communication is not a matter of convention or intention. It relates what is said to the event of saying. For him, reported speech is the paradigm of communication. While Austin claims that all saying is doing, Gandhi found saying in all doing. The clue lies in addressing.

Addressing is necessary and sufficient for communication. The act of addressing must imply both that S [speaker] wants A [addressee] to attend to S, and S's act must not be describable by A as S's trying to get A to notice S in some merely causal fashion.

> S addresses A if and only if S attracts A's attention to the fact that S is trying to attract A's attention to the fact that S is trying to attract A's attention to himself, i.e. to the fact that S wants A to attend to the fact that S wants A to attend to him. (Gandhi 1974, 39)

Addressing is the disavowal of the causal efficacy of communication. Telling someone something is a matter of "not really" trying to get someone to believe something or trying to get him to believe that the speaker believes something. According to Gandhi, to understand the notion of assertion—S telling A that P—is to understand how an action can both imply prima facie that: (a) S wanted A to believe P and (b) not imply prima facie that S was trying to get A to believe P. We can meet these contradictory demands by including "not really trying to do something" into the condition. "An ability to perform, and grasp the point of acts of "not really" trying to do to bring about something or the other is clearly a necessary presupposition of human communication." This "not really" is almost said without the force of assertion. This is the force frustrating gesture inherent to communication.

By granting priority to indirect speech, Gandhi agrees with Butler and Derrida who see citationality as constitutive of speech. In citationality, Gandhi sees speech's disavowal of force. Writing is prior to speech in so far as the former is silent. Silence addresses by abdicating all causal adequacy.

The mere saying of words is not sufficient for a speech act. It is not that something other than speech is required. The act here is internal to speech but irreducible to the transfer of information or meaning. Neither the presence of words nor adherence to conventions secures the uptake of a speech act. Let us take the speech act of warning. According to Austin, for the success of warning, the speaker should secure the uptake of the act as the act of warning. This means, there need not be any difference in the existing state of affairs as a result of that action. In cases like warning, the fact that the speech act does not produce any visible effect in the state of affairs may be a part of the intention. To warn someone I need to point out to him that he is in danger. In order to succeed in warning, I need to succeed in adverting to that fact. The uptake involves this event of adverting and not anything new in the state of affairs that can be represented as brought out by the successful performance of that act. In a case like warning, the change brought about by a successful speech act may just be the event or happening of the act.

How is warning different from a threat? A threat may be seen as a warning about possible harm or as a promise of possible hurt that will be caused. "I promise that I will kill you" is a threat. However, a threat is not a warning or a promise. To threaten to kill someone is not yet killing. It is speech that strives to get closer or appears to stay close to the act. The formal parallelism between promise and threat should not prevent us from noticing their difference. At the outset, we can see that promises are often accompanied with the declaration, "I promise" whereas threats are not prefaced by "I threaten you". While the success of a speech act does not depend on any specific string of words, the absence of an admission of the act in a threat says something about the nature of that speech act. While a promise contracts the speaker to a course of future action, a threat puts the burden on the listener. The aim of the threat is not to induce the listener to act but to force him to follow a direction. A warning brings some adverse factors to the attention of the listener and urges him to do something—or act freely to avoid their effect. A threat would like the listener to move only by the force of the threat. Here, we see the point of Habermas's claim that the speech act of threat has no illocutionary sense. It aims only at a perlocutionary effect. Threat achieves this by eschewing the "not really" clause of the address. A threat refrains from addressing and shuts off communication. Threat shares the linguistic features of interrogation identified by Elain Scarry (1985). During a torturous interrogation, the police force the victim to speak. However, this is no invitation to communication. It inflicts pain by suspending the very possibility of language.

Threat menacingly targets the listener's body. To see this, we need to acknowledge the role of the body in the speech act. The body enters the scene of speech act as a gesture. A gesture is not a communication-aid that accompanies speech. Nor is it a purposive action. For Gandhi, it is at once a miraculous and basic action. A basic action, as Danto (1965) defined, is an action about which we cannot ask "how did you do it?" Raising the finger is one such basic action.[4] A miracle is such a basic action. A miracle is miraculous even for the man who brings it about. Unlike a magician's trick, it does not incite your curiosity to get behind the action to seek an explanation. The agent is not the cause or initiator but a witness. A gesture, like a miraculous act, comes out of nothing. However, gestures are repetitive. They are simple movements of body parts and postures extracted from purposive and meaningful actions, recalled and presented on the body. Basic-miraculous-gestural actions invoke wonder and not curiosity because they wear their causal history on their sleeves.

What lies behind the action is neither a body nor a soul but only these basic actions and their self-intensifying repetitions. Gestures happen at once towards and away from the body (Gandhi 2002, 45).[5] According to Gandhi, as gesture speech itself addresses the speaker, speech begins by constituting the speaker himself as an addressee. Gesture opens up a space for all addresses to address the speaker. In this sense, a gesture is the locus of citationality in speech. A gesture is theatrical or staged. It is the non-seriousness that is constitutive of all speech acts.

According to Butler, the power of a proper name is an exemplary instance to study how speech can hurt. The subject is interpellated through naming. Naming fixes the addressee as a singular entity located in space and time. Butler emphasizes the other pole of singularity of the reference in the social character of the name. One can name only in so far as one is already named and that too without necessarily knowing how one was named so. The addressee of the name can also name others and be named by more than one name. For Butler, this socio-historical dimension preserves the resignifying potential of speech.

Butler is right in emphasizing that naming is also addressing. However, she commits the error that Kripke (1980) has warned us against when she locates addressing in the social dimension and leaves the referring function of name to fixing the singular as this or that. According to Kripke, a name is a rigid designator. We may use a description to secure our reference to the named. However, the name is not a description or a bundle of descriptions that the named object satisfies. Shakespeare is the author of Macbeth. One may secure the reference of the name with that description. Imagine that historical research has proved that Macbeth was written not by the person called Shakespeare, but by another person. We would not follow our description and call the "writer of Macbeth" Shakespeare but would only say that Shakespeare did not write Macbeth.

However, in hate speech, the name is used in a demeaning manner. Butler explains this by shifting the focus to the descriptive content that is used to fix the name. It is true that some demeaning descriptions interfere with the referring operation of the name. However, the hurting power of a name needs to be accounted for on the referential dimension that is proper to the name.

Vrinda Dalmiya proposes a framework to track the interference of hurting descriptions in the proper work of names (Dalmiya 1999). The "annihilatory model" she proposes for examining sexual harassment helps us in understanding the destructive work of hate speech. Harassment annihilates the victim by reducing her to the status of a thing. Dalmiya uses modal logic to uncover the logic of demeaning reference. A singular term normally has a purely referential function. A singular term could also attribute something to the referent. When I say "Smith's murderer is insane", I am referring to the murderer, but "Smith's murderer" is essential to what I say. I mean "whoever murdered Smith" is insane. The murderer of Smith, Alan, is Mary's brother. However, "Smith's murderer is insane" does not mean that "Mary's brother is insane". Though "Smith's murderer" and "Mary's brother" have the same referent, these clauses are not substitutable. Substitutivity of co-referential terms fails even if we know who Smith's murderer is and that he is Mary's brother. Here, the singular term or name enters into what is said. The term Smith's murderer if used purely referentially should have picked up Alan. However, it enters into what is said about Alan and makes that the condition for predicating insanity to him.

It would be sexually harassing to refer to Rita, who is a blonde, as "that blonde". "That blonde" enters into what I say about her. We refer to a person with the aid of some description and then attribute that description to her and make that a condition for making further predications. This, according to Dalmiya, erases the personhood of the named. The description, also being a name, makes the description the definition of the named. From the first-person point of view, this definition is not acceptable to the named. However, the issue here is not about using a false description. Being mistaken about others does not constitute harassment. An unacceptable description usurps the power of a name.

Dalmiya's account locates the harassing power of a name in the conflict of the interfering description with the self-description of the named. The violence, in this case, is caused by the content of the description. The ascription "the blonde" does not agree with the named ones self-description. It does not tell us how the description hurts as a name. Names do not conflict. Changing the self-definition of Rita need not blunt the hurting power of "the blonde". Being blond could very well be Rita's favoured self-description. Does that remove the demeaning nature of the name "the blonde"?

This problem is clearly visible in the case of stereotypes. Take the stereotypical use of "the Muslim" in India. The connotation, in this case, could be "the anti-national". We may try to enlighten the stereotypist by showing that the majority of Muslims are patriotic and there are many Hindus who are anti-national. The stereo-typist would readily agree with this as if this is obvious. However, the power of the stereotype lies elsewhere. The user may tell us that the majority of Muslims may be patriotic but there are some Muslims who are anti-national because they are Muslims. The Hindu anti-national are an accident of history. They are not anti-national by virtue of being Hindus. The availability of neither true nor authentic descriptions could counter the hate-name.

Zizek's Lacanian take on Kripke could be helpful here (Zizek 2008, 97). He notices that Kripke's examples (1980) of rigid designators are mostly objects of fantasy like unicorn and gold! Unicorns are fictional creatures. Imagine that we encounter an animal that satisfies all the descriptions we have about unicorns. According to Kripke, that animal will not be properly called by the name "unicorn". The name unicorn has something that is in excess of all descriptions of it. The name names this excess. Zizek holds that both descriptivist and anti-descriptivist approaches to naming miss this point. Both these approaches are based on their own founding myths. The anti-descriptivist holds that things receive their names in a primal baptismal ceremony and the reference is secured in a causal communication history where everyone uses the name as it was used before. The descriptivist uses the myth of a primitive tribe that bans the use of name after the person is dead. In such a tribe, names will refer without a causal history of use. For Zizek, both the descriptivist and the anti-descriptivist miss the radical contingency of name that is hooked on to an excess of descriptions. A name refers to the mere fact an object is called by that name. Even in the descriptivist's tribe, the name works just because it is the name. No knowledge of historical continuity that the anti-descriptivist's omniscient historical observer gathers is required to secure the name. The name has to be used as a name in order to be a name! The name refers to an object because this object is called that. The passive voice "is called" indicates the social dimension of naming as much as the natural/causal dimension. This call of being addressed cannot be interpreted as being called by empirical others. Everyone who uses that name takes it from a causal chain that begins with the contingent event of baptizing. The speech act of baptism succeeds if the uptake is a success— that means the name is repeated. (In many Indian cultures, during the naming ceremony, in addition to calling the child by the public name, a divine name—a name of Shiva or Parvati, depending on the gender—is whispered in its ears!)

Adorno notices the element of nature in names. Today, this natural-causal power of the name is preserved only in nicknames, which, despite being violent, make us laugh.

Even though laughter is still the sign of force, an outburst of blind and callous nature, it also has within it the opposite element: In laughter, blind nature precisely becomes aware of itself as such and therewith renounces destructive forces. This double meaning of laughter is akin to that of the name, and perhaps names are nothing but frozen laughter, as nicknames are today the only names in which something of the primordial act of name-giving lives on.

It is this power of nature that can be mobilized for resignifying hate-names. Already, Laughter is a counter speech. Butler locates the resignifying potential of speech in the constitutive failure of speech acts, the social dimension of names and the vulnerability of the address. However, she indicates a positive rendition when she quotes Shoshana Felman who says, "Failure (misfire) can be defined as what is sexual in every human act" (Butler 1997, 166). When an utterance misfires, the act is void and without effect. But this does not mean that nothing has been done. Much has been done except the purported act. For example, when a couple already married utter the formula for marriage-act, the speech act misfire, however, they have done many things including committing bigamy![6] This excess of the necessary infelicities ensure the gap between the speech and act and offer the possibility for restaging hate-speech.

To Love Our Brothers in Hatred

How can hate be transformed into love? What are the resources hate possesses to work on itself and to re-signify itself? Is there a passage between love and hate? Should we hate hatred the way we hate other things? Nietzsche and Spinoza in different ways pursued these questions. They both saw in hate something more than a mere negation of love. It is not a question of following the Christian advice to shift the target of hate from the sinner to the sin. It is also not an appeal to recognize the evilness of hate, feel guilty about it and stop hating. Both Nietzsche and Spinoza explore the possibility of a moral work of hate that can bring about transformation. For both, passions could think and trans-value themselves.

Nietzsche takes his lesson on the transformation of hate from Buddha! "Not by enmity is enmity ended; by friendliness enmity is ended:" These words stand at the beginning of the doctrine of the Buddha. It is not morality that speaks thus; this speaks physiology. (Nietzsche 1989b, I6/230).

Nietzsche clearly distinguishes Buddha from Christ. The Buddhist percept is very different from the Christian advice to love one's enemy. For Nietzsche, Buddha's is not a piece of moral advice but a physiological diagnosis. Buddha proposed more of hygiene than a religion. For Buddha ending enmity is overcoming ressentiment and the urge for revenge. Christian love is hatred and revenge in disguise. To be friendly with the enemy means to take pride in your enemy—not to treat him with contempt or with vengefulness (Siemens 2015).

Hatred is a quality of life. Enmity arises out of life's drive to assimilate that which is alien to it. Hatred is the feeling towards that which resists assimilation. The aversion towards alien blood exists at the level of a lower form of life. At the level of individuated life, such aversion is coordinated in creative ways so that hate seeks the blood of the aliens to feed on. This is precisely what morality refuses.

A genealogy of hate tracks its origin to the feeling of aversion towards the ugly. Reactive morality condemns the ugly as hateworthy and sinful and also celebrates it as the site of empathy and redemption. Morality makes us hate our aversion towards the ugly. It is not morally correct to despise anyone as ugly. We are taught to look for a beautiful soul in everything ugly. This is what the slave does with his hatred. On the one hand, we are trained to find ugliness everywhere, but, on the other, we are asked to elevate the poor, the weak and the ugly to the status of good. The priest, in his impotence, disguises his hatred in the form of love. The priestly hatred created a distinction between the sin and the sinner and made only the former and not the latter hate-worthy. By weakening the entity-directedness of hate and redirecting it to the features, the priest tames the power of hate to suit his own weakness. We are allowed to hate not the enemy but injustice. Self-hatred and self-denial are raised to the status of ideals. For Nietzsche, the war on hatred is the most deviously hateful war. The ascetic morality parades its own inability to take revenge as forgiveness. Nietzsche asks, "These cellar rodents full of vengefulness and hatred—what have they made of revenge and hatred?" (Nietzsche 1989a, I4/48).

Nietzsche sought the possibility of cultivating active hatred. He notices that hate is amenable to idealization. The priest uses this to serve his weakness. How can we master hatred by drawing upon its active and affirmative force? We need to protect it from the loss-making economies of revenge and contempt. We think that we can get rid of hate and fear but we do not try to get rid of other unpleasant drives like hunger, thirst or defecation. In any case, the Amoeba moves its pseudopods towards objects not out of hunger. Nietzsche tried to mobilize the life-affirming nature of such primitive attraction and revulsion for the transvaluation of hate. To affirm hatred means to take pride in one's enemies. We bring them under the condition of our success. We love our brothers-in-hatred not just our brothers in love.[7]

For Spinoza hate is a sad passion. "When the Mind imagines those things that diminish or restrain the Body's power of acting, it strives, as far as it can, to recollect things that exclude their existence" (Spinoza 1996, III, Proposition 13). Love is joy and hate is sadness both accompanied by the idea of an external cause. The movement from hate to love is a movement from sadness to joy and from the feeling of less power to more power.

Spinoza's ethics count on the occurrence of encounters with things and people. In these encounters, the relations that make us are composed of the relations that make others. Something is bad if it decomposes my relations. God asked Adam not to eat the apple because the latter would decompose Adam's body. Adam misrecognized his ignorance of a fact as a violation of moral law and this would sadden his soul in a manner more damaging than what the apple could do to his body. We hate something when we locate the cause of our pain in an external thing or person. We wish to destroy the cause to reduce pain. However, hate reduces the degree of power that I am.

Take the action of hitting someone or something.[8] I am affirming the power of my body when I close my fist and bring power to my hand. However, when I hit someone in hate my power gets into a bad relation with the image of my enemy. This relationship is bad because it destroys the relations that constitute the body of my enemy. I go through the same motions when I hammer a nail on the wall. Here the action is associated with the image of a thing whose relations agree with it. The good and the bad here are not a matter of utility or intention nor do they reside in the act itself. What matters here is the relation, the image the act has with the image of the object.

It is possible to conquer hate with love and such love is more intense than that if hate had not preceded it. However, this is no reason to hate someone so that we can love him more intensely later. If we desire to hate someone then we will have all reasons to hate him more hoping to increase love at a later date! Breaking the head of my enemy would make me happy. This joy is small compensation for the decomposition of relations. However, even such small joy can compose new relations. Indignation offers such a possibility. Indignation is the hate towards someone who has damaged another whom we love. If someone whom we love hates what we also hate then our hate will be intensified. We want those whom we love to love what we love and hate what we hate. All this could lead to everyone hating everyone else! However, indignation towards tyranny could be the path from hate to love.

In *Ethics*, Spinoza charts several passages between hate and love. Some of these involve "vacillations of effects". We may feel love and hate towards the same object. Just as there is no hope without fear and vice versa, there is no hate without love and no love without hate. These vacillations are the product of imagination. "If we imagine that a thing which usually affects us with the affect of sadness is like another which usually affects us with an equally great affect of joy, we shall hate it and at the same time love it". The constitution of the mind that arises from two contrary affects is called vacillation (Spinoza 1996, III, Proposition 17). This vacillation is the work of imagination. It is comparable to doubt which is also the work of imagination. The imagination that affirms the presence of its object is also affected by causes that exclude such a presence. The vacillation could be caused by the contingent relations of the object or by relations inherent to the mind. Imagination cannot sustain this posited presence of the object. With time it loses its focus and could wander towards other objects. However, reason can take over and sustain the work of imagination through common notions.[9] In doubt, under the power of reason, the mind vacillates but with more affirmative power. (Unlike Descartes, Spinoza does not see the doubt as hollowing itself out to reach certainty. Doubt occurs when imagination follows the sign of truth. Reason takes hold of doubt by focussing the mind on truth and not on signs of truth.)

Indignation is hate but under the power of love. It brings the indignant ones together. It is born out of a desire to be with others. Coming together to form common notions itself is a work of reason. Spinoza (1996, III, Proposition 45) makes a distinction between mockery and laughter. When hate dominates, indignation takes delight in the sad cruelty of mockery. Only a savage and sad superstition ascribes virtue to sadness and tears. This joyous coming together in laughter could free our indignation from the sadness of hatred. Spinoza insists that we need to eat and drink well and laugh with others. Then we are already on our way to joy and perfection. Generosity lies in repaying hate with love. This is not the same as loving one's enemy. We need to laugh with our enemy. This is how we forge "common notions".

The common notion is the knowledge-path between hate and love. Spinoza (1996, II Proposition 37–40) distinguishes common notions from abstract ideas. The latter is the work of imagination that generalizes based on some trait or other. A common notion is the representation of the composition of the relations between bodies affecting each other. We form common notions based on joyful encounters and these notions, in turn, engender active passions. Common notions secure agreements and also understand the reasons for these agreements. They understand affect in terms of internal causes. The transformation of hate to love involves the formation of adequate knowledge about the causes of feelings. Since this knowledge involves the composition of bodily states and images of these states it is not abstract knowledge but more a matter of physiology of emotions. Spinoza is clear; hate is bad and god can only be loved. The idea of god is already adequate knowledge and not a sign or a guarantor of knowledge and love. Since both love and hate involve inadequate knowledge in terms of external causes, in the idea of god one overcomes both love and hate.

He who rightly knows that all things follow from the necessity of the divine nature, and happen according to the eternal laws and rules of nature, will surely find nothing worthy of hate, mockery or disdain, nor anyone whom he will pity. Instead, he will strive, as far as human virtue allows, to act well, as they say, and rejoice (Spinoza 1996, IV Proposition 50, Scholium).

Against Hobbes, Spinoza holds that society cannot come out of the sad passion of fear. Nothing agrees with human nature than human nature itself! We attain perfection by forming a community. Hate is transformed into love in the collective construction of a community. Hate's wisdom is expressed in indignation towards tyranny and in hating solitude. We, the people, brothers in hate!

Let us note the profound agreement between Nietzsche and Spinoza on the nature of the wisdom of hate—it is at once physiology and hetero-phenomenology of emotions. Spinoza says

> So I've contemplated human affects—like love, hate, anger, envy, love of esteem, compassion, and the other emotions—not as vices of human nature, but as properties which pertain to it in the same way heat, cold, storms, thunder, etc., pertain to the nature of the air. Though

> these things are inconvenient, they're still necessary, and have definite causes, through which we strive to understand their nature.

Both these thinkers approach hate as an impersonal emotion. They begin with the body's response to stimuli of affinity and aversion. Emotions are diagrams that map these sensations. These maps are recorded and complied at multiple locations. At this level of sub-personal volitional formations that happen below the level of beliefs and desires, we do not encounter a self who is the owner of his feelings. The experiencer is not a centred subject but is woven by the threads of emotions themselves. Emotions are already management of our inner foreignness. The rational subject appears a bit late on the scene. No wonder, philosophers who try to guide passions and people end up writing satires instead of Ethics or Politics. The task of the reason is to upgrade our status as feelers from that of Nietzsche's impotent priests of reason to Spinoza's God.

Notes

1 An early version of this chapter was presented as a talk at the Centre for Languages, JNU, New Delhi. I thank Anomita Goswamy for reading, commenting and correcting the draft.

2 Che Guevara, Message to the Tricontinental. Available at https://www.marxists.org/archive/guevara/1967/04/16.htm (last accessed 18 February 2020).

3 For a discussion on the work of hate in the motherly love of the Greek character Medea, see Sanil (2010).

4 Arthur Danto, "Basic Actions," *American Philosophical Quarterly* 2, no. 2 (April 1965).

5 Ramachandra Gandhi, *Svaraj: A Journey with Tyeb Mehta's "Shantiniketan Triptych"* (New Delhi: Vadehra Art Gallery, 2002).

6

> Two final words about being void or without effect. This does not mean, of course, to say that we won't have done anything: lots of things will have been done—we shall most interestingly have committed the act of bigamy—but we shall not have done the purported act, viz. marrying. (Austin 1975, 17)

7 Nietzsche (1989b, I 14/48): "What there is left for them to love on earth is not their brothers in hatred but their 'brothers in love', as they put it, all the good and just on earth."

8 Deleuze discussed this example in his lecture on Spinoza. See Gilles Deleuze, "Lecture Transcripts on Spinoza's Concept of Affect". Available at http://www.webdeleuze.com/php/sommaire.html (last accessed 18 February 2020).

9 Common notion is a notion common to all bodies or minds. Being in motion or rest is common to all bodies. Love too is a common notion. According to Deleuze, Spinoza's common notion is affect-idea. Gilles Deleuze, "Lecture Transcripts on Spinoza's Concept of Affect".

References

Austin, J.L. *How to do Things with Words*. Edited by J.O. Urmson and Marina Sbisà. Cambridge: Harvard University Press, 1975.

Butler, Judith. *Excitable Speech: A Politics of the Performative*. London: Routledge, 1997.

Dalmiya, Vrinda. "Why is Sexual Harassment Wrong?" *Journal of Social Philosophy* 30, no. 1 (1999): 46–64.

Goswami, C.L., trans. *Srimadbhagavatam*, Vol. I & II (with text in Devanagari and translated into English). Gorakhpur: Gita Press, 1982.

Kripke, Saul. *Naming and Necessity*. Cambridge, Massachusetts: Harvard University Press, 1980.

MacKinnon, Catharine. *Only Words*. Cambridge, Massachusetts: Harvard University Press, 1993.

Nietzsche, Friedrich. *Genealogy of Morals*. Translated by Walter Kaufmann. New York: Vintage Books, 1989a.

Ramachandra Gandhi. *Presuppositions of Human Communication*. Delhi: Oxford University Press, 1974.

——. *Ecce Homo*. Translated by Walter Kaufmann. New York: Vintage Books, 1989b.

Rosen, Steven J. "The Reincarnation(s) of Jaya and Vijaya: A Journey through the Yugas Journal of Vaishnava Studies". *Religions* 8, no. 9 (2017): 178.

Sanil, V. "On Hating One's Own Children." In *Grounding Morality: Freedom, Knowledge and the Plurality of Cultures*, edited by Jyotirmaya Sharma and A. Raghuramaraju, 25–42. New Delhi: Routledge, 2010.

——. "On Rambling Wisdom." In *Ramchandra Gandhi: The Man and His Philosophy*, edited by A. Raghuramaraju, 8–24. New Delhi: Routledge, 2013.

Scarry, Elaine. *The Body in Pain*. Oxford: Oxford University Press, 1985.

Sheth, Noel. "Salvation Through Hatred," *Annals of the Bhandarkar Oriental Research Institute* 80, no. 1/4 (1999): 167–181.

Siemens, Herman W. "Nietzsche's Philosophy of Hatred," *Tijdschrift voor Filosofie* 77, no. 4 (2015): 747–784.

Spinoza, Benedict de. *Ethics*, edited and translated by Edwin Curley. London: Penguin, 1996.

Zizek, Slavoj. *The Sublime Object of Ideology*. London: Verso, 2008.

3

THE 'ISMOS' OF THE MANY

Shaj Mohan

Man has to awaken to wonder—and so perhaps do peoples.
—*Wittgenstein,* Culture and Value

'Populism' can be defined as politics conducted in an impoverished language about poverty.[1] The questioning of the realities of these two poverties—of thought and living conditions—whose provenance is the same, still retains the meaning of the more recent division of politics into the bio-spatial coordinate of right and left. The slick hierophants of the former tactfully assert that a reason is still being exercised in the impoverished language. The latter assuages, sugar coats, by comparing the fact of poverty with the scale of historic poverty and accuses us of exiguity of the desire to pursue radical changes, such as veganism and other moral determinations of everyday life, in other words, *hypophysics.* It is important to register that today the bio-spatial coordinates have a meaning only in relation to what is being called 'populism'. But before we come to reckon with the conditions under which 'populism' sustains itself—primarily the technological condition—it is necessary to understand what it means to call a collection of men 'people'. The mysterious value invested in this notion—'*the people is the good*'—has allowed confusions of concepts (for example, Heidegger on the 'volk' and 'dwelling') and the logics of miracles (Walter Benjamin's 'divine violence') to cover over the ground of politics. Instead of falling into the temptations of 'the people' (which helped to create 'Anna Hazare events' in India that led to the Hindu fascist ascension) one must ask 'what is a people?' in order to find out if there is such a thing. Further, one must examine the functional isolations through which men are determined as a people such that an 'ismos' assigns to them a state of being self-immured and according to which they come to be the end for which they alone are the means.

The Term

Populism says nearly nothing. When one defines a doctrine in accordance with a genus it would certainly delineate that which lies outside it, in the manner of recording a gentle contrariness as Aristotle would have thought. For instance when we consider 'Zoo-ism' it retains within it the possibility for something like a 'humanism' to be articulated as a species, although explicitly it merely separates itself from the 'non-Zoos'. The people implies a collection of men who are distinguished from a collection of petals, of stones, of prime numbers; more precisely the 'non-people'. That is, an 'ism' of the people does not say much, except that it is concerned with the abstracted people from the various determinate gatherings of men and that it is not concerned with any other animal. But it indicates an underlying condition; it is difficult today to define any 'ism' as such without some embarrassment, or that there is a consensus that we have found the end of 'ismos' (-ισμός). We resist witnessing the contours of what is now called the people because it may be a certain image which could force us to abandon all our familiar notions of politics and, we are forced to reckon through it with something other than 'man' (as that which makes 'the people') emerge in the determination of all values which is technological determinism.

But before we come to the new image of politics we have to have familiarity with the 'ismos'. The 'ismos' suffix is used to create abstract nouns that refer to something which is not a particular thing but that which may define a particular thing as that very thing, such as truth rather than something true, or Marxism rather than Marx. The abstract nouns derived through the suffix –ισμός tend to indicate something of a doctrine which corresponds then to a set of practices with regularity. For example, one would not speak of a 'pollen-ism', unless we had already derived a concept through analogy from pollens. On the other hand when we speak of 'Marxism' it refers to a set of doctrines derived from the corpus of Marx, from which one can then obtain a limited number of distinct regularities through the selection of groups from the given set of doctrines. The Marxism of Lenin, say, is distinct from that of Mao, although they are both Marxism*s*.

The practice of denoting states or defining regularities or creating abstract nouns through –ismos has had a theological passage and not a theological origin. Its early religious use was to denote doctrinally bound religious practices that could display regularity of conduct in the everyday life of the believer, including Judaismos and Christianism. The schoolmen would continue to derive abstract nouns to mark doctrines and distinct theological approaches such as Thomism and Scottism.

The secular usage of –ισμός came to be common from eighteenth century onwards, as we can see in the 'Spinozism' contests of Germany. Politics was soon defined as a battle of competing –ισμός which we often mistakenly called ideological battles.[2] The regularities of practices and regularized projects include socialism, communism, liberalism and situationism. We also found the extrication of doctrines from the corpus of individuals to derive –isms, the –ισμός of proper names—Leninism, Maoism, Trotskyism and Gandhism. It is well known that these constitutions of abstract nouns in politics that originated in the nineteenth century were reliant on the place of 'rumen', a room for turning over and over, vacated by Christianism. The 'rumen' was where Christian theologies determined human essence through the permutations of the relation between the creator and the creatures with respect to *being* in such a way that one could set a for-what or telos for man which in turn could be used to prescribe forms of regularity for familial civil life. For example, if one were to argue that the creature and the creator are determinations of something prior, say *being*, this would grant man the status of *a finite god* and for the creator the position of *the infinite man*. Following from that, people would be a collection of finite gods. There are versions of this problematic in both Duns Scotus and M.K. Gandhi. However, by the time Christianity vacated the 'rumen', the conceptual resources and the tendencies of thoughts had been the engines of the turning over of man—that is, the discoveries of various regularities of man with respect to the infinite man—were exhausted. Yet, in the political abstract nouns derived from proper names entertained the sense of a finite destiny which did not refer man to the creator or the infinite man, rather to man himself as something which could determine a historical bound for itself. We should note for now that the practitioners of all these political abstract nouns of the past would not deny that they were concerned with the people and only the people.

The proliferation of 'isms' in the last century denoted the confidence in the creation of new regularities while we must note that it was also the century which extended the critique of 'essences' towards the 'criticalisation' of –ισμός; a related but distinct group of activities of the latter kind came to have their own schools, and –ισμός including deconstructionism and existentialism. The –isms of the last century while proliferating it were, at the same time, relieving it of any 'essentiality' and in that they were 'anti-isms'.

To a political –ισμός belongs a man who is then the –ianus of it; the latter is the man who adheres to the doctrines named by the former abstract noun, such as a socialist is someone adhering to socialism—the model of doctrine and the adherent. The doctrine makes it possible for the adherent to constitute various regular relations within the milieu of the doctrine, such as 'friend and enemy', the blasphemer, the renegade and the dissident. One can observe this tendency in the doctrinal schools of philosophy too, where the followers of a certain doctrine would either designate other distinct and interesting doctrines in their neighbourhoods to be a species of their own or some other similar doctrines which are less interesting as belonging to the opposite doctrinal school. The little distinctions that make the greatest differences in philosophy thus remain hidden for the adherents.

The Use

We can now come to the beginning of our search for the –ismos of the people: populism or, people-ism, came to be when the –ισμός had already lost its provenances and for this reason in a crowd named as 'populist' one will not find an *–ianus* or the doctrine and the adherent. As we know Walter Benjamin sought to find the occasions and the conditions under which a crowd emerges through the screens of doctrines and laws that had established regularities for it. Benjamin's text, despite the efforts at remaining elusive, has a simple thesis: The regular forms of the people comprehended by law are maintained only through what he called mundane 'violence' and it is broken through a form of 'violence' which cannot be comprehended by the law that prescribes (and describes) the regularities of the people and for this reason he called it 'divine' that was his way of retaining a relation to the theological problematic of contingency and miracle as the conditions for the moral life of man. If this model could explain the people-isms of analog today then we will have arrived at the epoch of Benjamin-ism, and what we call 'populism' will be the beginning of the perpetual reign of divine violence. However, 'populism' may indicate something else altogether as we will find.

We know that this is not quite the case with almost any particular phenomenon we have been designating as populist. Rather, we find that most populist political formations resemble 'fascisms' and that the exceptions constituted by 'welfarisms' and 'socialisms' indicate that people have come to be something easily determinable, a collection of men with a propensity to any regularity whatsoever as long as it is not meant for a long time. In other words, programmability marks men in the era of populism. Martin Heidegger, while aligning with Nazism, was aware of the incipient forms of politics. Heidegger delivered a lecture course in 1934 at the University of Freiburg that was published later under the title "Logic as the Question Concerning the Essence of Language". The relation between the title of the lecture and the contents are not evident at first since the contents of the lecture are concerned with the determination of a people, of 'volk' and Nazism.

As with his other texts of this period, Heidegger was pursuing here something like a decline in the history of being. That is, the departure from the experience of being filled with the wonder found in the texts of the pre-Socratics was set aside by Plato's determination of being as 'Idea' which set aside the mystery of being in favour of the explanatory power given by the gathering of things under their 'aspect' led to the path marks through which metaphysics—the determination of being as a being—would lead to technology. The text refers to the original experience of logos as the comportment or being in the same milieu which unsettlingly differs with itself, as the gathering. The experience of coming to be in the milieu of 'the same' was eventually surrendered to logic as the rule-governed ordering of propositions—"It is the science of the forms of the fundamental structures and fundamental rules of the proposition".[3] Further, language too is found to reach the status of a mere domain of things to be ordered and organized in his time.

All of these changes—from logos to reason and language to linguistics—are found to be in a reciprocal relationship with 'the people' which Heidegger would explore later in his texts on technology. In 1934, Heidegger would expose something that remained mysterious about his own works and now unambiguously revealed in the recently published "Black Notebooks": We can call it the meaning of the community, 'the gathering', of being, which determines the meaning of being. Then, the question will be what is the community which is the ideal milieu which can be home to being's mystery? There are several divisions and distinctions throughout this text which explores 'the people' or 'the volk'. To obtain a sense of being of those days we will have to look at a lengthy passage:

> In a census, the *Volk* is counted in the sense of the population, the population, in so far as it constitutes the body of the *Volk*, the inhabitants of the land. At the same time, it is to be considered that in a governmental *order* of the census a certain part of the *Volk* is included, namely the part that dwells within the State's borders. The German nationals living abroad are not included in the count, [they] do not belong in this sense to the *Volk*. On the other hand, those can also be included in the count, *those who, taken racially, are of alien breed, do not belong to the Volk.*[4]

There is much to be understood from these passages for which Heidegger's own conceptual apparatus are inadequate, or perhaps their adequacy was always concerned with masking the quest for the community of being.

Two distinct logics are running through Heidegger's corpus which are deliberately left entangled. We can call them *analogy* and *homology*.[5] Analogy, as we know, finds the proportion a thing has with some other thing and the discovery of the form under which the proportion is distributed is the work of reason; in general, analogy is presented through the mathematical expression A:B and B:C which can often be described under field laws. Analogy allows us to move between distinct domains that may have no prior relation or the domains which are without something common between them and reason invents the ground on which these relations can be formalized. For example, the function of flight is analogous between a hummingbird and a drone. Analogy directs us towards the freedom for exchanging functions. Homology, on the other hand, is concerned with relations that reveal 'the pre-formal'[6] shared 'something'; what we often insufficiently call the materiality is that which is designated by homology. It is through homology that we find the constructability of something held in some other thing; the reed turning to the flute is possible through the discovery of homology. These two relations can be contrasted through the example of the 'population' of a typical Indian village. Two men from the same village without any familial ties will refer to one another as brothers since most of the functions of brotherly relations can be extended to neighbours and friends; and often they expect brotherly commitments from each other. At the same time when they are concerned with their land and property only 'the blood brothers' can enter into sharing arrangements. In the former the latter relation finds its analogue—the village is analogous to the home, although homology distinguishes the blood brother from the village brother.

In most senses 'Dasein', "the being for whom its own being is the question", is something prior to the faculties of analogy and homology. It is a being which witnesses in the nothing of the question—*Why there is something rather than nothing?*—the pressure of the unnameable plenitude which is its futurality; the nothing is the experience of more than everything. Yet, the abstract 'Dasein' which is both man and not-man, while experiencing in the 'something' homological powers and time as the freedom given by analogies, retains a particular determination of homology as 'race'. The 'Dasein' of a racial community is different from that of a band of men constituted by chance or of a motley crew. From here onwards, it is not a question of the precise nature of Heidegger's racism but the scale of values according to which peoples are ranked.

Heidegger's thought is on the one hand, like all those who are called philosophers, thought without any regard to a particular person. On the other hand, as we have found, he conducted himself like the worst of 'bourgeois thinkers' in the sense in which Wittgenstein used the term for Ramsay—"he thought with aim of clearing up the affairs of some particular community".[7]

Heidegger himself would remark on the two senses of 'race'—on the one hand, it merely indicates bloodlines and on the other, it also indicates a certain hierarchy or order of rank—"That which is racy embodies a certain rank, provides certain laws, does not concern in the first place the corporeality of the family and of lineage." As we know Gandhi undertook similar embarrassing argumentative steps to justify the caste order. The experience of *being* given for the people who are in this sense of a 'higher rank' is greater than that of the motley crew. Then, we can also argue that the history of being corresponds to departure from 'the people of rank' towards the motley crew—the decline. Even in the Heideggerian sense, the nature of such a process cannot be called metaphysical; that is, metaphysics is the determination of *being* as *a* being such that beings appear as that which is free for any logical organization.

Underneath metaphysics lies another science in the corpus of Heidegger which is hypophysics. According to hypophysics, nature as that which is originary is identical with value, or a thing is at its highest rank in its originary nature. That is, unlike metaphysics which actively finds all the possibilities of things encoded in a domain that is unlike the domain of things, hypophysics claims a passive reception of the conjoinment of value in nature. From a hypophysical point of view, physics and metaphysics are operations that denature nature or the practices through which one descends in an order of rank[8] towards the motley crew. The Greek men who were given the originary experience of being were not 'an arbitrary population and residents'. On the other hand, the Americans who are the objects of Heidegger's 'Introduction to Metaphysics' are precisely the arbitrary population, who signalled for Heidegger the pincer movement along with the Russians against the essence of the higher ranking Germans. Hence, a hypophysics articulates Heidegger's history of being and his interpretation of metaphysics from underneath 'the ground', or as the ur-ground.

Population Politics

Hypophysics led Heidegger to another discovery. Population, as counted by the census operations of the state, is indifferent to races of men and their ranks and the highest possibility of the State is to dissolve all orders of rank. That is, it reveals a certain epoch of freedom—both the voluptuousness of homologies and the unhomeliness of analogies—in such a way that thought is left disoriented, without a *right and left*[9] for it to recover its position in the darkest night. He would call a moment in this epoch without orientation as 'population politics'. Heidegger designated through 'population politics' the comprehending of a people as the single empty aggregation exogenously corporealized, described and organized through the regularities given by the laws of the state which was made possible by the decline from logos to logic. We can now designate something more than what Heidegger intended by this term; population politics[10] is the possibility of processing people as indifferent quantities through algorithms. That is, population politics is one of the limited possibilities of politics from the point of view of a new form of technocratic state that was anticipated by Heidegger and other thinkers. However, we are aware of another possibility that people can commune without the restricted homology of bloodlines. The idealized understanding of both America and Soviet Russia was something akin to it. Today this possibility is being realized and it implies that *everyone can be everywhere.*[11] It is perhaps the resistance to this possibility that dominates most political movements we call 'populist'.

It is here that 'populism' comes to be the symptom of a crisis in politics. The two tendencies that underlie politics are seeking to be the law which comprehends all organizations of people, and the very meaning of community and the common which is stasis of politics today. The tendency to constitute communities by relying on the regularities founded on hypophysical principles where the understanding of homology is limited to bloodlines is opposed to the tendency of constituting a motley crew of people, indifferent to their blood ties banding and disbanding according to no determinate rules nor principles other than the pursuit of this very freedom. Most versions of communism are restricted understandings of the latter possibility or the unhomeliness of man.[12] This notion that brings people together in uncanny ways without –ismos can be marked as *anismos*. In the communes and occupations of many of the protest movements today, the 'do it yourself' cultures which came with them, and the networks of sharing services which came up in Greece during the anti-austerity protests, one can sense the tendency of anismos. In the protests against the migrants, the hate crimes on the basis of bloodlines, in the events which began with Brexit and in the increasing calls for the technologization of borders we can sense the politics of *a* people or *Volk*. In other words, a process which surrenders freedom for the retention of bloodlines discards politics itself for its only objective is freedom.

The assumption that populism is the co-existence of these two tendencies—*anismos* and *Volk making*—relies on liberalism in its metaphysical sense. The metaphysics of liberalism asserts that all tendencies can co-exist in politics. For example, it is known to us through experience that Nazism and constitutional liberalism could not co-exist. Rather a tendency—say anti-corruption—in politics either dissolves other tendencies—such as secularism—or appropriate the competing tendencies—such as ethno-nationalism. Across the world, and in India, this particular form itself has been witnessed in the past decade of ethnocentric fascisms which assume moral positions.

Thus, instead of the pure presence of a people without determinations, we find that there are two tendencies which characterize 'populism' *Volk making* and *anismos* and we know that the former apparently dominates populism. This could be because the milieu of Volk making, of social orderings which are concerned with their ceremonial repetition such that bloodlines are conserved, is disappearing. Instead, the real contest in politics today is between *anismos* and population politics; that is, these two tendencies have already departed from the vanishing milieu of *Volk making*. Yet, as we found earlier, they share an important difference—while assuming the unhomeliness of man as that which is capable of freedoms which are incalculable, population politics seeks to determine people as something which can be algorithmically organized and mechanically regulated. Population politics is in preparation within what appears to be technologized border controls and biometric attested tracking of people in real-time.

The Fleeing Being

Earlier we indicated that our familiar concepts which delineated man, and hence people, are inadequate to think the new milieu of population politics. In what appears to be the immune reaction against refugees in the 'populisms' of most parts of the world, the very essence of man as the fleeing being is finally being revealed, despite the disastrous resistance to this idea, including the holocaust. The relation between the *refugee* and the *human* should be reconceived in such a way that we may not end up with a fetishism of the refugee. We conceive the human today as the complete subject of a state with all the rights it provides, and the refugee as someone who lacks it. Then, the problem is with the very notion of this *human* subject—*citizen* if you like—who has created its other in the *refugee*.

The word refugee comes from the Latin 'fugio', meaning 'to flee', to depart. Our 'species' is essentially the being which flees, or takes refuge, away from nature—the being which masters hypophysics in order to evade it. As Kafka said, the being which is always in search of the '*elsewhere*' or '*away from here*'. The migration of the human out of Africa is only an expression of this essential *fugio-ness* of man. When a human settlement, any stable arrangement, starts to crystallize we flee; when it is collapsing we flee. We are the species that can never be at home, at ease, or *we are unhomely of the earth*. Several religions express this unsettledness with the earth, the unhomeliness which projects another home in another domain. Most religions in this sense are the discourses of the refugee. Our literature and arts are the expressions of *fugio-ness*. Therefore, it is time for us to assert something fundamental—*the refugee is the ground upon which the human is standing* as a special moment. It will be calamitous if we will not begin to imagine and invent global institutions with this new fundamental towards receiving people as *anismos*.

Notes

1 See "L'entre deux: philosophe, une profession dangereuse [The Between: The Dangerous Occupation of the Philosopher]" Shaj Mohan Car il comporte "Intellectuels, philosophes, femmes en Inde: des espèces en danger", Revue du Réseau international des femmes philosophes parrainé par l'UNESCO, LE NUMÉRO 4-5 Editrice invitée : Divya Dwivedi, 2018.

2 See Simon Weil, *On the Abolition of All Political Parties*, trans. Simon Leys (New York: New York Review Book, 2013).

3 Martin Heidegger, *Logic as the Question Concerning the Essence of Language*, trans. Wanda Torres (NY: SUNY, 2009), 4.

4 P. Heidegger, *Logic as the Question Concerning the Essence*, 56; emphases added.

5 See Shaj Mohan and Divya Dwivedi, *Gandhi and Philosophy: On Theological Anti-politics* (UK: Bloomsbury, 2019).

6 It is possible to establish a relation between "das vorformale Etwas" of Emil Lask, Heidegger's early conceptions of intuition and homology.

7 L. Wittgenstein, *Culture and Value*, trans. Peter Winch (Oxford: Basil Blackwell, 1977).

8 We have called it the discipline which measures the hypophysical gradations of value "scalology". Both the celestial hierarchy and scala naturae are species of scalologies.

9 The ground of this question remains unexplored ever since Immanuel Kant asked the question "How to Orient Oneself in Thinking?" in 1786.

10 See forthcoming "Population Politics", Shaj Mohan and Divya Dwivedi, *Journal of Critical Philosophy of Race.*

11 These epochs cannot be understood through any of the versions of the universal. As Barbara Cassin remarked all universals are someone's universal. See ELOGE DE LA TRADUCTION: Compliquer l'universel

12 See "The Between: The Dangerous Occupation of the Philosopher," Revue du Réseau international des femmes philosophes parrainé par l'UNESCO, LE NUMÉRO 4–5 Editrice invitée : Divya Dwivedi, 2018.

CONJECTURES

4

BEYOND REASON: THE SUBJECT OF DESIRE AND ENJOYMENT IN POPULISM

Gautam Basu Thakur and Meghant Sudan

Introduction

'Populism' is defined, debated, and contested at multiple levels. Without entering the complexities involved in trying to define the term, this chapter takes as its point of departure the ideational approach staked by Mudde and Kultwasser in *Populism: A Very Short Introduction* (2017). According to them, populism is a "discourse, ideology or worldview" (Mudde and Kultwasser 2017: 5). It is a 'thin-centered ideology' which conveniently fuses with 'thick-centered' ideologies such as socialism and/or nationalism and "considers society to be ultimately separated into two homogenous and antagonistic camps, 'the pure people' versus 'the corrupt elite'" (ibid.: 6). But while Mudde and Kultwasser do an excellent job of laying down some of the critical terms underwriting the concept, namely, the people versus the elite, 'general will' (*volonté générale*) as separate from the 'will of all' (*volonté de tous*), and the cult of the charismatic strongman leader, their treatment lacks an interdisciplinary approach to the concept. But this is expected since, as John Abromeit correctly notes, academic scholarship on populism is commonly dominated by political scientists with few, if rare, contributions from sociologists, media scholars, and historians resulting in a general dearth of interdisciplinary and theoretical explorations of populism: "Insights into the socio-economic roots and social-psychological mechanisms that underlie populist movements" remain absent in current studies (2017: 177, 178). The attempt here will be to establish a partial corrective for this blind spot by introducing Freudian-Lacanian psychoanalytic theory for understanding some of the core concepts of Populism, but most specifically, by underlining the importance of addressing the issue from the perspective of the desiring rather than the discursive subject.

Barring Ernesto Laclau, whom we discuss later in the chapter, discussions of populism have mostly ignored psychoanalytic theory and when presented, these tend to be isolated references without any sustained engagement with the theory or application of theory to understanding the socio-psychological underpinnings of populism (ibid.: 180). This chapter will draw from Freud's writings and the seminars of Jacques Lacan, especially the 'later Lacan' or the Lacan post-Seminar XX, and such recent efforts to understand the social and the political through Lacan as pursued by the Slovene School, notably the works of Alenka Zupancic and Slavoj Žižek. Central to our focus would be an attempt to move beyond understanding 'the people' vs. 'the elite' distinction in terms of moral order and explaining it instead as the function of fantasy in relation to desire, ontology, and the other as a phantasmatic object. As we show below, the fantasy of the other's excessive enjoyment (jouissance) is the constitutive core of populism.

Recent attacks on progressive student movements in Indian universities by populist political parties of all ideologies demonstrate this well. Populist defense of and justifications for these attacks involve blaming the students for being anti-nationals, Maoists and foreign sympathizers, and additionally for being addicts, wasteful, and fornicators. Female students are principally singled out and chastised for being of loose morals, profligate, non-traditional and for having sexual independence. Whether waged from the Left or the Right, these populist attacks on the so-called elitism and moral corruption of India's progressive students betray anxiety over the other's excessive enjoyment, and violence against these students is characterized as necessary to purge the Indian society from anti-national, immoral, and excessive enjoyments. The other as an antagonist in populist discourses is always portrayed under the sign of excess. We should add that this is not to insinuate any false equivalence, when, for example, state-backed violence and its confluence with corporatized media and pliant institutions co-operate with one populist ideology against another. The question here, rather, is about the formation of the subject of populist ideology which takes place on a non-discursive plane of desire (see notes 1and 2).

In understanding 'the people' versus the 'elite-other' divide, it is therefore incumbent that we turn our attention to the role of the other's enjoyment, that is, the other's access to or ability to enjoy more and/or differently from the masses. Notwithstanding the symbolic reasons offered by populists to exchequer the 'elite-other' out of the ranks of the common people—nationalism and moralism—populist arguments on closer scrutiny almost always reveal concerns about the 'elite-other's' access to exclusive, unbridled, and surplus enjoyments and/or accuse the 'elite other' of stealing the dominant groups' right to enjoy. In other words, the populist charge against the other for enjoying privileges unavailable to or stolen from the common masses constitutes a fantasy narrative for the masses. This narrative explains to the masses that it is the elite other and their actions that are responsible for their plight and the erasure of privileges allowed to the elite other is the only way for recovering the masses from their abjection. This narrative, therefore, pushes out questions about governance, the economy, foreign policy, etc., by identifying a certain section of society as responsible for the lack of all-round national development. Building off these theoretical trusses, i.e., the function of fantasy in social discourse and the role of enjoyment in organizing fantasies about social relations, this chapter will propose a Freudian–Lacanian reading for understanding the function of fantasy in Populism via the case of right-wing Hindutva populism in India.[1]

Populism and Fantasy

Populism sustains itself by creating a fantasy or a series of interrelated fantasies, the most basic of which involves the imagination of the pure/real people as distinct from the corrupt elite as their antagonistic other. But we are not merely suggesting that the construction of this other is fantastic in the sense of being false or fabricated, but rather that fantasy understood in the Lacanian sense plays a pivotal function in creating and thereafter sustaining this self–other imaginary relationship. According to Lacan, fantasy is not detached from reality, that is, what is abstracted or outside of reality into which we might escape into (as Romantic poets strived to do) when overwhelmed by daily reality. Instead, fantasy is what helps us negotiate and navigate reality—the reality of our subjectivity as lacking/barred/castrated or desiring and the impossibility of the object satisfying our desire. Fantasy overrides this impasse by establishing a (impossible) relationship between subjectivity ($) and the object of desire (a). It is to denote this impossible paradoxical relationship between the subject and the object that Lacan writes the formula of fantasy as $ ⟨⟩ a: the diamond or the lozenge (as desire) representing the relation as one of "envelopment-development-conjunction-disjunction" (Lacan 2006: 542n17). Simply put, a *contraire* relationship (See, Leader 1997: 95).

Importantly, fantasy functions not simply to teach us what to desire but also how to desire (Žižek 1989: 118). And, herein lies its relation to ideology: Ideology is an unconscious fantasy structuring our social reality (ibid.: 33). Put differently, fantasy covers up a fundamental impossibility—the subject's (impossible) relation to the object—by staging ways for the subject to escape or evade this traumatic impasse. As such, ideology as fantasy masks the real condition of reality by appearing *not* to mask it. Thus, instead of forcing us to confront the impossibility of social relations or desire as hinging on a fundamental non-relationality, fantasy offers "an escape from [this] traumatic, real" by presenting (im)possible causes responsible for our abjection and suggesting that eradication of these causes alone can make us complete or whole (ibid.: 45). For instance, the populist fantasy responds to our dissatisfaction as a social group by identifying issues or others whose excision from the social can turn society back into a harmonious whole. To wit, populism invites the masses to take action, to be the change they desire to see in society by recognizing and then eradicating impediments sticking out against or challenging their desire for satisfaction, wholeness and plenitude. Instead of understanding the ontological reasons for civilizational discontent, populism introduces the intellectual elite or the freeloading minority as responsible for social ills—poverty, job insecurity, inadequate health care—and presents as a solution the removal of these excessive others for repairing all social ills.

The problem here is manifold. First, this ideology deflects questions about the government's responsibility in creating a better social space, which the government had promised to execute, by putting the onus of social change on the masses. Second, this ideology crafts an imagined Golden past that does not fit the present, and with this lack explains the subject's sufferings of the masses in the social rather than in terms of failed governance, capitalism, and, most importantly, divisive politics. In today's neoliberal technocratic democracies, populism is ultimately a managerial system of politics—it identifies, characterizes, and manages surplus enjoyment in the social, thus "obfuscat[ing] the possibilities of radical change [by] sustain[ing] illusory (but structurally necessary) hopes":

> [Populism] sustains the illusion that the democratic frame allows for radical changes (in the direction of welfare state) if only the majority votes for them . . . In short, to understand what actually happens we have to include what could have happened (but didn't)—betrayed hopes are part of a [populist] revolution. (Žižek 2019: 382)

Ideology as fantasy allows the subject/masses to come to terms with the reality of social non-relationality. But, instead of focusing on this non-relationality as an opportunity to engage in the politics of the impossible real, populist ideology teaches subjects/masses to identify social actors—the intellectual elite, the secular liberals, the minorities, etc.,—as responsible actors for restricting social unity (Zupancic 2017: 22).[2]

In today's India, the staging of 'pure people' versus the 'corrupt elite' makes use of two interrelated fantasies. The first is the fantasy of the other's enjoyment. This imagines the other is either imagined as being in possession of excessive enjoyment and/or guilty of stealing enjoyment that should have rightfully belonged to the dominant group and, as such, identified as threats to national security and society's (imaginary) moral–cultural values. The second is the fantasy of the new Father. Related to the first, this fantasy invests in the imaginary of an all-powerful exceptional (almost mythical) Father capable of rescuing the masses from the excesses of the other.

Fantasy I: The Other's Excessive Enjoyment

"It is always possible to bind together a considerable number of people in love, so long as there are other people left over to receive the manifestations of their aggressiveness," Freud noted in *Civilizations & Discontents* (1964: 113). The thesis presented in this sentence is simple yet complex: love for an object—nation, a person, a sports team—can unite a group of people but the collective thus formed will always distinguish itself from another group of people toward whom the former will direct nothing but hatred. The logic of this formalization, like all formalizations, involves as a minimum the identification of the other as standing against the imaginary of the self or community united by (object) love. Populism functions similarly by uniting one imagined community against an/the other by drawing symbolic lines of difference between the self and the other, that is, by imagining the self as one homogenous identity and the other as the abjection that must be distanced or rejected for this self to come into existence. What underwrites every symbolic discourse about the other's alterity—the other as criminal, the other stealing jobs, the other as anti-national—is an unconscious anxiety over the other's inassimilable jouissance.

As early as the unpublished *Project for a Scientific Psychology* (1895), Freud identified the *Nebenmensch* (neighbor) in terms of a distinct division between the familiar and what inhabits the familiar as its unknowable traumatic core. In his subsequent works, the notion of the traumatic in the familiar would be identified as the drive (*Trieb*) and human life explained as a constant struggle with the irredeemable drive. The social, consequently, would be explained by Freud as contingent on the management of drives—social ties are formed based on a shared jealousy of the primal Father's excessive enjoyments and culminates in the murder of the Father by the newly formed brotherhood. In the aftermath, paradoxically, social bonds are not freed from the pulsion of the drive, as the brotherhood remains impotent to access the enjoyments they envied, thereby requiring a constant figure of the other in whom or through whom the drive of enjoyment can be redirected against the imaginary of the social as means for consolidating identifications within the group. More specifically, the other's excessive enjoyment is underlined as the root cause for all social troubles including the people's failure to accomplish satisfaction or wholeness within their community. The other's unrestricted or unconstitutional enjoyment, we are told, is the reason why people remain deprived of satisfying their desires for wholeness and plenitude.

Material examples of this kind abound in populist discourses supportive of India's Hindutva parties. Extending from Jawaharlal Nehru's excessive thirst for power and him being a womanizer to minorities enjoying surplus opportunities (more than deserved), these discourses contend that titular figures of the INC and their elite secular liberal supporters are responsible for stymieing India's economic, (Hindu) cultural, and military growth. For the multitude suffering in India's neoliberal economy, the populists required a fantasy which, without questioning neoliberalism, would find scapegoats for explaining the economic insecurities ravaging the nation. The excessive other—the liberals and minorities—offer just that. They are foreign intruders or the enemy within whom different ways of life are identified as jeopardizing social and national harmony (Žižek 2008: 59).

Fantasy II: The New Father

Supplementing this first fantasy is the fantasy of the 'new' Father (figure) who is to deliver the people out of their dispossession. This fantasy, however, needs to be contextualized in relation to two moments. First, a socio-psychological moment represented by the replacement of the 'old' Prohibitive Father by the figure of the permissive Father; the latter does not prohibit enjoyment but rather insists that we enjoy more (Žižek 1994). The second is a temporal moment insofar as the move from the Prohibitive to the Permissive Father is specific to the twenty-first century, a movement that must be charted in direct relation to the spread of neoliberalism across the globe at the turn of the last century and experienced in the present as having resulted in a total collapse of symbolic authority.[3]

Presenting this arc Jacques-Alain Miller writes,

> We cannot fail to see that there has been a break, when Freud invented psychoanalysis under the aegis, as it were, of the reign of Queen Victoria, a paragon of the suppression of sexuality, whereas the twenty-first century is seeing the vast spread of what is called "porno", which amounts to coitus on show in a spectacle that is accessible to anyone on the web by means of a simple click of the mouse. From Victoria to porno, we have not only passed from prohibition to permission, but to incitation, intrusion, provocation, and forcing. [But] What is pornography but a fantasy [...] There is no better indicator of the absence of sexual relation *in the real* than the imaginary profusion of the body as it devotes itself to being given and being taken. (Miller 2016: n.p.)

The point to be noted here is that the move from prohibition to permission, from restrictions on enjoyment to the Super Ego's command to enjoy are far from allowing unrestricted enjoyment and satisfaction to individuals because they merely expose the emptiness of the symbolic order, the impossibility of the Real thus reinforcing the subjective need to remain in dissatisfaction.

Put another way, if the Freudian discovery insists on understanding subjectivity as contingent on remaining in desire—"the satisfaction of desire essentially consists of the preservation of [...] unsatisfaction, since a subject remains a subject only insofar as [...] he is a desiring [subject] that *wants-to-be*" —then, the impossibility of the object of desire either as the unreachable object (neurosis) or unsatisfactory object (hysteric), i.e., the object as the function of the big Other or Father's prohibition, allows for subjectivity. The subject remains perpetually suspended in desire, in pursuit of the object of desire, and in remaining incomplete or without the object of desire it *ex-sists* as subject (Chiesa 2007: 155). The move whereby objects of desire no longer remain prohibited and the subject no longer restrained from the enjoyment of objects, to wit is urged to enjoy more, presents the traumatic possibility of satisfaction of desire and end of subjectivity. Neoliberal emphasis on enjoyment disperses the subject in a world of free-ranging signifiers without a master signifier, the Father, guaranteeing the value or meaning of any signifier as privileged. This risks the collapse of the subject in face of a real possibility of being complete, of no longer being the subject of desire. Therefore, in order to arrest the continuous assault of signifiers, each promising more satisfaction than the other, the subject must reinvent the Law.

Since as subjects we do not desire the satisfaction of desire, the only way to negotiate the potential of unbridled enjoyment is by imagining newer restrictions against this enjoyment (Salgó 2013: 62). Today the subject has found a way around by reimagining the object as unsatisfactory because these objects are being leeched off by excessive others. Though the object in itself is no longer restricted, there are others who have an undue (historical) advantage when it comes to enjoying the object. Simply put, we are no longer limited by law to radical enjoyments but we have invented a way to remain in desire of the impossible object by creating a fantasy of the other whose unnatural enjoyment of the object renders the object less enjoyable for me. While not prohibited, enjoyment according to this fantasy scenario is stolen by certain actors operating within the socio-symbolic. In other words, the object of desire is not prohibited but enjoyment has become impossible due to others unconstitutionally extracting enjoyment out of objects that rightfully belong to the people. One cannot help notice as well how the idea of purity plays a crucial role in this logic. The object we wish to enjoy has been rendered impure by the other's excessive enjoyments, and it is only by returning the object to its former pristine glory that we can correct our subjective relation to the object and enjoyment.

In this context, the fantasy of the new Father further resecures the symbolic order by refitting it with meaning and purpose, i.e., desire. Simply put: The fantasy of the 'new' Father as capable of describing and arresting the lack of satisfaction in neoliberal societies is directly related to neoliberalism's failure to deliver its promise of all-inclusive prosperity. Except, this fantasy veils this reason deflecting attention to phantasmatic others identified for being responsible for the decay of social laws, mores, and desires.

Ironically, the fantasy of the new Father is a throwback to the 'old' primal Father who lays down strict laws of difference based on the logic of taboo and prohibition. The 'new' Father too demands that we sacrifice some of our own enjoyments for the greater cause—the eradication of others impending national development. At the same time, in spite of closely resembling Freud's castrating primal Father, the new Father is not imagined as an absolute figure of authority wielding uncompromising control over his children. In fact, he assures that sacrifice of enjoyment is temporary as a new dawn of wholesome enjoyment awaits the masses in the immediate future. As long as the masses abide by the calls for expunging those responsible for denuding national and (Hindu) cultural glories, they are guaranteed a share in this unforeseen happiness. Nor is the new Father unlike the people from within whom he hails. Instead, he was one of them but has since made personal sacrifices and wrestled with adversaries to secure for his children, the people and their right to enjoy. Thus, while in possession of a larger than life image, conscience, and physical strength, the new Father is also similar to us. He asks us to do what he has already done, and in making this plea, this demand, he also discloses his desiring subjectivity.

This is the brilliance of the Indian Prime Minister Narendra Modi's pre-election 2019 interview with Akshay Kumar: his benign admission to liking mangoes in this interview was widely criticized by liberals but Modi was scoring a point with his base. His articulation of desire and him as a desiring subject balance the fantasy of him being the exceptional One. This tempering humanizes the new Father making it easy for the masses to identify with him and believe in his promise to deliver them rightful enjoyments. Shaped by these twin fantasies, the base supporting Hindutva populism has lost sight of the Constitution, the history of the 'nation,' and are willing to remain undeterred by the facts of India's economic slowdown, joblessness, and market inflation, blaming instead the elite-other and the minority for their plight. Sadly, no exercise of telling them any of this matter for the "political position of the populist" is "immune to empirical refutation" (Müller 2016: 102).

Fantasy III: The Unknown Binding

The biggest mistake in opposing populism is made when appealing to facts. We believe that telling the truth or rationally establishing facts will blow away the cobwebs of populist fantasies. This appeal to facts, calling out fake news and returning to rationale empirical arguments, believe the masses are ignorant, lack political consciousness and are thus easy preys to populist politicians. But simply stating or restating facts have no effect on populist beliefs. Indeed, a sociological analysis of this phenomenon is possible as noted by Bruno Latour for instance. According to Latour, the world has changed and today there is 'an excessive *distrust* of good matters of fact disguised as bad ideological biases' (Latour 2004: 227). The reason facts do not matter today is because populist discourses have denuded figures of authority by characterizing them as part of the elite, therefore, disconnected from and/or against the masses.

But this sociological explanation repeats the same mistake made by those who think retelling of facts can counter populism. The problem is not that the masses do not know or they deride those who know, but, rather, that they prefer enjoyment over knowledge. It is a mistake to think of politics as a tussle between competing interests; politics is about organizing enjoyment through fantasies and populism succeeds by offering the masses certain fantasies that better structure their chances of gaining enjoyment in the society (McGowan 2019). This is also why the habitual belief that once populists gain power and themselves become elites they stand to lose the support of the masses is a comforting 'illusion' (Müller 2016: 42). In fact, as Müller notes, the argument that "antipolitics cannot generate real policies" fails in this case because the "[p]opulists in office continue to polarize and prepare the people for nothing less than what is conjured up as a kind of apocalyptic confrontation" (Müller 2016: 43): There is never a shortage of enemies who threaten the people with a state of continuous siege, and populists remain in power by confirming "what they have already determined [as] the will of the real people" (Müller 2016: 102). In other words, populism does not seek to realize their fantasies and by keeping them unrealizable enables the masses to enjoy their pursuit of impossible desire. Therefore, as counter-intuitive as it sounds, *the failure to deliver promises do not compromise populist appeal, but, paradoxically, extends their logic of governance*. Populist demand for eradication of excessive others is always a means and never an end in itself. By exploiting this continued state of crises, a populist government can both justify its governance—policies and executive actions—as well as continue to solicit support from the people on the premise that only sustained action can deliver the ever-elusive golden days.

To this, another point must be added. This deferment of enjoyment is necessary for sustaining fantasy as a defense against the Real. Insofar the core of the populist fantasy is occupied by the excessive other, any diminution of the other's excessive alterity can only collapse the fantasy and along with it the rationale for populist rule. Simply put: if populist demands for excluding or co-opting the other are carried out, whereby the other no longer remains an antagonist, then the phantasmatic support of populist rule—the people versus the other—ceases to function and the risks exposing the populist movement are revealed as a charade.

Like all fantasies, populist fantasies also function to structure social reality, make it appear meaningful and defend against the radical antagonism constitutive of the social. It cloaks this antagonism of social non-relationality by explaining non-relationality in terms of symbolic differences—the other's excessive enjoyment—and claims its divisive and repressive politics as necessary for eradicating the difference in enjoyment between the common people and the others. But this process is never complete, and the masses always remain short of satisfaction but never without being supplied another responsible for their dissatisfaction. In this context, it can be argued that Populism privileges a politics of the (im)possible. It is possible to be whole again or return to a golden past only as long as this becoming remains impossible. The indefinite deferral of populist promises *is* the true measure to populist power.

Theoretical Elements (I): Subjectivity

The structural elements of the populist frame of mind have been sketched in terms of desire, fantasy or ideology and their subjective arrangement. We can unpack this arrangement to explore the theoretical structure in greater detail. The particular elements to be examined are, first, the form of desiring subjectivity, and second, the temporal situation of subjects and objects. Aside from expounding particular details within the theoretical structure of populism, the larger interest of this discussion is to clarify how the psychoanalytic register of the story of populism has been dealt with here. This section takes up the first of the particular elements, the next section the second one, after which some features of Ernesto Laclau's similarly shaped and powerful account of populism account can be considered to address the larger interest at the end.

The story so far tells of the way the desiring subject relates to its object of desire or the way that it is at least moved into a certain apprehension of itself before its object. This form of the subject helps articulate the fantasy wherein the object is both in possession as well as in dispossession. The object is lost but also found, and the confusing shadows of its absent presence must be dispelled for the subject to take possession of itself. In resolving this quandary, the loving father has the object rightfully and the hateful other has the object wrongly, and the subject that was originally barred from acquiring its object of desire draws closer to the object by ensconcing itself between its two phases, to which accrue different subjectivities. This subject, surrounded by objects and other subjects, thus holds the whole thing together.

This game of apportioning objectivities in order to situate the self resonates with the Freudian theory of identification as developed in his *Group Psychology*, which Ernesto Laclau recounts (2005: 52–63) and uses as a 'point of departure' for his own account. Laclau hopes that his account does not remain only a 'Freudian venture', since he intends a certain 'intertextuality' involving a 'plurality of intellectual traditions' (ibid.: 63–64), and we will want to return to Laclau's intertextual handling later. For now it should be noted that the game of objects and selfhood also has something of the dialectic of recognition in it, the famous Hegelian story of self-consciousness that overcomes its empty formality to give itself content through life and desire and satisfaction in inter-subjective works. It will help to examine the Hegelian story with a particular eye to two under-appreciated points: the significance of corporeity and the failure of recognition. First, one should attend to the way that Hegel casts his story of self-consciousness in a *naturalized register* and not one of self-consciousness in a fully formed political condition by his lights. This creates a plane of analysis that is as much infused by animality, corporeity, sexuality, etc., as it is by the changes and exchanges proceeding at the level of consciousness and signification. Second, Hegel cautiously plants conditions for the *failure of recognition* in his story, which comprise, in various ways, degrees of fear, obedience, discipline, needs and wants, stages of *Weltgeist*, etc. Without the right conjuncture of these co-conditions, recognition is on the way at best or waylaid at worst.

Recall how Hegel develops his dialectic of recognition in his 1807 *Phenomenology of Spirit*.[4] We come to the question of self-consciousness after analyzing forms of consciousness in sensory reporting, perceptual uptake, and intellectual comprehension. In every case, the object has been dislodged from its purported substantive immediacy and absorbed into the dialectic of cognition. Now this dialectic is itself apprehended in the dialectic of recognition by seeing how consciousness involves self-consciousness, and self-consciousness, in turn, involves a certain inter-subjective frame of mind that Hegel calls *spirit*. Emerging in this way from consciousness and its loss of the immediately given object, self-consciousness is in a negative unity with otherness, those shapes of consciousness that it formally is, even as it goes beyond them. Thus, for Hegel, having the object and not having it in the course of seeking its own unity, self-consciousness is *desire*. This self-consciousness must recover the object with its own standing to be more than an empty form and it must develop this form to recover its own self-standing.

The object, for its part, is interwoven into the movements of consciousness and mirrors them. After its previous dialectical passage through the efforts of understanding the object as a causal center constituted through forces, the object is here taken as *life*, the processes of dissolution and articulation over space and time through living actual nature. The dialectic of recognition, which articulates the structure of self-consciousness, holds together the equal stakes of both self-consciousness and life. The well-known life-and-death struggle of recognition plays with these stakes. The structure of self-consciousness has three moments: (a) the simple 'I' as an immediate object; (b) the mediation that underlies this immediacy through the disappearance of the object in the form of desire; and (c) the recovery of this object, not as a given, lifeless thing, nor merely as a living thing (which, qua individual, cannot contain its negativity and is extinguished in the flow of life or which can merely express its being a determinate entity indifferently besides another), but as the living negativity that constitutes true content of self-consciousness in the form of another self-consciousness, 'a living self-consciousness':

> A *self-consciousness* is *for a self-consciousness*. Only thereby is there in fact self-consciousness, for it is only therein that the unity of itself in its otherness comes to be for it. The *I*, which is the object of its concept, is in fact not an *object*. But the object of desire is only *self-sufficient*, for it is the universal, inerasable substance, the fluid self-equal essence. While a self-consciousness is the object, the object is just as well an I as it is an object. The concept *of spirit* is thereby present and available for us. What will later come to be for consciousness will be the experience of what spirit is, this absolute substance which constitutes the unity of its oppositions in their complete freedom and self-sufficiency, namely, in the oppositions of the various self-consciousnesses existing for themselves. The *I* that is *we* and the *we* that is *I*. (Hegel 2018: §177)

In this way, the anxieties and disappointments over the object as the locus of satisfaction are resolved into an arrangement between subjects or an inter-subjectivity that affords satisfaction through the idea of freedom. We have not reached this idea yet, and, at this point, Hegel puts together only the preliminary steps for the freedom of self-consciousness. The dialectic of recognition thus outlines the basic elements of a freedom which will subsequently traverse thought and action, nature and morality, to develop the concept of spirit more determinately. It is important to stress that these 'basic elements of freedom' do not yet amount to a definition of will, let alone Hegel's particular resolution of the questions of overcoming the Hobbesian-Rousseauean differences over the unity and universality of a will to truly establish a political condition. Further, these basic elements are hard to simply list, however, and this is one of the reasons why Hegel's chapter on self-consciousness winds its way strangely through not only the fascinating details of mastery and servitude but also the symbolizations through Stoicism, scepticism, and the unhappy consciousness, and it is also the reason why it is never fully clear whether recognition is achieved in and only in the fact of the master-slave relation or if it is an interminable process sustaining all kinds of social life.

Another way of putting this point is that it is not the case that the dialectic of recognition moves in a linear way through the frustrations of the master and the slow subterranean revenge of the slave to produce three more shapes of consciousness in a progression. Rather, the dialectic of recognition assembles some pieces on a board in the detailed description of the deadly confrontation of self-consciousnesses, and the later sections illustrate alternative configurations of these pieces. In the deadly confrontation, we see, for instance, how desire is managed, when the master interrupts the cycle of consumption and desire by having the slave in the midst, or when the slave by working on the object both enacts another's will and desire and yet does so under the prior condition of hemming in its own desire as well as counteracting its desire-bound life of self-consciousness, etc. And, thus, later we can see Stoicism as *indifferent* to mastery or slavery and steadfastly pursuing the constructions of consciousness as reason or scepticism as *realizing* in forms of thought the acts of negation that appear in the master-slave relation as acts of desire and work, or we can see the unhappy consciousness as a multiform *joining* of the will of another with one's own, which is implicit in the master-slave relation.[5]

The point, in any case, is that the recognition dialectic does not simply resolve the master-slave relation. This relation persists alongside various configurations of the recognition dialectic that found social life proper or other developing forms of freedom as a constantly active cusp between life and self-consciousness, between the order of corporeity and the order of thought. At the same time, Hegel wants to give an account of how this stage is left behind in order to found the realm of reason—and this is clearer in the 'Phenomenology of Spirit' in his *Encyclopaedia*—to which realm belongs the systematic development of spirit as such through imagination and language. How these two levels—the primal scene of the living ego and the public sphere of freedom, inter-subjectivity, and universality; the mediated and relational structures of family-civil society-state and their compression or foreshadowing or over-determination into immediate and non-relational complexions in the realm of desire—are related calls for a deeper philosophical decision with the constitution of populist subjectivity at stake. [6]

To that philosophical decision it is pertinent how fragile the recognition order is for Hegel and how he describes it by way of planting conditions for its achievement rather than seeing recognition rolling out merely with the force of dialectical necessity. The latter feature comes out more prominently in the *Encyclopaedia*'s 'Phenomenology of Spirit', perhaps only because of its extremely compressed style. Although this is present in the 1807 version, it is made explicit in the *Encyclopaedia* §§ 428–430 that the process of recognition turns on the logical progression of singular-particular-universal endemic to Hegelian logic. For self-consciousness per se, or by its concept, is universal. But in its initial appearance as desire, it is singular just like the object in which it sees its satisfaction, although this is continually frustrated and is fleeting for just this reason. As self-consciousness, as universal, the object is annihilated and singleness is overcome, but true universality is not reached by itself due to the immediacy still affecting this stage, and so we only attain particularity or the duplication of self-consciousness, which *exists* only *for another* self-consciousness. Yet, the path to universality of self-consciousness—the *I* that is a *we*—is implicit here in the annihilation of singularity, and the complex unity of action[7] in embodied, particular self-consciousnesses drives on to such a stage. On this view, recognition proceeds, seemingly without life-and-death theatricalization, solely from the logical triad of singularity-particularity-universality, which is constitutive of the relations of self-consciousness on another plane.

On the other hand, there are at least two ways in which recognition is not only a matter of logical structure but is also affected by circumstantial conditions. First, because, as we have already seen, aspects and shadows and shards of the various details of the master-slave relation are seen lying about in different scenarios, allowing Hegel to pick through parts of Stoic and sceptical thought and the variety of devotional and ascetic practices in the postures of the unhappy consciousness. That these aspects are strewn around world history for Hegel to pick through means that various degrees of achievement of historical forms of recognition are given aside from the logical structure. Further, because Hegel explicitly states that not just any quality of fear and service qualifies for recognition but only a genuine experience of the absolute fear of death. Similarly, the shaping-forming activity of service too has to be pursued in a thorough or universal way for the negation of determinate otherness by its means to be effective in the right way (§196). Without the right kind of fear and the right kind of service and discipline, consciousness remains trapped in different types of vanity and (self-) servitude without rising to the new shape of self-consciousness, namely, reason, which alone enables the authentically universal form of inter-subjectivity or spirit to establish itself.

How we situate the constructions of fantasy and ideology as emerging from inherent tensions in the structure of desire or subjectivity as such affects our construal of the elements of populist subjectivity as either immanent to the order of reason entirely or as reaching beyond this. The fantasy-ideology can take particular shapes of apportioning certain types of objects, object-satisfactions or enjoyment, and subjectivities, to ease the inherent tensions and gaps, and populist fantasy-ideology would be a particular range of such easements and constructions that either entirely belongs to the constitution of the political condition or is operative in some displaced ways. The Hegelian story helps us to see how a prior loss of the object and making good of this loss belongs to the formation of collective experience, a formation that can often remain incomplete and shoddy and can appeal to projected unities and perfections of action and community, which fail to obtain in actual fact. The story itself, however, was never really about the perfect community, but, rather, about the formation of desiring subjectivity in various degrees and shapes, where, moreover, the spectral presence of primal life-forces and the fragile web of conditioning experiences and activities constantly motivate the inter-subjective arrangements and lead to easy or derivative or partial or badly formed claims of universality.

Theoretical Elements (II): Temporality

We have not yet thematized a striking feature of populist fantasizing in its apportioning of objectivities and subjectivities, namely, that these distributions carry a variety of historical charges. For despite the incredible or strictly fantastic nature of many populist ideologies, they are deadly earnest about history; about how things have come to be, about alleged historical facts carrying absolute truth, about the need to re-write history if only to read once again what was written for once and for all.[8] Some of this historical drive is no doubt to lend the fantasy a realistic urgency by pointing to a certain event or a certain time when an object was lost or stolen, thus inscribing the fantasy into the natural order of things, and recording it as a fact that has indeed already happened. Thereafter the fantasy projects the recovery of the object, often by stating that there is such a future that is at hand in which this object is returned or that this future is at the same time a golden past, and that, therefore, the re-possession has indeed already happened too. But is this only a question of rhetorical manipulation[9] or are there deeper grounds for these flights of historical fancy?

The Hegelian story did not decisively foreground any questions about these temporal elements to the fantasy construction, and so we must wonder whether they belong to the same framework of subjectivity arrangements explored so far or if these are added from elsewhere and alter the framework in some way? To be sure, the construction of self-consciousness on the plane of life and thus into a background of *natural existence* does provide grounds for including temporal elements into the arrangements of subjectivity, since this form of existence is premised on space and time as universals constituting objectivity at large. Although it was not explained how the dialectic of recognition incorporated these physical quantities, we can imagine it doing so via the negating acts of self-consciousness, especially, when, in the mode of servitude, and in the mode of desire hemmed in, it *works* upon the object, and, when, in the thoroughness of this service, self-consciousness chips away at every possible determination of the object until the work transcends the physicality of the object itself and begins to be directed upon the self as an object or starts shaping itself as reason, a new shape of self-consciousness determining objectivities in and of thought.

So, we are given direct clues for grounding the temporizing-historicizing moves within the same framework we have seen so far. An indirect consideration is provided by our own needs to sharpen the given theory towards application in terms of the various causal-temporal transactions involved in constructing fantasies about theft and recovery or the circumstantial deployments of these fantasies, let alone the grander historical horizons of capital and mythologies about identity that condition them. Thus there is a need to locate the temporal elements in the same recognitive framework to understand not only the internal construction of populist fantasies but to also account for how they ride upon or beside actual historical configurations, such as when populism is seen as parasitic on democracy itself[10] or as sharing fantasies with it, which was considered above in seeing the cohabitations of liberal democratic visions of social harmony with exclusionary populist assertions of social homogeneity. A parallel concern moved Habermas as he took up the task of accounting for the contemporary exhaustion of utopian energies and the worry whether this represented a shift within the *Zeitgeist* or the *Zeitgeist* itself was changing and shedding its inner character of being one that combined historical *and* utopian consciousness. Habermas chose to account for the depleted state of affairs as belonging to the same consciousness of modernity that represented its fuller moments,[11] for the variations in temporal elements, even when there arise questions of radical breaks with or into golden pasts, maintain the same secular circuits and the return of religion makes sense as a return (for it was always a part of the story of modernity) within the same structures of spirit (*Geist*) and its specifically temporizing character (*Zeit-geist*). Thus, in view of the political questions in our context about the failures, thefts or renewals of utopic imagination, we ought likewise to treat temporal elements in an internal way.

Since the Hegelian story is meager on this internal dimension we can look to phenomenological reflections on the constructions of selfhood and alterity and the role of time-consciousness in these. Husserl's *Cartesian Meditations* broaches the issue in the traditional philosophical vocabulary about solipsism and the problem of other minds. In that framework, we are given in perception material and not mental elements, bodies or embodiments rather than states of mind like cognitions, emotions, volitions, etc. So how do we know that there exist other selves or similarly cognitively constituted agents, especially if we don't want to accept that the presence of the other is merely a matter of inference or analogy? (Note that this does not even yet mention the unsettled ambiguity in the analogy itself, that is, whether the analogy takes us from one's mastery through thought over one's own body to another's mastery through *their* thought over *their* body or only to the master through *one's own* thought over *their* body.)

Now, while Husserl is happy to use that traditional language, his detailed exposition of intending the other clarify that he is not merely looking to prove the existence of a subject other than oneself, but, rather, he is looking to describe the constitution of a shared natural world which is as marked by organic life as it is by self-consciousness, and of a transcendental inter-subjectivity that can support this world. Thus, Husserl pursues here the basic questions of objectivity (of objective nature) as well as of subjectivity in the form in which Hegel himself had begun his chapter on self-consciousness: where consciousness conceives itself as being between, on the one hand, the movement of knowing (the dialectic of cognition), and, on the other, the same movement as a unity (the complex, reciprocal unity of the dialectic of recognition). Husserl too wants to understand the relation of the ego as a flowing consciousness and the ego as an intentional unity from within this flow, which leads to the examinations of an ownness-space, within which the ego finds an alter ego through animate, bodily pairings, before eventually firming up the spatiotemporal fields of nature, within which subjects can discover each other.

In Husserl's account, the intentional sense of the other as an embodied self-consciousness is developed through several layers of perceptual and agential presentations. But the main layer in this account of the complex movements of perceiving and filling-in is the sense 'natural world' as a system of constantly harmonized experience organized around the primacy of my organic body, and I always pass through this layer in order to transfer to other bodies, other places, the sense of lived materiality present in this layer. In each such transfer, the syntheses effected by consciousness are described by Husserl in terms of temporizing forms: first, in the case of simply projecting the other ego from within the primordial layer, and second, in the case of connecting the other with all others:

> Somewhat as my memorial past, as a modification of my living present, 'transcends' my present, the appresented other being 'transcends' my own being (in the pure and most fundamental sense: what is included in my primordial ownness). In both cases the modification is inherent as a sense-component in the sense itself; it is a correlate of the intentionality constituting it. Just as, in my living present, in the domain of 'internal perception', my past becomes constituted by virtue of the harmonious memories occurring in this present, so in my primordial sphere, by means of appresentations occurring in it and motivated by its contents, an ego other than mine can become constituted [...].
>
> If we return now to our case, the experience of someone else, we find that, with its complicated structure, it effects a similar *connection mediated by presentiation*: namely a connexion between, on the one hand, the uninterruptedly living self-experience (as purely passive original self-appearance) of the concrete ego – accordingly, his [its] primordial sphere – and, on the other hand, the *alien sphere*presentiated therein. It effects this, first, by its identifying synthesis of the *primordially given* animate body of someone else and the same animate body, but *appresented* in other modes of appearance, and secondly, spreading out from there, by its identifying synthesis of the same Nature, given and verified primordially (with pure sensuous originality) and at the same time appresentationally. In that way, the coexistence of my ego and the other ego...in short, a *common time-form* – is primarily instituted; and thus every primordial temporality automatically acquires the significance of being merely an original mode of appearance of Objective temporality to a particular subject. (Husserl 1995: 115, 127–8)

We need not enter the details of Husserl's inquiries and merely want to retain for our purposes the continuities stressed here between the temporizing acts and the constitution of the animate other in the living space of universal self-consciousness. This means that the temporal ordering is fundamental to apprehending not only the other but also claims of objectivity on this basis, and if ideology construction involves setting up identifications of objects and subjects, it implicates temporal constructions in this as well. This makes possible not only the temporized transactions between objects and subjects (theft/possession/recovery, historical circumstance/mythological projection), but, also, since this concerns the basic syntheses of ego and alter ego, between subjects as well (the *substitutability* relations between this father and the *new* one, the *virtuality* of the spatio-temporal field obtaining with these substitutions described earlier in the context of the second fantasy, and the *deferrals* of *promises* given to each other). On this extended view of desiring subjectivity in its natural settings, the temporizing-historicizing moves of consciousness condition articulations of contents that can serve populist fantasy construction and its theorization.

Conclusion

The central claim of this chapter, to set up an account of populism in terms of othering relations in regard to forms and objects of enjoyment and, in a principally psychoanalytic register, has already been stated in detail; the theoretical pieces at play in such an account have already been laid out. It remains to clarify the key cast of the theory itself in light of Laclau's treatment of populism, which should finesse the sense of some of those pieces. According to Laclau, "[p]opulism is, quite simply, a way of constructing the political" (2005: xi). It is not a particular or regionally delimitable set of beliefs, but, rather, the multiform structure of *any* process of community, where this structure is premised on discursive relations. Tensions between our view and Laclau's theoretical premises emerge at precisely this point, which was flagged earlier when speaking of Laclau's intertextual handling. For it is not clear precisely how Laclau accommodates the psychoanalytic register with the discursive structuration in his theory. As this is a shared problematic, addressing it will situate the present view as a result.

Laclau used the Freudian construction of the social bond through libidinal identifications to generate the aforesaid intertextual 'point of departure' for his own discursivity-based view. Although he explicitly courted the charge of eclecticism at this point,[12] we need to see how these two really come together in his view.[13] In fact, they do coincide for Laclau, but only because he unevenly absorbs the psychoanalytic register into the discursive one: by seeing, *on the one hand*, the discursive register as the deepest layer because, as a radicalized field of differential signs and representations, it basically yields a transcendental system of pure relations that constitutes objectivity as such, while the psychoanalytic register yields a determinate set of relations;[14] by seeing, *on the other hand*, the psychoanalytic register as itself a general ontology in order to imbue the formal system of representations with affective value.[15]

Now, although Laclau turns to psychoanalytic categories in order to provide affective heft to purely signifying forms, Laclau may still hold that questions of general ontology come after questions of the structure of objectivity as such to assert the primacy of the discursive register, and he can couple with this, in some appropriately downstream way, his stated view that affects and acts of naming are mutually dependent or intertwined (ibid.: 111). Does this not allow the said absorption of the psychoanalytic into the structural-political in an acceptable way, rather than the harder lines drawn by the present view that inscribes political formations on a psychoanalytic plane? Here, a second issue turns up, which we encountered in examining the theory's elements using the Hegelian recognitive framework, and it concerns the logical items of singularity, particularity and universality. Resolving *this* issue clarifies the previous one.

Laclau relies on a Gramscian notion of hegemony to uphold *both* the sheer particularity of demands from whose play the notions of democracy and populism are specified amidst the irreducible tension of difference and equivalence *and* the account of populism as a claim of the particular to stand for an impossible totality and therein reducing to singularity.[16] This position involves the crux of Laclau's theory of discourse, which rests on what he calls an empty signifier, as well as his disagreement with Žižek, which qualifies his adoption of a methodology supposedly not as 'eclectic' as Žižek's and hence qualifies the strategy of absorbing the psychoanalytic register into the structural-political one. The empty signifier is an ultimate condition of representation immanent to representation, and it signifies a "failed totality, the place of irretrievable fulness...an object that is both impossible and necessary" (ibid.: 70). According to Laclau, Žižek takes this (non) universal to truly denote a void, whereas, by subsuming it under hegemonic operations within representation, Laclau hopes to circumvent the concepts of void and plenitude altogether and, consequently, perilous Hegelian or Marxist claims of a true universality in stories of the state, capital or class, which make up one half (the other being psychoanalysis) of the 'incompatible ontologies' composing Žižek's theory (ibid.: 106–107). With his decision to construe the universal as an empty signifier, Laclau then claims to align himself more firmly with Lacan: "Although he [Žižek] is closer in this respect to Hegel than to Lacan, I think am closer to Lacan than to Hegel" (ibid.: 239).

If only, however, it were so easy to disregard the claims of universality built into dialectical systems, and, yet, at the same time, to make theoretical use of the idea of totality under various signs of negation or inflection.[17] This is where the present view diverges by taking the psychoanalytic register as central and self-standing. Consequently, our treatment of the Hegelian recognitive framework enables a philosophical decision (as we described this earlier), which delinks the form of self-consciousness as desiring subjectivity from the full unfolding of self-consciousness in the system of political will and right, to allow theorizing the former (psychoanalysis) as referring to the other (the metaphysical system) and to treat the universal as a pure emptiness that is part of its structure. This does not mean that either loses self-standing to become part of an eclectic absorption of incompatibles, for it is always possible for the latter to also have an ideology sustaining itself that can be described from within this primary structure. Thus follows the theoretical imperative to think populism from the standpoint of desiring rather than discursive subjectivity, that is, from desire, beyond reason.

Notes

1 This theoretical exercise does not claim the fantasies identified to be specific to right-wing/conservative or Hindutva politics alone, rather, as the last two decades have shown, the right, center and the left are all equally responsible for forging fantasies for their respective bases.

2 As used here, 'politics' is distinguished from 'the political' insofar as the latter describes the conditions of social (non-) relationality whereas the former, its obverse, seeks to build a better society (*polis*) on the premise that social relations are possible. The realm of *politics* is wider than the political in a sense, because to it belong many centers and layers of institutional structures, actions, and objects, whereas *the political* concerns a certain way of addressing objectivities available in the domain of politics and in other spheres of social life, so as to yield structures of desire and enjoyment and subjectivity through these.

3 Indeed, it can be argued that the fantasy of the 'new' Father capable of arresting a general experience of lack of satisfaction in neoliberal societies is directly related to neoliberalism's failure to deliver its promise of all-inclusive prosperity. Except, this fantasy veils this reason and deflects attention to others identified as responsible for all-round decay of social laws, mores, and desires.

4 Translations here are from Hegel, 2018, but for ease of reference, we provide Miller's paragraph numbering.

5 Again, it is worth stressing that this mere 'unity of purpose' or a will that is collective only in virtue of being directed to a common good satisfies neither Hobbes, who argues the need for a distinct, singular will at this point, nor Rousseau, who argues the need for conceiving the general will through a set of self-mediations at this point, nor, finally, Hegel himself, who argues for the need for several more folds or explications of self-consciousness to articulate a political condition or a system of right, even as a fundamental level of inter-subjectivity is already announced when, qua self-consciousness in the form of reason, contains the concept of the will implicitly.

6 Calling the decision 'philosophical' need not mean being imposed by 'philosophy' or in some other external manner altogether. It may be seen instead as a critical-reflexive moment within a given discipline, say, within a psychoanalytic account of populism. See Badiou's interview with Foucault for the historical-philosophical shapes and possibilities of such a moment in Foucault 1998.

7 The complex unity of action was described in abstract ways in the 1807 version by talking of the *reciprocal nature* of the actions of self-consciousnesses staking their own and the other's lives in the struggle for recognition and by talking of the *completeness* of the actions only when each does to the other what it does to itself as well as when each does to itself what it does to the other. In the *Encyclopaedia* version this complex unity is presented in more concrete terms by talking about the bodily existence of self-consciousness, which already opens paths to universality via use, tool-being, and signification, and by talking about the providential, acquisitive, preserving attitudes that develop in the course of using another body as means to mastery, and by talking, as did the 1807 *Phenomenology*, about the slave's work(ing) through absolute fear and through the implicitly general unity of will that holds over the particular distribution of actions, etc.

8 Whether this is thought in terms of the historiographical obsessions of dating oppression by invaders and contesting standard accounts with greater displays of precision or it is more revealingly heard in the flowing together of myth and history in tales of nuclear projectiles and plastic surgery in pre-historic eras, of sites of the mythical past recovered from under or within present monuments into the promised future, and even in the analysis offered in defense of CAA-NRC once heard at the Delhi Book Fair: the promises about the NRC, precisely because of their inconsistency, show that the NRC is not yet present, and so protest against an absence is nugatory; whereas the CAA is a provisional present for the divided India, which meant nothing in the past and will mean nothing in the future, both of these represented by an undivided India.

9 For Laclau, the denigration of populist 'logic' to mere 'rhetoric' is not only evidence of how 'the people' have been prejudicially viewed as a thoughtless mob but also an invitation to think of the construction of the category 'people' on a more structural analysis of discursivity as such. Discursivity, for Laclau, founds all objectivity, thus, presumably, historical objects too, although this feature is not explicitly addressed. This is a gap we aim to fill. We will later return to the topic of discursivity.

10 This is the classical worry about democracy as internally threatened by tyranny, which forms a central thread throughout Western political theory (see Roberts 1994). For Laclau 'democracy' names a distinct and fundamental alternative to populism, with which it co-constitutes a primordial space of sociality (2005: 125–128; see Chapter 6 for its connection with the conventional notion of democracy).

11 Habermas (1989: 52):

> [Perhaps] the exhaustion of utopian energies is not just an indication of a transitory mood of cultural pessimism but rather goes deeper. It could indicate a change in modern time-consciousness as such. Perhaps the amalgam of historical and utopian thought is disintegrating; perhaps the structure of the *Zeitgeist* and the overall situation of politics are changing. Perhaps historical consciousness is being *relieved* of its utopian energies: just as at the end of the eighteenth century, with the temporalization of utopias, hopes for paradise moved into the mundane sphere, so today, two hundred years later, utopian expectations are losing their secular character and once again assuming religious form. I consider this thesis of the onset of the postmodern period to be unfounded. Neither the structure of the *Zeitgeist* nor the mode of debating future life possibilities has changed; utopian energies as such are not withdrawing from historical consciousness. Rather, what has come to an end is a particular utopia that in the past crystallized around the potential of a society based on social labor.

12 "My hope is that this intertextuality does not make it unduly *eclectic* [emphasis added]" (Laclau 2005: 64).

13 It is ironical and symptomatic that Laclau diagnoses Žižek's mistakes by expressing almost the same problem we claim afflicts his own theory. Discussing his disagreements with Žižek he says, "What is, however, the true root of this theoretical disagreement? It lies, I think, in the fact that Žižek's analysis is entirely *eclectic* [emphasis added], for it is grounded in two incompatible ontologies: one linked to psychoanalysis and the Freudian discovery of the unconscious, the other to the Hegelian/Marxian philosophy of history. Žižek performs all kinds of implausible contortions to put the two together, but he is clearly far from successful. His favourite method is to try to establish *superficial homologies* [emphasis added]" (Laclau 2005: 235).

14 "Discourse is the primary terrain of the constitution of objectivity as such" (Laclau 2005: 68).

> We are not dealing with casual or *external homologies* [emphasis added] but with the same discovery taking place from two different angles—psychoanalysis and politics—of something that concerns the very structure of objectivity. The main ontological consequence of the Freudian discovery of the unconscious is that the category of representation does not simply reproduce, at a secondary level, a fullness preceding it which could be grasped in a direct way, but, on the contrary, representation is the absolutely primary level in the constitution of objectivity. (Ibid.: 115).

Two qualifying points: (a) Psychoanalysis as a 'point of departure' is one among many theories and, as Laclau often reminds us, a genetic rather than preferably a structural analysis. This accords a certain logical and methodological priority to the latter over the former; (b) Laclau himself resists the term 'transcendental'. We are using it simply to talk about the constitution of objectivity, especially when its stated ground is said to be representation.

15 "[P]sychoanalytic categories are not regional, but belong to the field of what could be called a general ontology" (Laclau 2005: 114). "The different signifying operations to which I have referred so far can explain the *forms* the investment takes, but not the *force* in which the investment consists.... There is no language in which the *value* relations would be established only between *formally* specifiable units" (Ibid.: 110–111).

16 Laclau (2005: 80–81; also see 68–71, 96–97, 106–107 and 115):

> I have shown that equivalence and difference are ultimately incompatible with each other; nonetheless, they require each other as necessary conditions for the construction of the social.... [A]*ll social* (that is, discursive) identity is constituted at the meeting point of difference and equivalence.... [T]otalization [on the side of the logic of equivalence that privileges populism in this co-constitutive play or tension] requires that one differential element should assume the representation of an impossible whole.

17 The use of frameworks like global capitalism would count as a concrete instance, but more plainly and inevitably, invocations of the logical difference between the particular and the universal that the same particular claims to be would count here too. The latter, in the context of populism, is, after all, an immediate assertion of the I that is We and—more importantly for Laclau—the reverse proposition "the We that is the I," that is, the ineffable singularity loaded with affectivity in acts of naming for Laclau. What is named here is produced through this act, namely, *the people* itself.

References

Abromeit, John. 2017. "A Critical Review of Recent Literature on Populism". *Politics and Governance*, 5 (4): 177–186.

Chiesa, Lorenzo. 2007. *Subjectivity and Otherness*. Cambridge: MIT Press.

Eszter, Salgó. 2013. *Psychoanalytic Reflections on Politics: Fatherlands in Mothers' Hands*. London: Routledge.

Foucault, Michel. 1998. "Philosophy and Psychology". In *Michel Foucault: Aesthetics, Method, and Epistemology*, translated by Robert Hurley, edited by James Faubion, 249–259. New York: The New Press.

Freud, Sigmund. 1964. "Civilization and its Discontents." In *The Standard Edition of the Complete Psychological Works of Sigmund Freud, Volume XXI*, 64–138. London: Hogarth Press.

———. 1966. "Project for a Scientific Psychology (1895 [1950])." In *The Standard Edition of the Complete Psychological Works of Sigmund Freud, Volume I*, 281–397. London: Hogarth Press.

Habermas, Jürgen. 1989. "The New Obscurity: The Crisis of the Welfare State and the Exhaustion of Utopian Energies." In *The New Conservatism*, edited and translated by Shierry Weber Nicholsen, Chapter 2, 48–70; here 52. Cambridge, M.A.: MIT Press.

Hegel, G.W.F. 2018. *The Phenomenology of Spirit*, translated by Terry Pinkard. New York: Cambridge University Press.

Husserl, Edmund. 1995. *Cartesian Meditations*, translated by Dorion Cairns. Dordrecht: Kluwer Academic Publishers.

Lacan, Jacques. 2006. *Ecrits: The First Complete Edition in English*, translated by B. Fink. New York: W.W. Norton.

———. 2007. *The Seminar of Jacques Lacan*. Edited by Jacques-Alain Mille, translated by Bruce Fink, [Reprint] ed., Book XX, *On Feminine Sexuality: The Limits of Love and Knowledge: Encore 1972–1973*, translated with Notes by Bruce Fink. New York: W.W. Norton & Company.

Laclau, Ernesto. 2005. *On Populist Reason*. London: Verso.

Latour, Bruno. 2004. "Why Has Critique Run out of Steam? From Matters of Fact to Matters of Concern" *Critical Inquiry*, 30 (Winter 2004): 225–248.

Leader, Darian. 1997. "Phantasy in Klein and Lacan." In *The Klein-Lacan Dialogues*, edited by Bernard Burgoyne and Mary Sullivan, 83–95; here 95. New York: Other Press.

McGowan, Todd. 2019. "The Price of Living Out Our Fantasies." Paper presented at the 2019 LACK Conference, Clark University, Worcester, Massachusetts, 9–11 May.

Miller, Jacques-Alain. 2016. "Unconscious and the Speaking Body." World Association of Psychoanalysis (WAP), X[th] Congress, Rio de Janerio. Web.

Mudde, Cas and C.R. Kultwasser. 2017. *Populism: A Very Short Introduction*. New York: Oxford University Press.

Müller, Jan-Werner. 2016. *What Is Populism?* Philadelphia: University of Pennsylvania Press.

Roberts, Jennifer. 1994. *Athens on Trial: The Antidemocratic Tradition in Western Thought*. Princeton: Princeton University Press.

Žižek, Slavoj. 1989. *The Sublime Object of Ideology*. London: Verso.

———. 1994. *The Metastases of Enjoyment: Six Essays on Woman and Causality*. London: Verso.

———. 2008. *Violence*. New York: Picador.

———. 2019. *Sex and the Failed Absolute*. London: Bloomsbury.

Zupančič, Alenka. 2017. *What Is Sex?* Cambridge: MIT Press.

5

AGONISM AND 'REVOLUTIONARY-BECOMINGS': MOUFFE, DELEUZE AND 'THE POPULIST MOMENT'

Raghu Menon Jayakumar

Introduction: The Agon and Political Theory

In *Homer's Contest*, Nietzsche identifies a quality that undercuts both Greek and Indian thought—the active recognition of life as a ceaseless struggle. Whereas most Indian philosophies renounced the struggle as unreal and advocated a life of renunciation, the Greeks, Nietzsche argues, embraced and revelled in the grind of worldly existence. The struggle, in other words, was 'the womb of everything Hellenic' and life became imbued with the spirit of the contest (*agon*)—over oneself, others and even the Gods themselves (Nietzsche 2006, 175). Though victories may be celebrated and extolled, the contest itself assumed greater prestige than the result.

In the essay, Nietzsche compares the violence and savagery of the pre-Homeric Greeks to the nobility and ambition of their successors. He attributes this change in Greek society to the ethos of the *agon* and the affirmative practice of envy it encourages. The ancient Greeks, he argues, understood envy quite differently from modern societies. It epitomizes the contest and nurtures ambition in individuals through burning jealousy: 'every talent must develop through a struggle' (Nietzsche 2006, 178). Most importantly, for Nietzsche, it ensures the perpetuation of the *agon*—and consequently, the 'well-being of the state'—by precluding a final resolution to the contest. He illustrates this point by recounting the story of the Ephesians who banished Hermodor because he was incomparably better than his peers: 'Amongst us, nobody should be the best; but if somebody is, let him be somewhere else, with other people' (Nietzsche 2006, 178–179). Hermodor is the transcendent and incontestable ideal that the Greek polity must resist at all costs; in order to guarantee a fair contest, and thus, sustain their way of life, the Ephesians are left with no choice but to ostracize the figure who portends the dissolution of the *agon*.

Although Nietzsche does not delve further into the agonistic nature of society at large, his brief account offers a suggestive paradigm to reframe political philosophy in light of the resurgent populist sentiment across the world. In recent years, owing to the works of political theorists such as Chantal Mouffe and Stephen Connolly, 'agonism'—albeit in a 'tamed' form—has emerged as an anormative-ontological model for certain theories of democracy (agonistic theories) that take issue with the 'deliberative school' of Rawls, Habermas and others. The latter conceives democratic society as a social space where consensus is attained through rational deliberation. For the agonists, the very act of consensus presupposes either an 'overpowering through compromise' or a wilful ignorance of 'opposing or dissenting' views (Turner 2006, 3–4).[1] As a result, deliberative theories end up repeating the same politics of antagonism from which they wish to move away. Agonists, on the other hand, reject any theoretical model that promises a 'consensus without exclusion', and revise Nietzsche's arguments to assert the ontological primacy of conflict and antagonism in the formation of social order (Mouffe 2000a, 15).

The issue at stake, for these thinkers, is the affirmation of plurality in a democratic society. In classical liberalism, the plurality constitutes 'a harmonious ensemble' in which, due to empirical reasons, we are forced to adopt only a few positions (Mouffe 2008, 8). The deliberative models attempt to circumvent the problem of plurality by setting up a 'tribunal of reason' which is capable of selecting the most rational and universal state of affairs (the consensus) from the many claimants.[2] Ironically, the liberal-democratic objective to herald a non-partisan 'post-political' social model often results in a gross centrism that displaces and subjugates opinions that diverge from the norm (Honig 1993, 133; Mouffe 2013, xvii; Mouffe 2018, 4). Indeed, pluralism, by its very nature, is conflictual due to the 'impossibility of reconciling all points of view' (Mouffe 2018, 92). It is no surprise then that the agonists are willing to embrace the myriad contests taking place at the heart of all things political.

The rise of right-wing populism in the last decade—as well as the perceived failure of traditional liberal thought to address this phenomenon—has urged some to propose agonistic correctives. Amongst these, Chantal Mouffe's arguments in favour of 'left-wing populism' offer a particularly compelling proposition. Rather presciently, the threat of a far-right revival appears as a recurring motif in her published works prior to the 2008 economic crisis (the development that spurred the current wave of disaffection with the establishment). In *The Democratic Paradox* (2000), for instance, she finds fundamentalism to be an inevitable consequence of 'the democratic deficit' internal to deliberative liberal-democratic models (Mouffe 2000b, 96). By replacing pluralism with a form of '*normative* rationality', she argues that these theories unwittingly facilitate dissension by attempting to evade it from the outset (Mouffe 2000b, 83). Similarly, in *The 'End of Politics' and the Challenge of Right-wing Populism* (2005), Mouffe unequivocally blames the neoliberal champions of the 'Third Way' ('neither left nor right') and 'all those who proclaimed the end of the adversarial model of politics' for the burgeoning appeal of far-right ideas. 'By constructing an opposition between "the people" and the "establishment", not only does right-wing populism shatter the consensual framework', she argues, 'it also brings to the fore the shallowness of the dominant theoretical perspective' (Mouffe 2005a, 51). Mouffe's diagnostic assessment of the right-wing revival has remained fairly unchanged over the years.[3]

Though Mouffe has often endorsed the idea of restoring the left/right frontier as a response to Third Way politics (Mouffe 2005b, 119), the nature of this undertaking had changed by the time she published her most recent work, *For a Left Populism* (2018). The text, which is, in many ways, a manifesto, calls for a re-articulation of the traditional left-right distinction following what she refers to as 'the populist moment'. By leaving behind all attempts to resuscitate classical socialist and social-democratic principles—a significant matter of concern in her previous works—Mouffe develops the tenets of 'left-wing populism' to counter the lure of the far-right.

The theoretical nature of this enterprise cannot be overlooked, as the present crisis is also partly a failure of political theory to move beyond spent ideas[4] (Mouffe 2018, 2–5). In what follows, I will critically examine Mouffe's agonistic arguments in support of left-wing populism and argue that the re-articulation of the political frontier must begin with the jettisoning of the loaded and overwrought left/right opposition. By drawing on Gilles Deleuze's political philosophy, I propose an alternative methodology to classify and evaluate responses to the populist moment.

The Populist Moment

The agonistic politics that Mouffe, Connolly, Honig and others put forward is, on the surface, vastly different from Nietzsche's original concerns. As Siemens notes, the problems of democratic politics that motivate these theorists are perhaps far removed from anything one may find in Nietzsche's canon. However, what brings them together, as we have seen, 'is the [ontological] claim that *antagonism, division and struggle are inherent to democratic politics*'. Furthermore, by restoring '*the original sense of democracy as incessant contestation*', they foreground antagonism as 'both a descriptive principle and an axiological principle' (Siemens 2013, 84; emphasis in original). As such, all claims or discoveries that attribute a 'natural' or 'final' order to society, be they from the left or right, remain oblivious to its contingent and conflictual nature. Every order, according to Mouffe, is temporary and 'an expression of a particular configuration of power relations' (Mouffe 2013, 2). The past few decades have witnessed the formation of a new hegemonic order that has brought forth a peculiar situation which she calls 'post-politics' or 'post-democracy' (Mouffe 2018, 16). The 'populist moment' which is fast defining our times, signals a crisis in this state of affairs.

According to Mouffe, the political upheaval witnessed recently across the world is 'due to the convergence of several phenomena that … have affected the conditions in which democracy is exercised' (Mouffe 2016a). The first significant phenomenon that she points out is the aforementioned 'post-political' turn which is a direct consequence of the consensus-based radical centrism outlined previously. The second phenomenon is 'the democratic tradition of equality and sovereignty' (Mouffe 2016a) that stands at odds with the 'tradition of political liberalism' (Mouffe 2018, 14).

The modern liberal-democratic practices have been fashioned by the confluence of two distinct positions that developed side by side. Political liberalism, with its emphasis on 'the rule of law, the separation of powers, and individual freedom' is naturally irreconcilable with the democratic tradition that privileges 'equality and popular sovereignty' (Mouffe 2018, 14). Mouffe draws this distinction from the Schmittian school which claims that such contradictions will inevitably lead to the dissolution of a pluralist liberal democracy. Though she accepts the argument that the two traditions operate on different logical registers, she, however, does not share the latter's assessment that they stand in contradiction to one another. On the contrary, she insists that 'the possibility of an 'agonistic' negotiation' has never ceased to exist in liberal democracies. Throughout its history, liberal-democratic politics has been shaped by 'a constant process of negotiation through different hegemonic configurations of this constitutive tension', conventionally understood in terms of the left-right paradigm (Mouffe 2018, 15).

In Europe, Mouffe claims, the right has generally inclined towards freedom, whereas the left emphasizes equality (Mouffe 2016a). The ongoing conflict between the two sides can only result in a temporary truce that establishes 'the hegemony of one over the other' at any given point in time (Mouffe 2018, 15–16). Although such sweeping generalizations of the left-right frontier are hard to make in the cases of countries such as the Philippines, Turkey and India—or even Europe, for that matter—Mouffe is right in reformulating the problem in terms of the tension between the different registers of liberal democratic politics.

If the tension between liberal and democratic traditions never ceases to exist, how does one then account for the present state of affairs?[5] Mouffe answers this by pointing yet again at the rational-consensus model of liberal democracy. By blurring the distinction between the left and right, and thus suppressing the natural tension between liberal and democratic logics, these policies attempt to subdue the agonistic discord necessary for a pluralist democracy and push society towards a 'post-political' milieu where such distinctions are no longer deemed necessary (Mouffe 2018, 15–16). Even though many neoliberals and deliberative theorists celebrate the diversity of discourses available in a democracy, they negate this plurality by constructing a collective 'we' that transcends differences. Notwithstanding that liberal-democrats like Rawls begin by accepting plurality and difference as 'social facts', Mouffe asserts that they 'proceed to find procedures to deal with differences whose objective is actually to make those differences irrelevant and to relegate pluralism to the sphere of the private' (Mouffe 1996, 246).[6]

In Mouffe's opinion, the elevation of liberal principles at the expense of democratic values has been the dominant trend of late in Europe. Although one may speak of democracy in Europe, it is meaningful only to the extent that it 'signifies the presence of free elections and the defence of human rights' (Mouffe 2018, 16). Though conditions undoubtedly vary outside that continent, it is tempting to agree with Mouffe's judgement that the 'populist moment' is a product of the disaffection of 'all those who oppose the "consensus at the centre"'—a feeling that is inescapable when the 'possibility of an agonistic struggle between different projects of society' is suppressed by the demands of 'post-politics' (Mouffe 2018, 17). She notes that the characteristic feature of all recent populist resistance is hostility towards 'a politico-economic system that is increasingly perceived as being controlled by privileged elites who are deaf to the demands of the other groups in society' (Mouffe 2018, 18). Denigrating or vilifying populism—including its right-wing expressions—hardly achieves anything, because, as Mouffe observes, one can recognize 'a democratic nucleus at the origin of many of their demands'. While it may be 'morally comforting' to smear and defame the populists by attacking them for their slavish devotion to 'irrational passions' or by questioning their 'lack of education', the demonization of this kind from those occupying the centre-left or centre-right is ultimately 'politically disempowering' (Mouffe 2018, 23–24). Though it may very well be the case that the right-wing populists will attempt to reinstate popular sovereignty, the problem with these ideologies, in Mouffe's view, lies in their interpretation of *sovereignty*. Often, this is conceived in terms of a 'national sovereignty', and, almost always, by the exclusion of a group (or groups) of people (Mouffe 2018, 26–27).

For Mouffe, the populist moment ought to be addressed by keeping in mind 'how the resistances to post-democracy are going to be articulated and how 'the people' is going to be constructed' (Mouffe 2018, 26–27). At the same time, the solution is not to construct a '*we* without a corollary *they*' but to develop a framework of 'we/they' that does not negate pluralism (Mouffe 2014).[7] It is in this context that Mouffe distinguishes between an 'enemy' and an 'adversary'. In deliberative theories, the discourses excluded by rational consensus ('they') assume the status of an enemy who must be repeatedly vanquished through dialogue and deliberation. In the kind of politics that Mouffe categorizes as right-wing populism, the social groups that are kept out by ideology assume a similar role. According to the agonists, in a true pluralism, rival discourses are not negated, but instead, contested; in other words, they are not enemies, but 'adversaries' against whom one competes in the active spirit of a contest. For Mouffe, this distinction between an adversary and an enemy is significant, as the adversary possesses a 'legitimacy' that the enemy always lacks (Mouffe 2014).

To believe that the conflict will have an end, or to assume that it can be negated through reason, is to misapprehend the ontological condition of pluralism. The agonistic solution is to replace consensus with adversarial respect.[8] Brandon Turner has aptly referred to this idea as 'liberalism with losers'—a model of liberal democracy in which discourses aim to offend, dispute, contest and emerge victoriously, but with an openness that acknowledges the possibility of their own contestation and defeat (Turner 2006, 29). It recognizes the unattainability of both objectivity and absolute consensus in politics and advocates the affirmation of democratic practice as the active contest between discourses.[9] Unsurprisingly, the brand of left-wing populism that Mouffe endorses is one that fits this account.

Mouffe's antipathy towards the 'essentialism' of left theories has remained unchanged right from her influential work with Laclau (Laclau and Mouffe 1985, 2; Mouffe 2018, 2–3). The bulk of left thought, in her assessment, is unable to move beyond an obsession with *a priori* categories like class and 'privileged agents' like the 'working class'. The populist moment is comprised of 'a set of heterogeneous demands' that cannot be adequately theorized 'merely in terms of interests linked to determinate social categories' (Mouffe 2018, 6). Furthermore, for reasons mentioned earlier, responses from the centre-left also remain ineffective, if not dangerous, in addressing these issues. Extreme-left, on the other hand, is chastised by Mouffe for their refusal to engage with people as they really are; instead, like revelationists, they relentlessly attempt to convince people of the 'truths' gleaned from their theories (Mouffe 2018, 55). Therefore, in Mouffe's opinion, to counteract the far-right, the left has no choice but to embrace a constructive form of populism.

Strictly speaking, she defines left populism 'as a discursive strategy of construction of the political frontier between "the people" and "the oligarchy"' (the latter being a broad term for the post-political elite; in other words, 'the establishment') (Mouffe 2018, 22–25). Such an approach is necessary, according to Mouffe, because most populist movements neither directly reject neoliberalism nor articulate their dissent in the manner outlined earlier. Though Third Way politics, neoliberal policies and deliberative theories have undoubtedly played a role in begetting disaffection among the masses, their protests are pronouncedly articulated in 'the language of democracy', and as a fight against the 'establishment elites'. Thus, for a left populism to succeed, Mouffe believes that it is essential to redraw the frontier in a manner that 'establishes a connection with the political values that are central to popular aspirations' (Mouffe 2018, 40). Such an endeavour will seek to promote agonist values by 'making…institutions more representative', thereby reviving the organic negotiations between the liberal and democratic registers (Mouffe 2018, 58). Furthermore, in keeping with agonism, it will neither circle around a pre-constituted idea nor assume a final order. Instead, it will be concerned 'with the creation of a hegemonic formation that will foster the recovery and deepening of democracy' (Mouffe 2018, 43).

Redrawing the Frontier: Deleuze and Mouffe

As a descriptive account of the populist moment, Mouffe's study is remarkable for tracing a common origin to the various forms of populism seen today. Provided one accepts the general viability of agonist ontology, as well as the criticisms levelled against the rationalist-deliberative model of democracy, it is hard to dispute her arguments in support of an affirmative model of populism. While it is indeed counterproductive to vilify or defame the supporters of the so-called right populism, the threats posed by many of these discourses to democratic practices are very real, as Mouffe reiterates. However, it is debatable whether a self-labelled 'left populism' could ever be successful in mitigating these dangers.

The arguments that Mouffe offers in support of a 'left' populism are often vague and arbitrary. Though she does accept the claim that many alternative prefixes—such as 'democratic', 'progressive' or 'humanist' populism—may well be equally suited to the task, she is, at the same time, determined to reinvigorate the 'left signifier [that] has been totally discredited' by mainstream discourses. (Mouffe 2018, 85). Nevertheless, she considers the likely criticism that the 'left' privileges the interests of only a section of the society to be a 'substantial objection'. Since Mouffe's 'populist strategy' centres around a common will or a collective 'we'—the 'people'—that emerges from 'the articulation of heterogeneous democratic demands' comprising the interests of various groups, qualifying it as 'left' defeats the 'transversal character' of the undertaking. However, she responds to this argument by stating that any vagueness over the political orientation of the strategy ought to be avoided due to 'the partisan way in which the "people" is constructed'. Furthermore, she justifies her use of the term by appealing to the 'axiological dimension' of leftist thought which is the emphasis on 'equality and social justice'. Broadly speaking, Mouffe holds it necessary to hold on to the leftist marker because contrary ideas of populism already exist with opposing ideological qualifiers: 'When it is recognized that the "people" can be constructed in different ways, and that right-wing populist parties also construct a "people", it is essential, for eminently political reasons, to indicate which kind of people one aims at constructing' (Mouffe 2018, 85–86).

By qualifying her position with one of the traditional ideological binaries, Mouffe fails to take into account the novelty and particularity of the populist moment, which, as she repeatedly emphasizes, has brought together heterogeneous demands from across the social spectrum in the form of a shared disaffection towards the establishment elites. The transversal nature of populism rightly demands a new intervention, but such an endeavour could be truly effective only if it achieves a certain degree of independence from loaded ideological signifiers. Though she stresses the importance of developing 'a different language' and 'a different vocabulary' to communicate these ideas, ultimately, she chooses to persist with the phraseology of the old Left (Mouffe 2018, 22). Throughout her oeuvre, Mouffe has stressed the importance of theorizing power without recourse to 'essences' or 'preconstituted identities' (Mouffe 1996, 247); yet, by recapitulating her political strategy through oppositions (agonistic or otherwise) such as left/right and people/oligarchy, her 'adversaries' are, in a sense, 'preconstituted' by their ideological history. Despite Mouffe's best efforts to revise and justify these markers, they ultimately thwart her project, as the 'preconstitutedness' of these terms nullify their agonistic dimension and, instead, render them as antagonists to be defeated by a revamped Left.

Mouffe is indeed justified in wanting to redraw the political frontier following the failures of other theoretical positions that attempted to blur such distinctions. The present study does not dispute either her ontology or her objectives; instead, it proposes a different methodology and an alternative vocabulary to construct this frontier. As Mouffe correctly points out, the conditions that facilitated the revival of populist discourses, both left and right, are largely the same, to the extent that they were born out of similar democratic demands. Though it is possible that many of these movements could stifle democracy 'in the name of recovering democracy', it would be a mistake to overlook the transversal nature of 'the populist moment', which is why Mouffe stresses that the new political frontier 'must be constructed in a "populist" transversal mode' (Mouffe 2018, 23–24). Yet, this idea of transversality is precluded by Mouffe's reluctance to move beyond the left/right distinction. Her assumption, for instance, that the ideas of equality and social justice are exclusive to the left appear erroneous and untenable when read alongside her own account of the populist moment. In fact, demands for justice and equality inspire most movements usually characterized as 'right-populist', even though such notions may be inherently exclusive in nature.[10] A better approach, I believe, is to move away from the charged (yet overwrought) dichotomy of left/right, and propose, in its place, an articulation of the frontier that takes into consideration the manner in which populist discourses organize social affects. To that end, I propose a dyadic (as opposed to binary) approach to the understanding of populism that draws on the political philosophy of Gilles Deleuze.

A certain recourse to dualisms is indispensable to the project of carving out a political frontier. Across Deleuze's corpus, one could find a number of such dualisms (molar/molecular, paranoia/schizophrenia, actual/virtual, reactive/active, state/nomad, major/minor, movement-image/time-image, etc.) that express the two tendencies or modes of 'becoming' in a body. In *Nietzsche and Philosophy* (1983), Deleuze offers a definition of the body in terms of forces and their relations:

> Phenomena, things, organisms, societies, consciousness and spirits are signs, or rather symptoms, and themselves reflect states of forces … We can ask, for any given thing, what state of exterior and interior forces it presupposes … every relationship of forces constitutes a body—whether it is chemical, biological, social or political (Deleuze 1983, 2, 40).

By defining bodies thus, Deleuze moves away from a representational model of philosophy, which seeks to determine a thing by its essence, towards a process-oriented approach that replaces the notion of a thing with concepts that express multiplicity and becoming (assemblage, machine, event). In so doing, Deleuze chiefly follows Bergson in understanding reality and experience as mixtures or composites. As Daniel Smith notes, the Bergsonian method of 'intuition' involves an attempt 'to seek out what is pure in any given mixture… and what is pure in a mixture are not elements but *tendencies*'. Though these tendencies ('pure concepts') do not exist on their own, 'it is only when we have isolated these pure concepts that we can begin to analyse the complexities of the mixtures found in any given social assemblage' (Smith 2012, 257 cf. Deleuze 1988, 91–94). Consequently, our theory of the frontier must involve an analysis of those pure forces (tendencies, flows, types and concepts) whose varying relations constitute its articulation and limit.

According to Fredric Jameson, if 'one can speak of Deleuze as a thinker of synthesis', it is because of his method of organizing thought in the form of dualisms ('the proliferation of thoughts and concepts by way of assimilation and appropriation'). Consequently, it is futile 'to search for … a central idea' in Deleuze, as he is more concerned with the task of transcoding 'a conceptual environment' into different 'force-fields' (Jameson 1997, 393). In *Nietzsche and Philosophy* (1983), for instance, Deleuze outlines an elementary processual principle, the 'will-to-power' which expresses itself in nature as a relation between two 'pure' forces—active (dominating) and reactive (dominated). Similarly, in *Anti-Oedipus*, it is the principle of 'desire' that is expressed in the sway between paranoia and schizophrenia. In *Kafka: Toward a Minor Literature* (1986), Deleuze and Guattari conceive language as a tension between major and minor modes. However, it is important to note that the major and minor modes 'do not qualify two different languages but rather two usages or functions of [the same] language … one of which consists in extracting constants from it, the other in placing it in continuous variation' (Deleuze and Guattari 1987, 103–106). Likewise, paranoia and schizophrenia do not indicate two forms of desire but the limit tendencies or the axes of the same principle. Broadly speaking, in Deleuze's philosophy, one could observe a basic process-principle that extends, on the one hand, towards an axis of structure, rigidity and hierarchy, and on the other, towards affirmation and relentless creativity.[11] As Jameson implies, this characteristic of Deleuzian philosophy indicates a 'drive toward monism'—will-to-power, desire, duration, etc.—'which is [also] paradoxically the source of ... [his] dualisms'.[12] The problem then becomes one of explaining how dualism emerges from this monism, as 'the very vocation of monism' lies in the 'rebuking of all those traditional dualisms' (Jameson 1997, 408).

In *A Thousand Plateaus* (1987), Deleuze and Guattari write that they 'make use of a dualism of models only in order to arrive at a process that challenges all models, ... [to] arrive at the magical formula ... PLURALISM = MONISM' (Deleuze and Guattari 1987, 20). Rodrigo Nunes correctly suggests that these dualisms ought to be read as 'dyads' and not 'binaries' (Nunes 2010, 104). According to Jameson, owing to their formal resemblance to ethical binaries, dualism always compels us 'to reinsert the good/evil axis to conceptual areas free of it, and to call for judgement where none is appropriate'. This, he believes, is accentuated in the case of Deleuze scholarship, wherein often one term of the dyad (schizophrenia, nomad, deterritorialization, molecular, etc.) is raised, or held as the standard, above the other (Jameson 1997, 409). The concept of a multiplicity, or the method of conceiving reality as composites or mixtures, is conceived by Deleuze to preclude a 'false choice' between one of the two dyads (Nunes 2010, 105).

Thus, populism—understood as a transversal principle of organizing heterogeneous demands—is dyadic, rather than binary, in nature. Consequently, populist discourses, as well as the 'people' constructed therein, are multiplicities (force-fields, assemblages, composites) that express major and minor tendencies in varying degrees of tension. By bringing a left/right binary into play, Mouffe's populist strategy inevitably privileges one term to the detriment of the other.[13] The frontier that Mouffe circumscribes is not merely an opposition between the left and the right, but also one between immanence and transcendence. If agonism is the basic immanent principle underlying her theory, it is so only within the purview of what she designates as the Left. Essentially, her populist model subordinates agonism to antagonism by pitting immanent agonistic acts against transcendent dogmas. Conceptually, this puts her political ontology at the risk of collapsing on itself (as agonism is meant to be the process-principle expressed in all forms of order) and threatens to derail the strictly immanent objectives of her earlier work. Moreover, it fails to account for the heterogeneous and rhizomatic nature of populist discourses that naturally resists categorization into such binaries.

In this context, how do we redraw the frontier given the dyadic nature of populism? The frontier, in my understanding, plays a role that is comparable to Hitchcock in the *Cinema* books (1986). The latter's films, in Deleuze's estimation, are 'movement-images' in the process of becoming 'time-images'. In the same vein, the political frontier may be conceived as the disjunctive synthesis that articulates the movement of 'paranoid-desire' in the process of becoming 'schizophrenic-desire' (molar-becoming-molecular, major-becoming-minor, reactive-becoming-active—the definition holds irrespective of the terminology of the dyads). It is a process that paradoxically connects and separates the two modes at the same time, thus affirming both their difference and distance as positive characteristics (Lecercle 2012, 18–19). Having reformulated the frontier in this manner, how may we theorize political agency in a model of agonist-populism? The answer lies in the distinction between the 'legitimate and illegitimate uses' of the agonist principle (Deleuze and Guattari 1983, 75). The former refers to its immanent application and the latter to its transcendent deployment. This is where the Deleuzian model differs conceptually from Mouffe's. Whereas the latter simply opposes immanence (agonism) to transcendence (dogma), the former conceives this distinction as a matter of praxis (and not as a mere opposition).

The problem of the legitimate and illegitimate uses of agonist-populism is perhaps best described in terms of the major-minor dyad. Broadly speaking, any discourse that privileges an identity, an ethnicity, a state, a form, a structure or a belief-system as the transcendent standard by which differences are measured (and subsequently removed) employs an illegitimate use of the agonist principle—we may refer to this as the major mode. On the other hand, any synthesis that actively creates something new by affirming and connecting differences from within the major mode (thus perpetuating the *agon*) operates legitimately—we may call this the minor mode. No discourse or practice exists exclusively in any one of these modes; instead, they express varying relations of tension between the major and the minor, with some leaning more towards one pole than the others. As noted previously, the theoretical preference for one side of the dyad in Deleuze scholarship is a consequence of treating these terms as binaries rather than as the two axes of the same process. As Schrift points out, 'becomings take place between poles; they are the in-betweens that pass only and always along a middle without origin or destination'. Consequently, the emphasis must be on 'the active process of assembling rather than hypostasing or reifying the endpoint to be assembled' (Schrift 2000, 152). In a similar vein, Nunes writes that 'there is no choice between the *two poles*, because one can only ever choose in between them'. This approach to Deleuze is what he refers to as 'politics in the middle' (Nunes 2010, 120). If there are two logics at play here (liberalism-democracy/paranoia-schizophrenia/active-reactive), as Mouffe suggests, their negotiations are dyadic, and not binary, in nature.

If there is a normative element to Deleuze's political philosophy, it is only to the extent that it grants 'an axiological as well as ontological priority to processes of deterritorialisation, becoming and metamorphosis' (Patton 2005a, 50). However, as Nunes acutely points out, 'to affirm deterritorialising power does not mean saying yes to all deterritorialisations, but knowing how to select'—because certain deterritorializing movements 'can turn out bad, either because they find paranoid reterritorialisations, or because they become isolated and turn in upon themselves ... it is never a matter of fleeing, but of constructing an active flight' (Nunes 2010, 123). It is a matter of realizing the difference between the 'history of revolutions' and 'revolutionary-becoming' (Deleuze and Negri 1990); if the former conveys the idea that any 'fixed' notion of identity, value or truth is nothing but 'a momentary strategy' open to unpredictable and violent change (Schrift 2000, 154), the latter expresses an 'intervention'—the fact that 'in every *here* and *now*, there are *potentials* that can be *acted upon*' (Nunes 2010, 121). For Deleuze and Guattari, the Marxist concept of revolution involves an 'absolute deterritorialization' (Deleuze and Guattari 1994, 101), whereas the idea of 'revolutionary-becoming' or 'becoming-revolutionary' expresses an ethos of constant and continuous 'relative deterritorializations'. 'Revolutionary-becoming' is both a matter of knowing that the subject-position that we occupy is 'not an ontological necessity' and of affirming other positions that 'are possible in terms of the contingencies of the present moment' (Schrift 2000, 154).

As Paul Patton notes, Deleuze and Guattari endorse 'revolutionary-becoming' as 'the path toward a new Earth and a people to come'. It calls for a resistance to all 'existing forms' of democratic practice, but only as a means to realize a 'becoming-democratic that is not to be confused with present constitutional states' (Patton 2011, 122; Deleuze and Guattari 1994, 113). According to Patton, the emphasis that Deleuze places on the relation between 'becoming-democratic' and 'becoming-revolutionary' is his most significant normative contribution to contemporary democratic thought (Patton 2005a, 56–66; Patton 2005b, 185–194; Patton 2011, 122–126). If 'agonist-populism' is understood dyadically as tending towards the two poles of paranoia and schizophrenia—and as being characterized by major and minor modes—the kind of 'politics in the middle' that we are advancing here must emphasize acts of relative deterritorialization, or 'revolutionary-becoming', as the normative principle most qualified to resist and mitigate its illegitimate uses.

The two concepts—'becoming-democratic' and 'becoming-revolutionary'—converge on the principle of 'becoming-minoritarian'. Patton refers to the latter as 'a vector' of 'becoming-democratic' (Patton 2011, 123). Minority here is not understood in numerical terms but as a 'nondenumerable' concept. As Jameson notes, 'it may be numerous or even infinite ... like a majority'. In the case of the majority, 'the relationship within number constitutes ...a complete or infinite ensemble ... that can always be denumerated or counted'; on the contrary, minority, as a nondenumerable ensemble, is characterized by 'connections'. Consequently, the 'role of the minority is to bring out the power of the nondenumerable even when it consists of only one member (Jameson 1997, 12). As this view appears to subordinate numerical majority to a concept that is more affective in nature, writers like Mengue (2003) tend to dismiss Deleuze as a theorist of democracy. However, as Patton points out, the idea of 'becoming-minor' does not necessarily translate to an outright dismissal of consensus or public opinion. It is instead a recognition of the fact that consensus and opinions themselves often reflect 'the cynical perceptions and affections' of certain privileged groups (Deleuze and Guattari 1994, 146; Patton 2005b, 188). Becoming-democratic/becoming-minor, for Deleuze, is to challenge 'the "considered" opinions that determine the nature and limits of public reason' and to critically engage 'with existing opinions about what is just or acceptable' (Patton 2005b, 189). He is not opposed to rights or jurisprudence, but instead, contests their reification as transcendent, eternal and abstract values. Rights and laws are, according to Deleuze, contingent and historical, and must respond to singular problems in a given milieu: 'There are no "rights of man", only rights of life, and so, life unfolds case by case' (Deleuze and Parnet 1996, translated in Patton 2005a, 60). It is this 'case-by-case' approach to problems of democracy that 'introduces movement into abstractions' and makes it an agonistic process of 'ongoing and open-ended' creation (Patton 2005a, 58–61). Furthermore, such a political stance acts as a deterrent against the concentration of power in the hands of an individual or an ideology; in other words, a 'minoritarian' attitude could prevent any illegitimate deployment of democratic-populism by keeping at bay the reterritorialization of politics around an identity or essence.[14]

In many ways, Deleuze's political philosophy emphasizes active lines of flights over conflicts. While his idea of the 'micropolitical' incorporates a Nietzschean ontology, the politics of affirmation that he is attempting to develop must inevitably dispense with the notion of conflict. Instead, he explains the agonist process as an ongoing interplay between deterritorializating and reterritorializing movements. His political philosophy is 'populist' in the Mouffian sense as it affirms the plurality of demands and interests that constitute the 'socius'. This heterogeneity can be immanently realized in practice only if it is accompanied by acts of 'revolutionary becomings'. As Patton writes,

> it is a matter of knowing that the majority is an abstract and empty representation of an ideal identity that is linked to particular systems of power and control and of knowing that there are minoritarian becomings in which everyone can be engaged and which have the power to disrupt and transform these systems. (Patton 2005a, 57)

As such, to 'become-minor' or to 'become-revolutionary' is to 'become-Ephesian'. It is a matter of knowing and seeking out the many Hermodors, not to banish but to 'disrupt and transform'.

Notes

1 According to Bonnie Honig, the problem with the idea of consensus is its tendency to exclude voices or leave 'remainders' (Honig 1993, 5).

2 A useful point of comparison is Sandel's (1982) critique of Rawls and his 'original position'.

3 In a recently published interview with Iñigo Errejón (2016), she repeats these arguments almost verbatim: 'To me it's a consequence of neoliberalism, and that is why it's accurate to say that we are living in 'post-democratic' societies. Furthermore, the consensus at the centre that we discussed previously has contributed to the discrediting of left-wing politics' (Errejón and Mouffe 2016b, 119).

4 Mouffe acknowledges as much in an earlier essay:

> An important part of my argument will be of a theoretical nature because I am convinced that in order to understand the appeal of right-wing populist discourse, it is necessary to question the

> rationalist and individualist tenets which inform the main trends of democratic political theory. (Mouffe 2005a, 51)

5 Although Mouffe occasionally makes statements that appear to claim that 'the agonistic tension between the liberal and democratic principles … has been eliminated' as a result of neoliberal hegemony (Mouffe 2018, 16), I have chosen to overlook them as they are inconsistent with the ontological premise that the *agon* never ceases to exist in 'the political' (Mouffe 2013, 2). One must presume that such statements have been aims for hyperbolic appeal rather than theoretical consistency.

6 While older theories of democracy and politics, in general, were conceived in relation to absolutes ('the good life'), the emphasis on pluralism as a 'social fact' and as a sign of the 'dissolution of the markers of certainty' is a discovery of the liberal-democratic model (Mouffe 1996, 246). It is, however, the failure to account for this 'fact' that Mouffe and other agonists bemoan. Though I have drawn chiefly from the works of Mouffe to substantiate my arguments, it must be noted that agonists such as Connolly and Honig tend to disagree with her on the specific nature of an agonistic democracy. Nevertheless, the critical objective of all their works is to theorize a model of pluralism that does not exclude or negate differences through collective abstractions.

7 In *Democracy, Power and the Political* (2005), Mouffe writes that only 'when *différance* is construed as the condition of possibility of being' can a truly pluralist idea of democracy ever be realized (Mouffe 1996, 246). Variants of this idea lie at the heart of all her works.

8 William Connolly refers to this idea as 'agonistic respect' (Connolly 1991, 14).

9 Objectivity is impossible, Mouffe argues, because we already find ourselves in a social order conditioned by hegemony. The social is 'constituted by sedimented hegemonic practices' and is the 'battlefield where hegemonic practices confront each other without hope of a final solution' (Mouffe 2007).

10 Right-populist movements often tend to bring up a perceived historical oversight or a form of racial/ethnic essentialism to advance their demands for justice and equality. Both concepts are inextricably linked in their rhetoric: While justice is often demanded as a corrective action to either reverse or universalize preferential policies and reforms implemented for the welfare of a minority or a group of minorities, equality is established as the basis or ground of this justice. Equality, in these discourses, is defined as the rightful claim of a group or class to the identity of a nation, culture or state on essentialist grounds. These claims tend to begin with the premise of an undeserving or unworthy 'outsider' who misappropriates the ethos of a culture. The objective of the populist movement, in these discourses, is to re-establish what they argue to be the most 'natural' and 'authentic' state of affairs pertinent to a region. Furthermore, although these discourses affirm the difference of a privileged group from the rest, they nonetheless negate this difference by demanding an equivalence

between all groups. This equivalence, however, often entails an exclusion of certain claimants from the public sphere or merely amounts to a homogenization of rights and demands according to the terms set by the revolting majority.

11 This expression of the process-principle articulates 'the univocal or immanent plane of a Nature conceived of as process of production' (Zourabichvili 2012, 163).

12 Jameson eloquently articulates this idea by referring to the principle of desire:

> For the principle of desire itself would be a monism … everything is desire; there is nothing which is not desire, nothing outside of desire. This means, of course, that fascism is a desire … that bureaucracy is desire, the State is desire, capitalism preeminently desire, even the much maligned Oedipus complex has to correspond to a certain desire in order to take on its inveterate authority. (Jameson 1997, 408)

13 This is the case also with any political model that applies to a Schmittian friend/enemy binary. This applies not only to those populist ideologies that demand national or ethnic sovereignty but also to the very distinction between a right and left populism. While Mouffe may disagree by pointing to the difference between an enemy and an adversary or by restating the problem in terms of agonistic respect, the fact of the matter is that a trace of 'the enemy', as well as a hint of antagonism, persists in her call for left populism. Mouffe demands a left intervention precisely because there is perceived right-wing populism and because the latter poses a threat. The project of working out an affirmative and agonist-pluralist populist model can never be truly validated if it is constituted by an original act of negation.

14 It is so because of the temporal nature of the praxis in the dyad and it relates back to the ontological accounts of time Deleuze provides in *Kant's Critical Philosophy* (1984) and *Difference and Repetition* (1994). According to Deleuze, classical Western philosophy till Kant is characterized by the subordination of time to movement. Irrespective of whether time is understood as 'the extensive [and divisible] movements of the cosmos or the intensive [and subjective] movements of the soul', pre-Kantian philosophy, for the most part, demanded the postulation of an 'originary time' (the eternal) against which all other times (the orders of change) could be measured and evaluated (Smith 2019, 33). As Smith notes, these systems were driven by the need to safeguard philosophical thought from 'aberrant movements' (Smith 2019, 36). The possibility of '*derived* time' that threatened to slip away from the rule of the originary time was a matter of concern in both the extensive and intensive domains. Kant attempted to solve this problem by inverting time's relation to movement, such that all movements—be they cosmological or psychological, originary or

derived—occur 'within time'. In other words, these movements are now understood as '*modes* or *relations* of time itself'. Whereas previously, 'time had been defined by succession, space by coexistence and eternity by permanence', in the first critique, they came to stand, respectively, for the rules 'of what is in different times… at the same time, [and] for all times'. Effectively, time becomes 'the pure and empty form of everything that changes and moves' (Deleuze 1989, 271; Smith 2019, 39). Deleuze revises this argument by stating that the pure form of time is 'a form of what is *not* eternal'. Furthermore, it is also 'non-chronological', as succession and simultaneity are simply modes of time and not constitutive of it. Neither is it permanent because if it were, it would be perceivable through sensation. Time is 'rendered ordinary' through a series of syntheses that are processes 'brought to bear, not on time itself, but on the modes of time, in order to render both being and knowledge possible' (Deleuze 1984, vii–viii; Smith 2019, 39–40).

In the first critique, Kant equates the passivity (of sensibility) to a simple receptivity and attributes synthetic powers only to the activity of the Understanding. Deleuze, on the other hand, argues that sensation itself is constituted temporally by a series of passive syntheses (Deleuze 1994, 86–87). As Williams notes, what is unique about Deleuze's theory of time is the emphasis it places on 'the caesura or split in time' that accompanies any event. This 'irrational cut' is also concurrently an 'assembly' of time as well as a 'production of the new': every event splits the time into two—'the past before the event and the future ahead of it'—however, we still 'decode the past and the future through this event, which is therefore adequate to the whole of time' (Deleuze 1989, 71; Williams 2012, 35). As subjectivity is necessarily fractured in time—'I is another', as Deleuze says, quoting Rimbaud (Deleuze, 1984: viii)—all claims regarding the essence and eternality of an 'authentic' identity, history or culture are necessarily contingent and untenable.

Bibliography

Connolly, W. 1991. *Identity/Difference.* Ithaca: Cornell University Press.

Deleuze, G. 1983. *Nietzsche and Philosophy*. London: Continuum.

——. 1984. *Kant's Critical Philosophy.* London: The Athlone Press.

——. 1986. *Cinema 1: The Movement-Image*. Minneapolis: University of Minnesota Press.

——. 1988. *Bergsonism*. New York: Zone Books.

——. 1989. *Cinema 2: The Time-Image*. Minneapolis: University of Minnesota Press.

Deleuze, G. and F. Guattari. 1983. *Capitalism and Schizophrenia: Anti-Oedipus*. Minneapolis: University of Minnesota Press.

——. 1986. *Kafka: Toward a Minor Literature*. Minneapolis: University of Minnesota Press.

——. 1987. *Capitalism and Schizophrenia: A Thousand Plateaus*. Minneapolis: University of Minnesota Press.

Deleuze, G. and A. Negri. 1990. 'Control and Becoming: Gille Deleuze in conversation with Antonio Negri.' *Anterieur I* (Spring 1990). Translated by Joughin, M. Futur. Available at https://www.uib.no/sites/w3.uib.no/files/attachments/6._deleuze-control_and_becoming_0.pdf (last accessed 16 June 2020).

Errejon, I. and C. Mouffe. 2016. *Podemos: In the Name of the People*. London: Lawrence and Wishart.

Honig, B. 1993. *Political Theory and the Displacement of Politics*. New York: Cornell University Press.

Jameson, F. 1997. 'Marxism and Dualism in Deleuze'. *The South Atlantic Quarterly*, 96(3): 393–416.

Laclau, E. and C. Mouffe. 1985. *Hegemony and Social Strategy*. London: Verso.

Lecercle, J.J. 2010. *Deleuze and Badiou Read Literature*. Edinburgh: Edinburgh University Press.

Mouffe, C. 1996. 'Democracy, Power and the Political.' In *Democracy and Difference*, edited by S. Benhabib, 245–256. Princeton: Princeton University Press.

——. 2000a. 'Deliberative Democracy or Agonistic Pluralism'. *Political Science Series*, 72: 1–17.

——. 2000b. *The Democratic Paradox*. London and New York: Verso.

——. 2005a. 'The "End of Politics" and the Challenge of Right-Wing Populism'. In *Populism and the Mirror of Democracy*, edited by F. Panizza, 72–98. London: Verso.

——. 2005b. *On the Political*. London and New York: Routledge.

——. 2008. 'Art as an Agnostic Intervention in Public Space'. *Open* (14): 6–15.

——. 2013. *Agonistics: Thinking the World Politically*. London and New York: Verso.

——. 2014. 'Agonistic Democracy and Radical Politics.' *Pavillion Journal for Politics and Culture*, 2014. Available at https://www.pavilionmagazine.org/chantal-mouffe-agonistic-democracy-and-radical-politics (last accessed 16 June 2020).

——. 2016a. 'The Populist Moment'. Available at: https://www.opendemocracy.net/en/democraciaabierta/populist-moment (last accessed 12 November 2019).

——. 2018. *For a Left Populism*. London and New York: Verso.

Nietzsche, F. 2006. 'Homer's Contest'. In *'On the Genealogy of Morality' and Other Writings*, edited by K. Ansell-Pearson, 174–181. Cambridge: Cambridge University Press.

Nunes, R. 2010. 'Politics in the Middle: For a Political Interpretations of the Dualisms in Deleuze and Guattari'. *Deleuze Studies*, 4: 104–126.

Patton, P. 2005a. 'Deleuze and Democratic Politics'. In *Radical Democracy: Politics between Abundance and Lack*, edited by L. Tønder and L. Thomassen, 50–67. Manchester: Manchester University Press.

Sandel, M. 1982. *The Limits of Justice*. Cambridge: Cambridge University Press.

Schrift, A. 2010. 'Nietzsche, Foucault, Deleuze and the Subject of Radical Democracy'. *Angelaki: Journal of the Theoretical Humanities*, 5(2): 151–161.

Smith, D. 2012. *Essays on Deleuze*. Edinburgh: Edinburgh University Press.

——. 'The Pure Form of Time and the Powers of the False'. *TijdschriftVoorFilosofie*, 81(1): 29–51.

Siemens, H.W. 2013. 'Reassessing Nietzsche's Radical Democratic Theory in the Light of Nietzsche's Ontology of Conflict'. In *Nietzsche and Political Thought*, edited by K. Ansell-Pearson, 83–106. London: Bloomsbury.

Turner, B. 2006. 'The Thrill of Victory, the Agony of Defeat: The Nietzschean Vision of Contest.' Proceedings of the Annual Meeting of the American Political Association.

Williams, J. 2012. 'Difference and Repetition.' In *The Cambridge Companion to Deleuze*, edited by Daniel W. Smith and Henry Somers-Hall, 33–54. Cambridge: Cambridge University Press.

Zourabichvili, F. 2012. *Deleuze: A Philosophy of the Event Together With the Vocabulary of Deleuze*. Edinburgh: Edinburgh University Press.

6

ON THE DECONSTRUCTIVE LOGIC OF POPULISM[1]

Samir Gandesha

Introduction

Can there be little doubt that one of the most important political developments in the past decade has been the rise of Left populism? This political formation is, as Chantal Mouffe has recently argued (2018), a type of 'radical democratic' politics entailing an immanent critique of liberal-democracy—the attempt to make its institutions live up to their normative promises. Left populism aims at the genuine expression of the will of the 'demos', constituted via an antagonism with the 'oligarchy', yet within the framework of the rule of law and constitutional 'checks and balances'. Mouffe argues for a "'radicalization' of the ethico-political principles of liberal-democratic regime, 'liberty and equality for all'" (Mouffe 2018, 39). Left populism, along with its authoritarian counterpart, emerges with the shattering of the 'post-political neoliberal consensus' in the aftermath of the financial crisis of 2007–2008. The notion of 'consensus' refers to the widespread acceptance virtually across the entire political spectrum, from nominal social-democratic to conservative parties, of a neoliberal market-based agenda of privatization, deregulation, upward redistribution of wealth and appropriation by dispossession—the four constitutive dimensions of neoliberalism according to David Harvey's concise definition (Harvey 2005). Differences between the parties are generally taken to be over style rather than the actual substance of social and economic policy. This often reflects not just lack of political will per se but institutionalized limits, for example within the EU, on deficit spending.

In contrast to the technocratic consensus, Left populism reinjects antagonism and conflict back into the ossified liberal-democratic institutions of the Western world by emphasizing the opposition between the demos or the people, on the one hand, and the oligarchy or the powerful, on the other. While not all political movements and tendencies would accept the designation, it is possible to identify in Bernie Sanders' bid for the Democratic Party's 2016 Presidential Nomination, reiterating the opposition identified by Occupy Wall Street between 99 per cent and the 1 per cent, in the Corbyn-led British Labour Party emphasizing a politics 'For the many and not the few', and in Podemos, with its inflection on the opposition between the *gente* (people) and the *caste* (elite), forms of Left populism according to Mouffe's theorization (Errejón and Mouffe 2016). Indeed, in the latter party as well as in Mélenchon's *La France Insoumise* (Unbowed France), we see the direct influence of Laclau and Mouffe's attempts to develop the idea of 'populist reason' (Desmoulières 2016).

While the aforementioned Left populist movements and parties are the source of tremendous hope for a very different kind of politics, another example provides a somewhat more sober lesson in some of the not-inconsiderable structural constraints facing them when they have formed governments and sought to exercise power (see Žižek 2019). Such practical failings may, in turn, expose certain theoretical shortcomings or blind-spots in Laclau's 'deconstructive' account of populism. Laclau's account of populism is deconstructive insofar as it is the very heterogeneous and, therefore, the undecidable nature of the social that constitutes the, as it were, 'groundless ground' of hegemonic politics. The theoretical shortcomings to which I alluded may be identified as a failure to fully grasp the economic logic underlying the populist shattering of the technocratic consensus. By 'economic', I mean both the objective structures of neoliberal capitalism grounded in deregulation, privatization, accumulation by dispossession and a massive upward redistribution of wealth, on the one hand, and the production of a form of subjectivity, on the other, understood along 'entrepreneurial' lines (Foucault 2010) that entail ever-greater personal responsibility for one's success (or failure). This is the process of a remaking of the figure of *homo politicus* into that of *homo economicus* (Brown 2015). In other words, the consensus has to do with the power of finance, financialization and debt as quasi-objective processes that lie very much at the heart of our neoliberal present as well as the psychological mechanisms or 'personality structures' or what Erich Fromm calls 'social character' (Fromm 1994) or the quasi-subjective conditions that are socially reproduced that ensure the maintenance of given social order. It is necessary to attend to the relation of social character in the context of contemporary neoliberal society to ascertain both the continuities with and departure from the previous form of capitalism, specifically with respect to authoritarian tendencies that, as we have seen, in the recent decade or so have risen to the surface. This is what I refer elsewhere to as the 'neoliberal personality' (Gandesha 2018). The affectively charged nature of the populist challenge to the neoliberal cannot be properly grasped without understanding the nature of the contradictory relations between these objective and subjective dimensions. Laclau's deconstructive account of populism, I argue, is, unfortunately, not fully up to the task of doing so.

These failings can be attributed to Laclau's understanding of the social as marked by increasing contingency rather than a necessity which begins with the relative autonomy of politics and ideology from the 'economic instance' in Althusserian or structuralist Marxism. In such a form of Marxism, as Althusser states, 'From the first moment to the last, the lonely hour of the 'last instance' never comes (Althusser 1977, 113). Laclau then advances to an account of the social as characterized by a deconstructive logic of undecidability, 'radical heterogeneity' and the 'madness of decision'. It would seem that, for Laclau, the logic of the social is one of all or nothing: *either* reductionism and economism *or* radical heterogeneity; the tension within political theory from Machiavelli through Spinoza, Kant, German Idealism, Marx, Gramsci and Arendt, among others, between necessity and freedom, appears to have been annulled. Yet, in the actual practice of politics, no question is more important than those related to the limits and possibilities of political action.

Neither sophisticated forms of Marxism nor psychoanalysis submit to such an either/or logic. Laclau's insistence on the radical heterogeneity of the social makes it impossible to recognize the power of historically elaborated structures deeply at odds with the understanding of the social as characterized by an 'ontological' openness and contingency. It could be retorted, however, that the structures themselves can be understood as contingent. Yet such a rejoinder is ultimately unconvincing insofar as structure is typically understood as embodying necessity, not contingency. This does not mean that structure and agency are to be understood as antithetical. We can understand such logic in both sociology and psychoanalysis.

In respect to the former, class structure manifests a form of necessity that is reproduced in the specific actions of individuals within the specific context of the family, schools and universities, medical and psychiatric institutions. With the respect to the latter, the compulsion to repeat has to do with a response to the trauma of loss which is reproduced in the life of the analys and until its specific nature is brought to light through processes of transference and counter-transference relations within the course of analytical treatment and worked through. Paradoxically, Laclau's account emerges out of the idea that the political and the ideological instances are relatively autonomous from the economic and culminates in the view that the political, itself, institutes 'the social.' But, what we see in the Greek case is precisely the foundering of the 'political' on the shoals of the social, that is to say, the overwhelming power of finance capital. The structure of my argument is as follows: (I) I first sketch in broad brush strokes the key moves in the development in Laclau's theory of populism, before (II) suggesting some criticisms in his account of politics before (III) zeroing in more specifically on his engagement with Marxism and (IV) concluding with some reflections on the Greek case.

I

Laclau's initial theorization of populism arises out of a structuralist—or Althusserian—reading of the Italian Marxist Antonio Gramsci. Gramsci is best known for his understanding of the Russian Revolution as a 'revolution against *Capital*' and for his critical stance towards the Third International's inability to address the problem of the 'national-popular' forms of political mobilization in unevenly developed social formations such as Italy. Such societies were marked by a profound and enduring 'combined but uneven development' leading to the split—one which is still very much reflected in the politics of the current governing collation partner Lega (formerly Lega Nord)—between an industrialized north and a largely agrarian south (Gramsci 1978). As an attempt to address both problems, Gramsci seized upon Lenin's idea that in the context of the particular agrarian conditions of Russia the working class was not the sole agent of political transformation but rather had to play a leading or 'hegemonic' (*gegemonia*) role. The October Revolution's slogan 'Peace, land and bread' was not, of course, exclusively proletarian in content. It included the demands of other social classes, namely the peasantry—a class that Marx once argued was objectively reactionary because its members were isolated from one another, working in small groups on lord's *demesne*, rather than in large numbers in urban industrial factories (Marx 1979). For both Lenin and Gramsci, the politics of hegemony entailed the transcendence of what Lenin in his pamphlet 'What is to be Done?' called 'trade union consciousness' (Lenin 1969, 17) through organization. As we shall see, the capacity of populism to incorporate heterogeneous demands within the constitution of 'the people' will form the core of

Laclau's conception. The logical unfolding of this conception entails a progressive decentering of the working class, to the point where social structure dissolves in a radically contingent play of signification that can only be provisionally and incompletely arrested to yield fixity and stability. For Laclau it becomes the very essence of the hegemonic logic of the political.

For Gramsci, the working class in Italy could play a hegemonic role by virtue of its claim of addressing the condition of unequal development by assuming a leadership role within the nation. That is to say that, while in other countries—paradigmatically France—it was the bourgeoisie that unified the country under the auspices of the nation-state, for Gramsci, in Italy it would be the working class that would assume the mantle of 'national-popular' leadership. The Communist Party, specifically, would play the role of what Gramsci called the 'Modern Prince' and echo Machiavelli's call in the closing pages of *The Prince* (Machiavelli 2003, 82–85) for Lorenzo de Medici to unify Italy. For Gramsci, hegemony represents the 'cathartic moment' whereby the working class transcends its narrow 'trade union' interests and becomes capable of integrating the interests of other 'subaltern' classes into its political project. It is easy to see the attraction of the Italian author of a text entitled 'Some Aspects of the Southern Question' (Gramsci 1978, 441–462) for a figure like Laclau who was profoundly attentive to the unique semi-peripheral status of his native Argentina.

Laclau (1977) approaches Gramsci through a structural lens, which means that he seeks to interpret him through the idea of *structural* as opposed to *expressive* totality. For the latter, most clearly outlined in the early work of Georg Lukács, totality was understood (at least according to Althusser) as *expressing* a single underlying contradiction within the realm of the economy between the relations and forces of production, that would prioritize the working class as the agent of revolutionary change (Althusser 1979). From the standpoint of the expressive conception of totality, class determinations that arise out of this contradiction can be located at every level of society as a whole; state and politics, culture and ideology. For example, Lukács famously argued that proletarian consciousness provided an answer to some of the most complex and intractable philosophical questions arising out of German Idealism (Lukács 1971, 83–222). Writing decisively against Lukács, Althusser developed a notion of structural totality between different instances of the mode of production, each of which was relatively autonomous from the others, although the economic was ultimately the determining aspect or instance, as noted previously. While for the Lukácsian conception of totality secondary contradictions simply reflect principal contradictions, for the structuralist conception of totality, Althusser argues 'the secondary contradictions are essential even to the existence of the principal contradiction, that they really constitute its conditions of existence, just as the principal contradiction constitutes their condition of existence' (2006, 205). The relation between the different elements of a mode of production, for Althusser, is established via a notion of *articulation* (Althusser 1977, 202).

In the 'Theory of Populism' essay included in the volume *Politics and Ideology in Marxist Theory*,[2] Laclau argues that Lukàcsian Marxism seeks to understand politics and ideology—and populism by extension—on the basis of reductionism. Refusing to reduce them to the class positions, Laclau seeks to understand politics and ideology in terms of *articulation*. Laclau conceives of populism as an 'antagonistic synthesis'; a synthesis of heterogeneous elements with no necessary class belonging, that plays a role in a given antagonism between the 'people' and the 'power bloc' or state. In other words, the contradiction between proletarian and bourgeois at the economic level took the form of an antagonism between 'the people' and the 'power bloc' at the level of politics and ideology. Moreover, there was no necessary relation between the two. The content—what makes a given ideology democratic or authoritarian—has to do with its precise *form of articulation* (Laclau 1977, 143–199).[3]

In his hugely influential yet profoundly controversial subsequent work with Chantal Mouffe entitled *Hegemony and Socialist Strategy*, Laclau seeks to develop his analysis of populism so as to generate a new post-Marxist politics. In other words, Laclau is developing in a British context (he is now based at Essex University) a political strategy that is germane to a context that has seen the rise of what Stuart Hall called 'authoritarian populism' (Hall 2017, 172–186) in the form of Thatcherism. Laclau and Mouffe's *Hegemony and Socialist Strategy* (1985) differs from Laclau's earlier work in at least two ways: (a) it breaks with Althusserian Marxism, particularly that of Nicos Poulantzas (2014), insofar as it no longer accords the working class a privileged role in social transformation; and (b) it provides a discursive account of the social. The continuity, however, lies in the fact that Laclau insists upon the centrality of the concept of hegemonic articulation of heterogeneous political demands as the basis of a leftist political strategy (1985).

Hegemony and Socialist Strategy was widely criticized by the Marxist Left. One of the most notable of such critiques was issued by so-called 'Political Marxist' Ellen Meiksins Wood. Wood argued that Laclau's and Mouffe's position represents a step in the wrong direction, that is, it was a form of 'New True Socialism' that Marx and Engels criticize in the *Communist Manifesto* (1986). But what Wood and other Marxist critics failed to acknowledge was the importance of thinking through the *specificity* of the political in a manner started by Gramsci who does so through a brilliant appropriation of the 'Machiavellian moment' (see Gandesha 2018). Indeed, it comes as no surprise that Gramsci referred to the Italian Communist Party as the 'Modern Prince', as previously stated. At the same time, it is impossible to understand the specificity of the political outside of socio-economic relations as Theodor W. Adorno suggests in one of his rare public lectures on politics: Adorno implicitly invokes Marx's claim against Hegel, that the anatomy of the State was to be located in *bürgerliche Gesellschaft*, by suggesting that politics cannot be understood as a 'self-enclosed, isolated sphere…but rather can be conceived only in its relationship to the societal forces making up the substance of everything political and veiled by political surface phenomenon' (Adorno 1998, 282). I shall return to this further in the chapter.

In *On Populist Reason* (2005) Laclau develops the basic notion of populism in terms of an equivalential articulation of differences in relation to an 'antagonistic frontier'. For Laclau, as becomes apparent in his excoriating criticisms of Hardt and Negri's concept of the 'multitude' and what he calls Žižek's 'Martian politics' (Laclau 2005, 232–239), all democratic politics are populist. In other words, if we assume that society is inherently heterogeneous, politics must entail the hegemonic articulation of multiplicity of political demands in a manner that is always provisional and infinitely open to revision. A given hegemonic equivalential articulation of differences is always shifting and temporary and is based on the logic of the empty signifier. Whether society can be understood in terms of such heterogeneity is a question I take up further.

The key difference from his previous work is Laclau's attempt to conceptualize the affective dimension of politics via Lacanian psychoanalysis. John Kraniauskas (2006) understands this as the articulation of a Gramscian Lacan in contradistinction to Žižek's Hegelian Lacan. While the latter takes as its point of departure the understanding of the 'desire of the Other' (the impossible-because-unattainable desire for intersubjective recognition), the former can be understood in terms of *political* desire. For Laclau political desire is geared to what Lacan calls the 'objet petit a', meaning a partial object that is a fragment of the Real (the order that eludes symbolization yet is caught within the symbolic order). The 'object petit a' is often symbolized by the bountiful breast; and as such promises a return to an originary plenitude prior to the symbolic order based on differentiation and non-identity between signifier and signified. Political desire, then, is established through the Name or the coincidence of signifier and signified that is only set retroactively. The key point Laclau is making here is that this Lacanian understanding of political desire enables us to understand desire in a way that provides an alternative to Freud's, the latter being mass politics grounded in the love of an authoritarian leader who represents the Imago of the father. In contrast, political desire grounded in the utopic logic of the 'objet petit a' is characterized by the horizontal relations between brothers (although it's not clear if this includes 'sisters').

II

Several problems can be identified with Laclau's approach to populism. Critics have drawn attention to its formalism stemming from its reliance on structural linguistics in which signification is understood by way of a system of differences with no positive terms. This formalist premise is the basis for his understanding of the figure of the *people* as an empty signifier that can take on radically divergent contents. What the approach seems to elide is the diachronic continuity of this figure. The idea of 'the people' (*demos*) has a rich and semantically charged history stretching from fifth-century Athenian democracy through the Roman Republic to the bourgeois revolutionary experiences and then onto the radical Black tradition with the Black Panthers' slogan 'All Power to the People'. Such semantic richness does not, however, imply the kind of semiotic openness proposed by Laclau. While in *Hegemony and Socialist Strategy*, Laclau provides (with Mouffe) a genealogy of the concept of hegemony, in *On Populist Reason* he avoids providing the kind of account of the people that is, for example, sketched by Giorgio Agamben in *Homo Sacer* (Kraniauskas 2006).[4] Relatedly, while Laclau quite rightly takes up a sceptical attitude towards class reductionism, it simply does not follow that this necessarily implies, as Laclau seems to suggest, an account of the social as marked by radical contingency. It seems that Laclau thinks *either* we must conceive of necessity in terms of a Hegelian or Marxian philosophy of history that offers the possibility of a closed historical totality in terms either of Absolute Spirit or Communism *or* the social dissolves completely into an infinite, deconstructive play of radical differing and deferral of meaning (Derrida 1982, 1–28).

Laclau, strangely, overlooks the materialist core of psychoanalysis according to which, for example in *Civilization and its Discontents*, class-divided societies are based on repressive mechanisms which, themselves, produce surplus frustration and aggressiveness. These can subsequently be directed at 'out-groups' or 'others.' The necessity of producing and reproducing the conditions of human sociality are not merely *contingent* but *necessary* features of all forms of society. The tension between Eros and Thanatos, unity and destructive aggression, is, for psychoanalysis, inescapable for class societies. Central to these is the necessity of the production of surplus product and societal reproduction. And, of course, the irony is that the relations of objectivity and subjectivity—as Marx argued in the *Grundrisse*, an object is produced for a subject, but also a subject for an object—forms one of Gramsci's key insights. This premise is irreconcilable with Laclau's depiction of the social as characterized by a logic of radical heterogeneity.

Laclau's engagement with Marxism largely avoids Marx's own texts such as the *Civil War in France* or his particularly timely writing on slavery, the Irish and national questions (see Anderson 2016) and so forth. It is especially difficult to maintain that the *Eighteenth Brumaire of Louis Bonaparte* is an exemplar of 'economism' or 'class reductionism'. Rather, it is a particularly nuanced understanding of the class struggle that 'brushes against the grain', in the Benjaminian sense, of any straightforward progressivist philosophy of history. And in this case, we see, far from the radical heterogeneity of the social and the logic of 'empty' or 'floating' signifiers, an all-too overwhelming, inescapable semantic fullness of the sign. 'History', Marx famously observes, 'weighs like a nightmare on the brains of the living' (Marx 1979). The (modernist) production (*poeisis*) of new signs is a necessary requirement for any socialist movement with a future and cannot be accepted simply as a given. *In other words, Marx's question is precisely how is heterogeneity or, more specifically, semantic difference possible?* Marx's call for a 'poetry of the future' is a call for such difference. The homogeneity of dead labour weighs all too heavily on the potentiality of living labour. It comes as little surprise, then, that debates within Marxism in the 1920s and 1930s are centrally preoccupied by questions of art and aesthetics (Gandesha and Hartle 2017; Jameson 2006).

In the *Brumaire* we see in the bourgeoisie's fixation on the heroic signifiers of the alternatively Roman Republic and Roman Empire, the traumatic realization of its situation, of being poised between the old which cannot die and the new which cannot yet be born; between the heroic bourgeois revolution of 1789 and the incipient though, of course, failed proletarian revolution of the Paris Commune in 1871. What better description of the nephew of Napoleon than 'morbid symptom'. Marx's style is provoked to such brilliant rhetorical intensity precisely out of the realization that history was less to be understood in linear narrative terms that would deliver a revolution in the modern sense—the 'new'—as in the *Communist Manifesto*, but rather was understood in the ancient sense, conceived as the inevitable cyclical rise and fall of political regimes as in, for example, the Book VIII of Plato's *Republic*. That the fixation with the master signifier of Rome transcended the heroic bourgeoisie's tragedy and proletarian comedy ('Communism as the solution to the riddle of history') and discharges in a farcical repetition compulsion (see Gandesha and Hartle 2017).

While providing an 'ontological' understanding the 'logic of the political' in a somewhat inflated way as the '*institution* of the social', Laclau curiously downplays the actual 'ontic' role of institutions in historical change and continuity (Mouzelis 1978). Laclau's account of the social is deconstructive insofar as it bears striking similarities with Derrida's own early engagement with structuralism in the human sciences, in particular the anthropology of Levi-Strauss, which emphasizes temporality in the form of logic of deferral of meaning, the 'play' of signification and the role of reading in stabilizing the meaning of an inherently contingent and open-ended text (Derrida 1978, 351–370). Laclau understands this in terms of the exigencies of decision on the horizon of an inherent 'undecidability'. As Laclau explains

> From here we can move straight to the question of the decision. I think that the matter can be put in the following terms. To deconstruct the structure is the same as to show its undecidability, the distance between the plurality of arrangements that are possible out of it and the actual arrangement that has finally prevailed. This we can call a decision in so far as: (a) it is not predetermined by the 'original' terms of the structure; and (b) it requires its passage through the experience of undecidability. The moment of the decision, the moment of madness, is this jump from the experience of undecidability to a creative act, a fiat that requires its passage through that experience. As we have said, this act cannot be explained in terms of any rational underlying mediation. This moment of decision as something left to itself and unable to provide its grounds through any system of rules transcending itself, is the moment of the subject. Why call it a subject? We will approach the matter by considering the constitutive dimensions of any decision worth its name. (Laclau 1996)

Or as he puts it in *Emancipation(s)*, hegemonic formations are always 'unstable and undecidable' (Laclau 1996, 15). Laclau goes on to argue for a deconstructive form of subjectivity insofar as the subject is, itself, defined in utterly formal terms as the distance between a field or horizon of undecidability and the decision. This is supplemented by a Lacanian understanding of the subject as constituted by 'lack.'

Derrida's reading itself can be regarded as a decisionistic version of what Nietzsche called 'Will to Power' or the 'imposition of the aspect of Being on becoming' (Nietzsche 1968, aphorism 617; Gandesha 2019, 168–170). A key difference, though, is that like Machiavelli and Gramsci, Nietzsche emphasizes institutions such as those of Academic philosophy (Platonism) and the Church (Christianity) in elaborating 'hegemonic' interpretations of the teachings of Socrates and Jesus respectively as the most effective and enduring instances of such 'will to power' (Nietzsche 1990) the early Derrida and the later Laclau tend to elide the role of institutions.[5] This becomes especially clear in Laclau's emphasis on the radical heterogeneity of the social. Can we understand the mechanism of articulation other than through institutions such as the family, the state, political parties, trades unions and the whole host of organizations and associations that comprised what Gramsci called 'civil society', which was, for him, the terrain of a 'war of position' or a cultural-ideological struggle?

III

Finally, and most importantly for our purposes, the questions mentioned previously are raised by the Freudian/Lacanian psychoanalysis upon which Laclau depends to ground his account of populism, in particular, to rescue populism from the 'denigration of the masses' of figures like Gustav Le Bon. However, Laclau's engagement with Freudian social psychology must be regarded as a missed opportunity, since he ignores the problem that occupies such an important role in *Group Psychology and the Analysis of the Ego*, namely the phenomenon of the regression of the group to the primal horde. As John Kraniauskas (2006, 51) argues:

> In Laclau's populist version, the former is no longer the authoritarian Father but just another brother, one among equals, and, as a model for thinking the hegemony of one equivalential claim among others, it is the means through which populist political identity is produced.

The possibility of regression marks a key feature of psychoanalysis that Laclau struggles with in his account of populism, namely the manner in which the 'past weighs like a nightmare on the brains of the living' and the closely related problem (for both Freud and Lacan) of the compulsion to repeat. Surely, to understand populism today (particularly its authoritarian form) it is necessary to come to terms precisely with such phenomena. In other words, from both ontogenic and phylogenic perspectives, psychoanalysis must be understood not merely as a formal model by which the equivalential articulation of differences is possible but also substantively in terms of a method for working through the stubborn persistence of effects of past traumas which is profoundly at odds with Laclau's seemingly voluntarist emphasis on the radical *contingency* of the social.

Laclau's twin engagements with Marxism and psychoanalysis are also thrown into a new critical light in the wake of the publication of Samo Tomšič's important but flawed book *The Capitalist Unconscious* in which the author argues that in Lacan one can find not one but two returns to Freud. The first is through the structuralist linguistics of Saussure and the second is through Marx's structural critique of political economy through which Freud is revealed to have developed a labour theory of the unconscious. In other words, Tomšič shows the 'homology' of the two 'negative' logics of a Marxian and a Freudian economy. Tomšič identifies the way in which, in a late capitalist society, even the unconscious is colonized by the logic of capital. Yet, at the same time, Tomšič makes the critical error of failing to distinguish between labour (*Arbeit*) and labour power (*Arbeitskraft*) and, therefore, misses the key component of abstract labour which is homogenous discrete, quantifiable *time* itself. Capital is none other than congealed surplus labour time. Yet Freud argues that the unconscious is characterized by neither time nor space (Freud). And, indeed, this is what preserves the non-identity of the unconscious—that it doesn't enter into concepts without disruptively leaving a remainder. But what remains valuable in Tomšič's reading is his emphasis on the disavowal of treating either psychoanalysis or Marxism as simply 'world-views' (Tomšič 2015).

This finds an important echo in the so-called new readings of Marx (*neue Lektüre*) that focus on the 'value-form'. that emphasize that Marx's writings ought not to be understood as a kind of alternative world-view of the political economy of the working class, and therefore a form of class reductionism, but rather a rigorous and self-reflective 'critical theory' (Heinrich 2012). In contrast, instead of taking labour as a trans-historical category, the [value-form] approach analyzes the specific form of labour in capitalist society—abstract labour which expresses itself as value and, as such, is the means by which the structures of capitalist society are produced and reproduced. Rather than articulating a critique of capitalism from the standpoint of concrete labour and emphasizing labour processes and exploitation, the new reading of Marx emphasizes the standpoint of the totality of the moments or elements of capitalist society mediated by abstract labour or value as such. And rather than emphasizing a materialist political economy against the Idealism of classical German philosophy, this second reading emphasizes the importance and irreducibility of the idea of 'critique' understood as the de-fetishization of the categories through which capitalist society understands itself, including the one-sided understanding of concrete labour. It entails a critique of forms of subjectivity as well as of objectivity. The point is not to advocate a more equitable distribution of value but rather to overcome the expression of wealth *as* value. In other words, the Marxian critique of capitalism isn't simply articulated from the standpoint of 'concrete' labour—which would be the object of Laclau's attack as 'class reductionism' and 'economism'—but is a critique that aims precisely at the relation between concrete and abstract labour.

Laclau's theorization of Left populism takes its point of departure from economistic and class reductionistic forms of Marxism. However, it is far from clear that such an account can do without a 'critical theory' which is both a critique of the categories of political economy and a critique of its prevailing libidinal economy. Political and libidinal economies converge in the idea of what Erich Fromm calls 'social character'. As he explains:

> Character in the dynamic sense of analytic psychology is the specific form in which human energy is shaped by the dynamic adaptation of human needs to the particular mode of existence of a given society. Character in its turn determines the thinking, feeling, and acting of individuals. (Fromm 1994, 278)

Fromm uses the concept of social character to account for the way in which the German labour movement which was strong and confident prior to the rise of the Nazis was so quick to capitulate once they were politically victorious. While socialist and communist ideas were widely accepted amongst German workers, they didn't reach particularly deep. Therefore, Nazism was not met with the kind of steadfast opposition one would have expected from the working class. According to Fromm, 'Many of the adherents of the leftist parties, although they believed in their party programs as long as the parties had authority, were ready to resign to support the right when the hour of crisis arrived' (Fromm 1994, 280–281). According to Fromm, because of the deep-seated authoritarianism stemming from Calvinistic and Lutheran traditions, they opted to subordinate themselves to an authoritarian form of rule rather than struggling for self-determination in the form of revolutionary activity.

The concept of social character, the specific concatenation of the logic of political and libidinal economy, explains the ease with which the Nazis were able to seize power. Far from confirming the radical heterogeneity of the social on the basis of which the Nazis were able to forge a new 'equivalence of differential demands'; those of, say, industrial capital, the petty bourgeoisie and large swaths of the working class, in relation to the 'antagonistic frontier' of Jewish financiers, Council Communists, 'back-stabbing' politicians, 'Versailles', etc., what we see is all-too-much homogeneity or identity over the difference that can be traced back to the earliest origins in the 'spirit' of capitalism. Laclau, like Left-wing German political leaders, to use Fromm's own language, overemphasizes the 'range' as opposed to the 'weight' of Left-wing ideas. But the key thing isn't just the weight of the ideas themselves but the manner in which they become powerful in a particular socio-historical conjuncture. As Fromm explains, in contrast to the picture of the political leadership of the Left,

> our analysis of Protestant and Calvinist doctrines has shown that those ideas were powerful forces within the adherents of the new religion, because they appealed to the needs and anxieties that were present in the character structure of the people to whom they were addressed. In other words, ideas can become powerful forces, but only to the extent to which they are answers to specific human needs prominent in a given social character. (Fromm 1994, 281)

In a sense, what Fromm is identifying is precisely what Marx referred to in the *Brumaire* as the weight of history. Insofar as the French bourgeoisie was faced with an increasingly restive proletariat, when push came to shove, it acquiesced to the leadership of Louis Bonaparte and the 'party of order'. Such 'Bonapartism' would, of course, anticipate the rise of fascism as a response to the devastating crisis of overproduction and under-consumption and the rise of the spectre of communism. Without grasping what the German historian, Arno J. Mayer, called the 'persistence of the old regime' (1981) both in political economic and psychological terms, it is not possible to adequately come to terms with populism. After all, so many forms of right populism, rather than directly and explicitly advocated inequality and subordination (the antithesis to Left populism's emphasis on equality and freedom), make an implicit, affective, appeal to an idealized past. This is, of course, no more crassly and directly expressed by President Donald J. Trump's slogan: 'Make America Great Again' which suggests not only the economic imaginary of industrial jobs and the family wage but also a libidinal imaginary of authoritarian, racialized social order before substantial non-European immigration, an order in which African Americans, women and members of the LGBTQ community knew their subordinate positions in the social hierarchy constituted as a form of 'authoritarian populism' (see Hall 2017, 172–186). It is, as it were, a repetition compulsion prompted by a traumatic transformation of post-industrial America.

IV

Laclau's account of the radical heterogeneity of the social seems to be clearly belied by the case of Greece and this is important to recognize precisely at a moment in which Italy's new right-populist government has had its own budget 'rejected' by the European Commission for the second time because of severe financial sanctions. Hit particularly hard by the reverberations of the global financial crisis that originated in Wall Street (Tooze 2018) leading to spiralling sovereign debt crisis, Greece was forced to turn to the Troika for bailout funds or risk economic collapse and a possible GREXIT. The Syriza Prime Minister, Alexis Tsipras, called for a Referendum on whether the Greek people would accept such conditions or not. On 5 July 2015, the answer was a resounding Oxi! or NO! (61.31 per cent to 38.39 per cent). But this was simply not acceptable to the Troika. As Merkel's Finance's Minister, Wolfgang Schäuble, put it with arrogant candour: 'Referendum results cannot interfere with economic policy.' So, not only was Greece forced, contrary to the popular will, to accept austerity conditions, these conditions were even harsher than those first proposed.

In return for successive instalments or 'tranches' of bailout funds, the country was forced to comply with the monetization of valuable assets for the creation of an independent fund from which Greek banks could be recapitalized, although as a Deutsche Bank strategist made clear this move was less about meaningful recapitalization and more about furthering privatization. The pensionable age was pushed back to 67 and the highest VAT rate (23 per cent) was extended to cover more goods and services. The government was also made to put into place quasi-automatic spending cuts in order to generate a budget surplus. The Troika ruled out restructuring or 'hair-cuts' and therefore insisted upon keeping 240 billion euros on the books. The austerity measures also included further liberalization of labour market as well as energy and financial sectors and a shrinking of the state (*Guardian* 13 July 2015).

But what is the significance of this? The IMF took a more lenient position with respect to Greece than the other two members of the Troika, as it was convinced that austerity was ill-conceived and counter-productive insofar as it was premised upon the 'household fallacy' or the idea that the state's finances ought to be modelled upon that of the 'oikos'. The fallacy lay in the obvious fact that in that the latter ruled out deficit financing, while the former often entailed it in order to stimulate economic growth and eventually to generate a sufficient tax basis so as to replenish government coffers.

What lay at the heart of such a fallacy was not purely technical rationality, that is of economic efficiency, but a moral imperative—a policy that ought to be undertaken for its own sake. In other words, the EC and ECB wished to teach Greece (and perhaps other member states) a lesson irrespective of the dire consequences for the country and its citizens. The household model is precisely where the political and libidinal economies intersect in an interesting way. It is in the psycho-dynamics of the household, which is to say, the family, that the super-ego is formed by way of the Oedipal complex which functions by way of a two-fold repression: of desire for the mother and murderous aggression directed at the father. The complex is successfully negotiated when the male child accepts the prohibition on incest and turns the aggression initially directed at the father inwards in the form of an internalization of morality. As Nietzsche says, in his account of the ascetic ideals 'all instincts that do not discharge themselves outwardly, turn inward' (Nietzsche 1989, 84). This is precisely the formation of a guilt complex. And as Maurizio Lazzarato has shown in his analysis of the Greek debt crisis, debt is a means of governance by creating 'indebted' and therefore *guilty* subjects (Lazzarato 2012, 2015).

What happened in Greece can be understood of a playing out of ambivalence towards the European Union that, of course, represents the very embodiment of paternal(istic) authority. As Tooze recounts in his thorough account of the financial crisis of 2007–2008, the vast proportion of Greece's debts accumulated in the 1980s and 1990s when both PASOK and New Democracy 'lured voters with the promise of West European modernity and affluence' (2018, 323–324). Insofar as the Troika had made it amply clear that a refusal of the austerity conditions would not only mean no more bailout funds but also would be a possible prelude to a Grexit or Greece exiting the Eurozone. It is, therefore, possible to discern here a playing out of crucial ambivalence for Europe on the part of Greece. On the one hand, there is a convincing rejection of the terms of austerity imposed by the Troika in which the European Commission and European Central bank took up the position that Greece (and other profligate states) needed to be taught a lesson, while the IMF took a more forgiving position. On the other hand, we witness an attachment to what had become a mere fantasy, the idea of a 'social' Europe. This was an image that had long been dispelled by a succession of laws such as the Single European Act (1986), Maastricht Treaty (1992) and treaties such as the Stability and Growth Pact (1997) that reconstituted the European project along firmly neoliberal lines. At the end of the day, such an intersection of political and libidinal economies constituted the conditions whereby the Greek 'people' far from being able to engage in an antagonistic political struggle against the 'oligarchy'—both within Greece itself as well as within the EU as a whole—identified with the imago of the father, that is, with the *aggressor* which is to say with the cold rationality instituted by a punishing and unforgiving neoliberal Europe. The irony of the putatively radical democratic party, Syriza's backtracking on the referendum results, clearly under the duress of the Troika's threat to suspend its membership in the EU, is that democracy was being subjected to an unendurable crisis in its very birthplace. It was a deeply ironic and painful reversal of what E.M. Butler (2012) called in 1935 the 'tyranny of Greece over Germany'. To use Mouffe's language, the oligarchy or the powerful had not merely dominated but had effectively crushed the *demos*. One wonders whether on the basis of Laclau's quasi-deconstructive account of populist reason, it would have been possible to see this coming.

Notes

1 This chapter builds on and develops a chapter of *Critical Theory and Authoritarian Populism* entitled 'Understanding Right and Left Populism,' in Jeremiah Morelock (ed.) (London: University of Westminster Press, 2018), 49–70. I wish to thank Lasse Thomassen for very helpful comments on a previous draft of this chapter. An earlier version was published in a special section on 'Populism, Feminism and Popular Culture' in *Scenari: Revistasemestrale di filosofiacontemporanea* 11 (2019): 396–416.

2 What's also important, and brilliant, about Laclau's first book on populism, is his argument that early twentieth-century socialist parties focused too narrowly on the working class as the subject of revolution and ignored the progressive traditions of nineteenth-century democratic movements which left it to the fascists to appropriate these traditions in their own perverted ways. Schmitt's appropriation of Rousseau or

Gentile's appropriation of Mazzini are exemplary in this regard. The left needed a politics that was both socialist and democratic.

3 John Kraniauskas, 'Critique of Pure Politics,' *Radical Philosophy*, 136 (March/April 2006): 51.

4 This is the key point of contention between Derrida and Foucault.

References

Althusser, Louis. 1977. *For Marx*, translated by Ben Brewster. London: NLB.

——. 1979. *For Marx*. London: Verso Press.

Brown, Wendy. 2015. *Undoing the Demos: Neoliberalism's Stealth Revolution*. New York: Zone.

Butler, E.M. 2012. *The Tyranny of Greece Over Germany*. Cambridge, U.K: Cambridge University Press.

Custer, Olivia, Penelope, Deutscher, and Samir Haddad (eds.). 2016. *Foucault/Derrida Fifty Years Later: The Futures of Genealogy, Deconstruction, and Politics*. New York: Columbia University Press.

Derrida, Jacques. 1978. *Writing and Difference*, translated by Alan Bass. London: Routledge, Kegan & Paul.

——. 1982. *Margins of Philosophy*, translated by Alan Bass. Chicago, Ill.: University of Chicago Press.

Desmoulières, Raphaëlle Besse. 2016. "Chantal Mouffe, la philosophe qui inspire Melanchon," *Le Monde*, 26 January 2016. Available at: https://www.lemonde.fr/politique/article/2016/12/26/chantal-mouffe-la-philosophe-qui-inspire-melenchon_5054023_823448.html (last accessed 27 February 2019). The article was translated by David Broder and posted on the Verso website.

Errejón, Innigo and Chantal Mouffe. 2016. *Podemos: In the Name of the People*. London: Lawrence and Wishart.

Foucault, Michel. 2010. *The Birth of Biopolitics: Lectures at the Collège de France 1978–1979*. New York: Picador.

Fromm, Erich. 1994. *Escape from Freedom*. New York: Henry Holt.

Gandesha, Samir. 2018. "Identifying with the Aggressor: From the 'Authoritarian' to the 'Neo-Liberal' Personality," *Constellations* 25 (2018): 147–164.

——, 2019. "Aesthetic Politics of Hegemony," *Studi di Estethica: Italian Journal of Aesthetics* anno XLVII, IV serie N° 13(1): 151–171.

Gandesha, Samir and J. Hartle. 2017 *Aesthetic Marx*. London: Bloomsbury Press.

Gramsci, Antiono. 1978. 'Some Aspects of the Southern Question,' *Selections from the Political Writings*, translated by Quentin Hoare, 441–462. London: Lawrence and Wishart.

Harvey, David. 2005. *A Brief History of Neoliberalism*. Oxford: Oxford University Press.

Hall, Stuart. 2017. 'The Great Moving Right Show.' In *Selected Political Writings: The Great Moving Right Show and Other Essays*. Durham: Duke University Press.

Kraniauskas, John. 2006. 'Critique of Pure Politics'. *Radical Philosophy* 136 (March/April).

Laclau, Ernesto. 1977. *Politics and Ideology in Marxist Theory: Capitalism, Fascism, Populism*. London: New Left Books.

———. 1996. *Emancipations*. London: Verso.

———. 2005. *On Populist Reason*. London: Verso Books.

Laclau, Ernest and Chantal Mouffe. 1985. *Hegemony and Socialist Strategy: Towards a Radical Democratic Politics*. London: Verso Books.

Lenin, V.I. 1969. *What is to be Done?* New York: International Publishers.

Lukács, Georg. 1971. *History and Class Consciousness*. Translated by R. Livingstone. Cambridge, Mass.: MIT Press.

Marx, Karl. 1979. 'The Eighteenth Brumaire of Louis Bonaparte.' In Collected Works Volume 11, Karl Marx and Friedrich Engels, 99–197. London, U.K.: Lawrence and Wishart.

Machiavelli, Nicollo. 2003. *The Prince*. London: Penguin.

Mouzelis, Nicos. 1978. 'Ideology and Class Politics: A Critique of Ernesto Laclau,' *New Left Review*, I/112 (Nov/Dec): 45–61.

Mouffe, Chantal. 2018. *For a Left Populism*. London: Verso.

Nietzsche, F. 1968. *Will to Power*, translated by W. Kaufmann. New York: Vintage.

———. 1989. *The Geneaology of Morals and Ecce Homo*, translated by W. Kaufmann. New York: Vintage.

———. 1990. *Twilight of the Idols and the Antichrist*. New York: Penguin.

Poulantzas, Nicos. 2014. *State, Power, Socialism*. London: Verso.

Tomšič, Samo. 2015. *Capitalist Unconscious: Marx and Lacan*. London: Verso.

Tooze, Adam. 2019. *Crashed: How a Decade of Financial Crises Changed the World*. New York: Viking.

Wood, Ellen. 1986. *Retreat from Class: The New True Socialism*. London: Verso Books.

Žižek, Slavoj. 2019. 'I Believed in Syriza, But Their Election Defeat Was Secured the Moment They Caved in to the Forces of Capitalism,' *The Independent*, 8 July 2019. Available at https://www.independent.co.uk/voices/syriza-greece-election-tsipras-new-democracy-troika-austerity-varoufakis-a8993811.html (last accessed 17 September 2019).

7

POPULISM LITE

Prasanta Chakravarty

Consider the following lines by the Hindi poet Ramkumar Chetankranti

> हम नए विचार वाले हैं
> मॉब लिंचिंग के सख्त खिलाफ
> इसलिए मार नहीं
> अकेला छोड़ रहे हैं
> सुधर जाना

> We are progressives
> Strictly against mob-lynching
> So shall not kill you
> But leave you free
> Rehabilitate yourself

These enigmatic lines are part of a longer verse to which we shall return later. But the reason to begin with this key section is to set the tone of the subject. It takes us straight into the heart of the behavioural core of a particular tribe: *concerned citizens*. Who are the people that speak against vigilante justice and in what manner do they conduct their business? What do they seek instead in terms of governance and political morality? Indeed, what is the nature of their sanity? What are their *concerns as citizens* in times of sharp political polarization and civic unrest? What might *leaving* someone free in order to be rehabilitated mean?

Liberal humanism, when smuggled within radical aspirations, promotes the following dilemma: How to accommodate the rights of man and demands of civility with corrosive mass mobilizations and methods of strategic terror. The dilemma gets further aggravated if it becomes increasingly difficult to distinguish between aims and motives of genuine egalitarian change and those conditioned by or devolving into the white rage of righteous paranoia playing itself out in a massified and congregationist manner. Observe historian William Sewell's brief appraisal of the events that unfolded in 1793–1794 in France: "This was the period of the 'reign of terror,' when the Parisian sections and the Committee of Public Safety horrified Europe by their intrepid cruelty and miraculously saved the Revolution from what seemed certain defeat" (Sewell, 1980). One could read the observation in two ways. Words like 'cruelty' and 'horrified' show the uneasiness with which Sewell acknowledges human brutality, deployed to correct supposed vice, decadence and oppressive power. On the other, it is clear that he is simultaneously relieved and awed that such 'intrepidity' was the only recourse to 'miraculously save the revolution.' The ideas of the miracle and intrepidity in populist and virtuous mutinies, alien to the thoughtful and constitutionalist mind, find support since one part of it wishes to project its tacit contribution to change and transformation through 'action.'

Isaiah Berlin's celebration of the fox variety of human beings, as opposed to the hedgehogs, is perhaps the most potent metaphor for describing the liberals. To be a fox would mean having the capacity to remain flexible or pragmatic in all negotiations, decision-making and institution-building activities. Since modern ideas of liberalism are connected to the enlightenment notions of championing diversity, melliorism and freedom from bigotry and prejudice, it has acquired a special kind of status among its votaries and detractors alike. Though avowedly respectful of the sanctity of the individual, modern liberals have sometimes played with positive forms of collective existence (communitarianism and egalitarianism, for instance) and given in to subjective forms of moral behaviouralism right from its inception. Instead of eradicating faith and belief from the *civitas*, liberals have often placed those in the private domain. But from Kant to Rawls, orthodox liberals have been indeterminate and inconclusive about the nature and role of the public dimension of faith, irrationality and 'affective' impulses. Therefore, from time to time liberals indulge in a kind of defensive and embarrassed form of 'sophisticated' quasi-hysterical populism that goes directly against their most vaunted tenets of the rule of law, objective evaluation, diversity and communicative reason. The result is that at such times liberal actors can neither fully join the populists nor can they be true to the classical tenets of liberal thought which in themselves are thin and non-ideological. Sandwiched thus, this association with fideism breeds a certain kind of *pathos* in its wake among liberals. The inherent *aporia* within liberalism then propels it to a continuous and difficult balancing act: between its communicative-rational aspirations, the underlying framework of behavioural-moral sentimentalism and its secret awe at supposedly active and transformative politics. The real but elusive tussle is between the 'will of the individual' and the 'will of the collective'. The difficulty lies in bringing together liberty (an individual motivation), equality (a horizontal hope for collectivization) and fraternity (a vertical, loyal communitarian given) within the same scope of radical politics. This dithering and elusive balancing act fosters curious negotiations in times of cascading mass outrage.

In order to appreciate the politics, attitude and tonal quality behind the Chetankranti lines mentioned at the outset, the chapter shall rather take an unexpected avenue. I shall look at sections of two central documents that helped formulate the tenets of the liberal credo: John Locke's *Second Treatise of Civil Government* (1689) and the ruminations of Third Earl of Shaftesbury about virtue, taste and morality, collected in *Characteristicks of Men, Manners, Opinions, Times* (1711). While I would like to read Locke in order to shed light on the questions of political breakdown and the nature of mass uprising in defining Whig politics, through Shaftesbury, I would seek to unearth the relationship between sentimentalism and rationality in forming and informing the liberal ethos and its particular sense of moral judgment. The chapter shall conclude by making some observations about the nature of liberal resistance within the current scenario by bringing these two strands together. The reason for focusing on Locke and Shaftesbury is to address some basic tenets and contradictions woven within classical liberalism that are yet to be resolved. The non-resolution of certain political tenets has grave implications for the manner in which socially concerned liberals conduct themselves in times of heightened and extreme political mobilizations such as ours.

By bringing together certain fundamental tenets of classical liberalism and by drawing attention to their relation in dealing with rage and despair, loyalty and loneliness, tact and silence, especially during times of acute social polarization, I would like to arrive at a particular disposition and way of negotiation in public life. This I call *populism lite.* Populism lite maintains certain specific traits. Foremost, its votaries wish to keep the zone between the social process and its breakdown amorphous and malleable. Second, it helps foster and maintain a climate of severe behavioural-moral boundaries functioning within bonds of loyalty by *allowing* freedom to individual agents. In this sense its operations are blithe and breezy—hence lite. But the very deftness of moral and political negotiation makes such a brand of populism one of the most ominous and oppressive forms of social interaction. *Ruthlessness wrapped in decorum* is its essential bedrock value. In this deeper sense populism lite is actually its very opposite: its ways and effects are most leaden and devastating in public life.

Purposeful Vacillation

Chapter XIX, the final and the last chapter of John Locke's *Second Treatise,* pertains to a single and singular issue: *Of the Dissolution of Government.* This chapter contains statements that must closely associate Locke with the events of 1688–1689, though some of the speculations may have happened in the early years of the decade. Locke often shows little faith in the power of the majority in his many writings and yet maintains the right to resistance in particular cases. With respect to the question of revolt and resistance against an established authority, it is important to note how far and in which manner Locke is ready to grant extra-constitutional rights to the majority to foment and carry forward such a revolt and topple the government. Certain corollary questions would follow: (a) whether Locke suggests dissolution only of the political form of the government or of the civil society *per se* (b) once dissolved whether human beings return to a state of nature or does a state of war now prevail within the formations of the civil society (c) what is the role of conspiracy and factional politics during popular revolts (d) how often can such revolts be repeated.

Early on in the chapter, Locke confronts two kinds of situations when a government can be dissolved—with the inroad of some foreign force and when the existing legislative is itself broken from within owing to some internal disquiet. Locke begins by asserting that anyone who wishes to speak with clarity about dissolving a government (and by implication, any established order) must 'distinguish between the Dissolution of Society, and the dissolution of the Government' (Locke, 1960, 211). But few lines on, he controverts himself by saying that only when a society is dissolved and humans who had previously come together to form that society, now moves either to a new order or to the state he was before (nature?) could the government get dissolved: "that where the Society is dissolved, the Government cannot remain; that being as impossible, as for the Frame of an House to subsist when the Materials of it are scattered, and dissipated by a Whirl-wind, or jumbled into a confused heap by an Earthquake" (Locke, 1960, 212). The general confusion and dissipation are highlighted in the case of foreign invasion. In such circumstances, the 'arbitrary will' of the monarch takes over. The same is true when people lose faith in internal arrangements of the legislative which have dishonoured 'publick will' and have squandered the delegatory power of that will earned through a common contract. The society now not being "intire, free and independent" people dissolve the original legislative body and "everyone is at the disposure of his own will" (Locke, 1960, 218). It is a situation of breakdown and a time of absolute subjective and massified decision-making.

To begin with, we are left unsure as to whether and at what point the society alters and accepts a new legislative body. Is there a hiatus between its reverting to a state of nature or is it that in the interim there remains radical uncertainty and people find themselves in an internal state of war within some uncivil state of breakdown? The contingency is much more pronounced in the latter case when people revert to being a 'confused multitude'. Moreover, in these circumstances, society seems to be able to survive without a government. We can draw a fundamental conclusion about the liberal mind as he addresses resistance: that he is unsure when given to choose between the political and the natural condition of man. In times of civil war, populist uprising, internal revolt or external aggression, liberals will give in to the natural instincts of people's power to resist what it considers tyranny. But at the same time, they will look for a peaceful and legislative means whereby there could be a seamless shift from one legislative order to another without any violent rupture. It is to this contradiction that Leo Strauss has drawn our attention:

> Locke teaches, on the one hand, that society can exist without government and, on the other hand, that society cannot exist without government. The contradiction disappears if one considers the fact that society exists, and acts, without government only in the moment of revolution…The revolutionary action thus understood is a kind of majority decision which establishes a new legislative or supreme power in the very moment in which it abolishes the old one. (Strauss, 1953, 232)

Nathan Tarcov has rightly shown that at the instant of resistance, Locke summons the peaceful state of nature in order to justify people's resistance to tyrants and yet calls it a warlike situation in order to condemn the tyrants who may have fomented the dissolution of the government (Tarcov, 1981). And yet the resistance actually takes place within the trappings of a political society. Resistance, therefore, becomes a kind of preventive and thoughtful act. How can resistance by dissolution be peaceful? How is it that tumultuous acts of dissolving a set legislative structure still happen within some peaceful state of nature? It is evident that the reason Locke is not ready to call people's resistance violent is to at once keep the category called 'people' pristine and also to put the blame for the warlike state of exception entirely on the magistrates and tyrants.

This brings us to the crucial part of the chapter, often ignored by Locke scholars: the internecine struggle/civil war. Locke has an evocative, organic metaphor for this state: 'intestine broils' (Locke, 1960, 227). Such broils erupt within people themselves even as they resist an unlawful monarch or a foreign force. It is here that we see the liberal mind flinching from the real cost and tragedy of a dissolution. Locke is aware that at such times often opportunists and mercenaries will take advantage of the melee, and resort to subterfuge, violence, backstabbing and robbery for invading their neighbours. This awareness is inconsistent with the noble cause of defending one's right or ensuring security as reasons for revolt. Locke refuses to deal with the darkest side of resistance when resistors themselves turn rapine and oppressive and large forces clash with each other. Yet there are moments in the chapter that acknowledges a more complicated picture. At one point he begins to caution against populist usurpers who, taking advantage of lawful resistance, shall play mischief. These creatures he castigates as "busie heads and turbulent spirits" (Locke, 1960, 229). These are the people who stir passion. But in the same breath Locke pronounces,

> I grant, that the Pride, Ambition, and Turbulency of private Men have sometimes caused great Disorders in Commonwealth, and Factions have been fatal to States and Kingdoms. But whether the mischief hath oftener begun in the People's wantonness, and a Desire to cast off the lawful Authority of their Rulers; or in the Ruler's insolence, and Endeavours to get, and exercise an Arbitrary Power over their People; whether oppression, or Disobedience gave the first rise to Disorder, I leave it to impartial History to determine. (Locke, 1960, 231)

This is a classic instance which depicts the actual dilemma within the liberal when confronted by a revolutionary circumstance. Looked carefully, we shall notice three distinct movements in the aforementioned statement and the author is confident that he can accommodate all three within a single framework! First, the acknowledgment that private men could be very much prone to pride, ambition and turbulency (all subjective excesses) and therefore could become agents of causing political disorder. Besides, such tendencies have led to factionalism which is fatal for any stable government. But such mischief can be excused for the greater cause. The onus rather lies with those who wield arbitrary power over people. But when asked to choose a side, we see the real nature of the liberal response: removing oneself from judgement and handing it over to History which is supposed to be impartial. This is what is at the heart of the idea of *concern* in the liberal citizen. She can forever remain concerned about social ills without having to take any firm position or advancing political vision. Handing over one's principled position to History is a remarkable positivist hope. What history is ever impartial? How and what actors pass judgement in and about history? Locke skirts the question of responsibility for factionalist and schismatic politics which inevitably must give all politics of authenticity and spontaneity their proper location in times of churning. No wonder Locke's *purposeful vacillation* has been sharply contrasted with the democratic radicals taking part in the Putney debates.

Locke also reserves a serious judgement about the inertia of the masses—"the frame they have been accustomed to" (Locke, 1960, 223). The majority principle (which anyway is in this case about 'freemen' with holdings and not all 'free men') to him effectively means reference to the will of the majority with a serious mistrust for its capacity to discern and decide upon circumstances objectively. The real trick is to secure the required popular support so that a right-minded minority can take decisions about resistance. Locke assumes that the people are 'slow' and indifferent and are likely to endorse the monarch's prerogative and action: the people stir "till the mischief be grown general, and the ill designs of the rulers become visible, or their attempts sensible to the greater part" (Locke, 1960, 230–231). The multitude is primarily more disposed to suffer, since "the people being ignorant and always discontented" (Locke, 1960, 223–224). Besides, they are callous towards the sufferings of others: "the examples of particular injustice, or oppression of here and there an unfortunate man, moves them not" (Locke, 1960, 231). So, there must be others who ought to lead the majority against tyranny. Freemen and property holders like him? And yet action can only come through a spontaneous uprising of the majority. There is always a fear in the mind of the classical liberal that the majority, at once slow to action and turbulent in mind and as such prone to join the wrong-minded initiators of revolt and factious malcontents, might eventually help the enemies of the people—the tyrants and fascists. But at the same time she feels that whether people are inveigled to action by false prophets or they end up fomenting unjustified revolts, they ought to be given that right. This is the second conundrum for the liberal: to try and merge thought and action, considered means with revolutionary zeal during the time of mass mobilization.

A related issue is the nature and frequency of revolts. Locke is again evasive. He begins with his pessimism about people: that people usually *see* things but do not revolt. They usually overlook "little mismanagements", "slips of human frailty" or even "great mistakes" (Locke, 1960, 225–226). But there are limits of toleration even for the base multitude. They would "rouze themselves" when a "long train of abuses, prevarications and artifices" makes the "design visible to people" (Locke, 1960, 226). At the root of the revolt then is a certain build-up that leads to outrage and then to outburst. A new legislative ('a new form') may come to being but the original impulse is the outrage when *things come to a head.* For a brief period, the people "continue the Legislative in themselves" (Locke, 1960, 243). Here, Locke is quite optimistic about people's wisdom and decision-making capacity in being outraged. The only thing he tells is that a new legislative body must be formed soon enough. But what if an underlying politics of outraged paranoia conditions the new organs of governance? Or worse: if a body of paranoid and victimized people begin to run a parallel network of governance along with and in tandem with the freshly formed official legislative body?

Feeling, Sense, Outrage

Let us consider a slightly different but related strand: the deep personal and intellectual relationship that Locke shared with Anthony Ashley Cooper, Third Earl of Shaftesbury. Locke was the tutor of young Shaftesbury. They were almost complementary in thought and action, save their differences on the questions of individualism and sensualism. Politically they found themselves in the most dangerous situation during the early 1680s (in the wake of repeated defeats of the Exclusion Bill and Whig fear of the Popish Plot) and both were involved in the Rye House Conspiracy of 1683. Both men were disaffected with the government and shared a remarkable closeness in class, colonial thinking, religious outlook, morality and culture. At the heart of their camaraderie is a shared enthusiasm about a specific bourgeois idea of natural law (again, contrary to the Levellers on one hand and Republicans on the other). Considering the nature of this powerful friendship takes us closer to appreciating the ways in which modern civil society was conceived in its initial phases and the reasons for its lingering in imagining and encountering whatever erupts as uncivil, ominous and tangled from within its own belly.

Shaftesbury claims moral sense is innate in human beings. But are dispositions innate or are they actually complex products arising out of customs and education? Social affection, which fosters virtuous sociability, is the key to his scheme of things. Is sociability innate or do social habits foster politeness at the very dispositional level? This is a circular logic. It has been rightly deduced that by fusing liberty with politeness, Shaftesbury gives a new direction to the civic tradition. The bedrock principles of civic republicanism—heroic austerity, public-mindedness, martial qualities and independence, turn into a blend of decorous and conversible urbanity by the early eighteenth century. *Politeness itself becomes a form of liberty.* The important thing to note is that there is something common in Locke and Shaftesbury: one makes resistance serviceable to the Whig ideology while the other does the same with politeness. *In ordinary times such porous serviceability is masked. But during populist mass politics, these two subtracted ideas of civic virtue and civic resistance collide with each other and keep the liberal in a perpetual limbo.* Consequently, the 'liberal revolutionary' fumes, stutters, practices strategic silence and begin to support clandestine resistive measures without taking responsibility for the bloodletting and loss involved in times of purging. She also cannot entirely celebrate the purge, for violence she is supposed to shun. And yet she cannot fully absolve herself for veering away from scepticism, tolerance and reasonableness for she is betrothed to the 'bright side of human nature'. Consequently, she stops short of espousing revolution as a belief in conducting experiments of social transformation. Again, ordinarily such motivations remain shrouded. But during times of political polarization, the reasons for a liberal for not being able to imagine any clear road-map and vision of politics becomes glaring.

But how is Shaftesbury able to conjure up a scheme about freedom for the emerging genteel class without shouldering the burden of civic responsibility? More importantly, is the neat scheme of sentimentalizing feeling compatible with the demands of human frailty, calls of desire, contradictions of will and the complex dynamics of relationality, especially during times of heightened political polarization?

The first populist measure that the sentimentalist takes is to confuse feeling for philosophy. J.B. Schneewind, while delineating the fundamentals of eighteenth-century moral sense insists how "everyone can just see what morality requires bears on both moral and epistemological concerns" (Schneewind, 1988) especially since such a claim is epistemologically projected against scepticism and value neutrality. Based on such certainty Shaftesbury makes this extraordinary claim that a "Sense of Right and Wrong ... [is] as natural to us as natural affection itself" (Shaftesbury, Vol. 2, 2001, 25). Even the "wickedest Creature living must have a sense...it must consist in a real Antipathy or Aversion to Injustice or Wrong, and in a real Affection or Love towards Equity and Right, for its own sake, and on the account of its own natural Beauty and Worth" (Shaftesbury, Vol. 2, 2001, 24–25). Sense of justice arises out of our natural beauty and worth. The moral distinction thus becomes coterminous with affection. What Shaftesbury inaugurates, and what would be taken forward by the likes of Hutcheson and Hume, is the implication of the moral within the epistemological, mediated through a meliorating inter-subjective exchange of feeling. In this framework, votaries must reject uncertainty about human knowledge outright; especially anything that may count as ambiguous or unsavoury knowledge about our interlocutors and associates. There is, of course, a staggering claim in demanding the self-evident consensus about the phrase: 'everyone can just see'. Here is the slippery slope that forecloses all queries about the very ground of such a framework by enjoining certainty to moral claims. The claim not only ignores thoughtful scrutiny about its nature and origin but also precludes variations of sense perception, tricks of memory and ways of idea formation in formulating such claims. All it does is to shield inter-subjective exchange of virtue, mediated through feeling: as if the workings of sympathy and politeness are readily observable and reliably operational in human interactions. The immediacy of feeling, as it were, could be discerned with an inward eye. The further claim is that feeling travels and is reciprocated perfectly. In this context, Nancy Yousef makes an acute observation that for Shaftesbury, the term natural is used in the dual sense of being innate and inborn and also as a product of aesthetic education and discipline (Yousef, 2011). Nature is at once a species attribute and a motivation that is imparted through inculcating virtue and taste which is a 'natural' outcome of a fundamental sociality.

The problem arises when we notice that the moment of certainty actually arises out of an extreme sense of vulnerability and moral crisis. Confidence and anxiety about human affability and capacity to inculcate taste are inextricably intertwined. Indeed, the more anxiety is relegated to the domain of untrustworthy knowledge and fellow feeling brought to the fore, the more tentacles of doubt begin to take root. Fragility of intimacy, dragnets of kinship ties and intricate dynamics of human interaction make it incumbent to declare the self-evident nature of amiability and collegiality with more vigour. The very obviousness of stressing on observable mutual feeling shows the delicate nature of its workings and the contingency that lingers within such assertions. Towards the conclusion of *Enquiry on Virtue and Merit*, Shaftesbury deals with the Hobbesian isolated persona, whom he tries to caricature as a misanthrope. The existential nature of that isolation is indeed empirical in nature and the persona has to confront psychic individuation. The misanthrope is averse to even communicate, let alone share affability with other humans. The return of sceptical despair happens with vengeance every single time he wishes to amplify affability and fellow feeling. Similarly, in *The Moralists*, Shaftesbury sharply brings into relief the opposed qualities of misanthropy and sentimentality. Innate feeling does not ensure bonding among the civil members. Rather, it seems one must inculcate and have faith in intersubjectivity in order to take refuge in the certainty of sentimentality. The framework works as a shield of safety, cocooned within a kinship structure. But the anxious pall of estrangement hovers around affective relations all the time. We can doubt everything around us but not our natural quality of affection and sympathy, says Shaftesbury. But the 'feeling passes within' and it does not actually matter whether love and pain of others are realities or illusions. At its root feelings feed our narcissistic selves. Social disclosure is the emptying out of interiority. And hence, we remain forlorn in our sociability. This self-regarding ruthlessness about moral sentimentality is at the heart of Shaftesbury's anxiety about asserting behavioural affability.

There is a similar disciplining strain in Locke's idea of education which is complementary to the halting and staggered formulations of his right to resist as discussed earlier. Public order and self-government demands moral citizens who must naturalize custom and habit and rein in the wayward strings of desire. Governance of conduct is the key to this new mode of citizenry. There is a strong element of 'inverted quarantine' in Locke, by means of which *concerned citizens* self-discipline their conduct by inculcating habit, not right reason. In fact, Locke is refining a pedagogical scheme of natural ethics already inaugurated by the likes of Thomas Cranmer and Richard Hooker a few decades ago: reason married to custom. He is remarkably close to Shaftesbury in defining the ambit of the moral citizen in spite of their differences on issues of empiricism and processing of sense data. One is free to the extent that one follows a path of behavioural virtue propounded by the civil society. Such a mode of governing conduct makes James Tully observe that, "moral error [for Locke] is not so much misjudging relative to one's habitual relish but acquiring a relish that does not lead to the greatest or true happiness" (Tully, 1988, 53). Relish is, therefore, an acquired act of judging people and situations with moral discrimination.

So, what has organizing of sensation into sentiment mediated through a certain aesthesis to do with the liberal revolutionary persona that we had encountered earlier in the final chapter of Locke's *Second Treatise*? More importantly, what do all these have to do with the populist ethos and temperament? We are trying to get at the genesis of a certain provisional and unsettled fraternizing of the modern liberal with fervour and spontaneity that righteous indignation demands during populist outbursts by managing to conjoin that resistance with feeling and right sensation. In such a pattern of dealing with indignation, it is crucial to clearly outline *the triangulated network among moral sense, a mitigating aesthetics and the right to resist*—a filigree that informs this particular persona. The starting point of class compromise for the small landholder and the emerging market entrepreneur is to resist tyranny and violent mutiny alike and emphasize law and rights, failing which to go ahead with resistance but with a deep suspicion about the masses. Inwardly the class loathes addressing the inertia and the divisive nature that characterizes the populist mob. At the same time, its moral framework hinges around exchanging feeling and taste and a concomitant sense of guilt about moral scepticism and human vulnerability. Therefore, such a mode requires constant shielding of what it considers to be vice and evil by mobilizing a loyal club of ostensibly civic individuals. Within such a setup, one of the opportunities that *populist massification of outrage* provides to the liberal persona is to allow channeling of feeling through indignation. Politeness and indignation go hand in hand. This compound helps create a resistance theory primarily erected upon sensation and humane pathos reserved for the inferior classes and other unfortunate souls. Robert Markley has clinically delineated the use of such monological idea of sentimentality as tact and performance in Shaftesbury (Markley, 1987). On the other hand, securing an assured place for resistance within the rights discourse by the likes of Locke provides the seeker of behavioural virtue like Shaftesbury with a possibility to consider a group of traumatized, virtuous and entitled individuals as harbingers of change and transformation. The outrage of feeling can replace all structural change at the ground level as long as the right signals of resistance are offered to the sufferers. *Populism lite* can only thrive by commoditization suffering.

The Honourable Mob: A Case in Point

The nature of the polite and righteous liberal, so carefully crafted by the likes of Locke, Shaftesbury and Hutcheson, is brought into sharp relief when the mob begins to show its collective retributive side, directly challenging the tactful character that we have been trying to delineate. At the appointed moment the mob names its enemies: marking what it designates as elitist and/or pluralist power centres/personalities which it wishes to overthrow and annihilate summarily. Monstrosity erupts from the middle of the polity and hovers like a pall over it. The response of the progressive liberal is to delve further into the recesses of her personality: simultaneously drawing inward into her stuttering, studied self who does not wish to confront vice and violence and yet hopes to come across as morally upright by standing by the side of the populist mass as a fellow traveller. She shuns all structural and legal paraphernalia of governance and wonders how to deal with virtuous violence without being fully engulfed by the flames. We are now in a position to look into the full scope of Ramkumar Chetankranti's poem which we had mentioned earlier. The poem captures the very method and the various shimmering shades with which the righteous middling hordes strike in order to remain relevant in times of political and moral vigilantism.

कितनी घृणा हुई होगी तुम्हे मुझसे
(सोचता हूँ और काँपता हूँ)

जब मेरा नाम लेकर उन्होंने
तुम्हें कोंचा होगा
तुम्हारा उपहास किया होगा

तुम्हारे समूचे अहसास को चिन्दी चिन्दी किया होगा
रोंदा होगा कूद कूदकर नाच नाचकर

तुम्हारी एकाग्रता पर टूट पड़ी होगी भीड़
('उग्र भीड़' जैसे अब कहने लगे हैं अखबार सम्मान के साथ)

मुझे पता हैं
तुम्हें कितनी नफरत हुई होगी
पहले मुझसे

फिर खुद से

वे मुस्कुराते हंसते चीखते लांघते फलांगते छप छप
कांय कांय करते करते आये होंगे

मोटर साइकिलों से करों से घोड़ों से रथों से

बस यह बताने
कि तुम कितनी और किस किस तरह गलत हो
कि तुम्हारा होना एक प्रश्न है
कि हम समझ नहीं पा रहे कि तुम कौन हो क्यों हो क्या हो

और यह
कि प्यार करने का हक़ अब नहीं है तुम्हें
तुम्हें स्वीकार किया जा चूका है
अपना लिया गया है तुम्हें

तुम पानी की तरह हिली होगी
साफ पवित्र पानी की तरह

हैरानी से
आँखें फाड़े खामोश
कांपती हुई
जनहीन पृथ्वी पर अकेली
लबालब एक झील की तरह

जीतकर
जब उन्होंने
अपने तीस इंच के महामार्ग पर झंडे लहराते
कूच किया होगा
कहते हुए की हम नए विचार वाले हैं
मॉब लिंचिंग के सख्त खिलाफ
इसलिए मार नहीं
अकेला छोड़ रहे हैं
सुधर जाना

तुम कितने अकेले ढंग से
अकेली खड़ी रही होगी—सुन्न

How much must you have loathed me
(I think and I shudder)
When they took my name
And impaled you
Scorned you

Must have shredded your whole existence
Trampled all over it, vaulting, hopping, plunging

All over your thrall the crowd must have thronged
('radical crowd' is its honourable name)

I know
How much hatred you must have felt
First for me
And then for yourself

Laughing chortling sniggering climbing leaping
Hissing growling they must have arrived
on bikes and cycles, in cars, on horses and chariots

Just to tell you
How much and in what ways you have erred
That your very being is a question
That we cannot fathom who and why and what you are

And that
Henceforth you no longer have the right to love
You have been accepted,
Chosen and received

Like water you must have stirred
Like water, clean and sacred

Bewildered and
Wide-eyed, silent and
Shaking
Alone on this desolate earth
Like a lake brimming over

Victorious
On their thirty-inch highway
When they conducted a flag-march

Announcing we are progressives
Strictly against mob-lynching
So shall not kill you
But leave you free
Rehabilitate yourself

How forlorn you must have felt
How lonely and forsaken—numb

It is a triangulated scene. The speaker is trying to portray a situation in which a horde of people (radical crowd) has descended upon a woman, trying to forcefully caution her against the speaker and by doing so, puts a question on the very basis of her relationship with him. The mob is also raising a doubt about certain decisions that she must have taken on her own. The poem tells us less about the reasons for such mass outrage but more about the nature and psychology of the parties involved. A strange negotiation is underway and several things become clearer as we go along.

The most instructive part is the nature of the crowd. The crowd is boisterous. It is a mob that would brook no argument. It is relentless and is formed by a conglomeration of people who arrive in all kinds of vehicles, modern and ancient. The only thing that it is interested in is to teach a lesson to the woman. The erring decision that the woman has taken has something to do with the speaker, exemplified by this early hint, "When they took my name/And impaled you/Scorned you." To the seemingly irrational crowd, the speaker must have done something abhorrent. And perhaps the woman too. Both are implicated and yet the crowd has descended upon her. At the primary level, the brunt is borne by her. The speaker imagines the scenario and is tormented. The lines are really an intimate conversation, a letter meant for the bereft woman. The vulnerability of the situation is converted into a poem and is shared with us by the speaker-poet. As voyeurs, we become privy to a conversation that happens at several levels.

Once we have a sense of the coordinates, we begin to delve deeper. This is certainly not an ordinary horde that has descended. Its overtly noisy and clamorous nature has another curious dimension. The nature and reactions that are produced by the woman are the direct fallout of the way the crowd behaves with her. The crowd, though rough and boisterous initially, seems to be dealing with her quite unlike itself, that is to say, as an ordinary crowd. Is it trying to negotiate rage? But who can possibly be reasonable with anger? To begin with, the crowd questions her very being ("cannot fathom who and why and what you are") and questions her right to love. But the method of their thwarting of her right to affection is unique. They do not directly force her so that she would renege from her position. Instead, they foreclose her options by making her understand that she has "been accepted,/Chosen and received." This is indeed in keeping with a far more clever way of manufacturing consent by hinting that she cannot but accept their guardianship and security since she has been already chosen and received by the tribe. It is a deterministic scenario. Cold, brutal velvet gloves are being offered to her and she can only refuse the refuge of the tribe at her own peril. We immediately realize that the warfare is happening at a subterranean and psychological level. The nature of the curious crowd is further and finally clarified when we are told that this horde is a new and progressive one. An oxymoron is at play: it is a *thinking feeling crowd: the horde of concerned citizens*. It is fitting to remind ourselves here as to how Locke had thought to create this particular category in the *Second Treatise*: not only by imputing rationality to the resistance and violent mob but by seeking the source of such rationality to feeling: "Are the people to be blamed, if they have the sense of rational creatures, and can think of things no otherwise than as they find and feel them" (Locke, 1960, 231)? Since the mob is at once thinking and feeling, the most important sign of its progressive credential is that it does not believe in mob-lynching. In fact, it is strictly against such practice. Instead, this particular mob does something quite canny instead of killing its victim. It leaves her free.

What kind of thumping mob lets its victim walk free? We understand that the price of that freedom is rehabilitation. That is the ransom she must secure: the trap the civil society lays for her. The highway of outrage is barely thirty inches though. The victory march is a travesty. But the diktat is smooth and ostensibly liberating. The cage is gilded though and the victim of such a lite mode of populism is left forlorn and wandering. She is left bewildered, angry at the speaker and at herself for she now has no choice left but to correct her errancy. Errancy will not be allowed. The progressive mob, therefore, is the wiliest when it tries to operate within the framework of a *sensus communis*. Whoever will not play by its rule will be deposed and purged if she does not go through a process of acceptance and forced rehabilitation. The tribe thus redirects violence through a skilful guiding of moral conduct. This is the liberal tribe's contribution to populism proper.

The speaker, at one remove, deftly characterizes the inner turmoil that the victim who is put to ransom by the forces of *populism lite*. There is no scope for manifestation of anger. There is also no opportunity for any meaningful dialogue among the parties. Anger is garnished tastefully and then sublimated only by one side—*the thinking feeling horde*. As a result, the lite mode of populist righteousness makes the victim bewildered and silent: 'brimful like a lake.' She is now truly a pariah, a living dead within the bounds of civility. The civil mode of extracting populist revenge can only make a spectre out of the victim, hanging in stupefied awe.

The poem ends with the telling condition that the speaker is trying to express: numbness. It is eminently evident that such topography of engagement is far from transformative. Nowhere is the slipperiness of the term populism more evident than when it plays itself out by combining angst with sly moral righteousness. But the manifestation of this very tactfulness always happens through a language of generosity, acceptance and silence. Populism lite, therefore, can be defined as *the very instance that liberalism does not wish to talk about, made stark during times of heightened political polarization. Populism lite resides in the gap between the modern man's inviolable trust in the processes of social contract and the aesthetic-moral sediments of outrage and panic that lie beneath such seeming trust.*

Coda

In this context, William Arthur Galston has tried to caution liberals about their keeping company with the populists, especially when readymade solutions are sought for complex social and personal problems. He puts the blame on natural human tendency which prefers to fall back on community comfort rather than take individual responsibility during times of crisis:

> But citizens often crave more unity and solidarity than liberal life typically offers, and community can be a satisfying alternative to the burdens of individual responsibility. Preferring those who are most like us goes with the grain of our sentiments more than does a wider, more abstract concept of equal citizenship or humanity. So does the tendency to impute good motives to our friends and malign intent to our foes. Antipathy has its satisfactions, and conflict, like love, can make us feel more fully alive. (Galston, 2018)

At the core of the liberal ethos is security. Hence, all the tact and suasion, every gesture of cautious silence and strategic voluble thumping that happens as time and scope demands.

The Locke–Shaftesbury legacy renders people into an empty supplement. The older ideas of the political spectrum are made deliberately foggy in times of populist outbursts that often feed on certain politics of social segmentation, *schadenfreude* and *ressentiment*. The evisceration of democratic norms may happen owing to a sense of distributive injustice and/or loss of status or influence for a section of society. It could simultaneously be the fallout of extreme narcissism, entitlement and possessive individualism. In fact, a sense of inheriting a subtracted life-world is often entwined with pure self-regarding motives. Hence, full-grown resentful populist gestures are often defensive-offensive in nature. The liberals try to gauge this particular mood and metamorphose accordingly. They realize that there is always a gap between liberal constitutionalism on one hand and the robust republican public sphere on the other. The only way to bridge that gap is by taking us back to the tactful world of politeness when threatened by either side.

Jean Comaroff has summed this specific incarnation of populism well with her remark that, "When mobilizations invoke the people as alibi, they conjure with a fetish that exists at some distance from social reality—a fetish with two faces: one progressive, the other reactionary" (Comaroff, 2011). Our current mass-mediated populism of the so-called post-humanist uncivil times is a cocktail of several factors which feed into each other: a certain liberal class privilege and a politics of ally-ship/kinship ties up with the mood in order to signal participating in politics of resistance (following Locke's Chapter XIX) along with socially identitarian and economically precarious groups. Anger is then personalized and channelized through moral empathy and outrage, which is sought to be tamed from time to time in remembrance of constitutionalism and civility. Populism lite, with its unique blend of merciful revolution and traumatized morality, helps truly blur the distinction between democracy and demagoguery. Ironically, more the *concerned citizens* try to play the populist game lightly more the chasm with the mass increases. Jean Cohen has aptly given us the reason to this ambivalence:

> None can close the gap completely or render democracy or the people fully determinate. Claims to do so destroy rather than deepen democracy. The gap exists not because representative democracy is insufficiently direct or participatory. Rather, it exists because the construction of the demos (who belongs and votes), the receptivity of democratic construction of the demos (who belongs and votes), the receptivity of democratic processes and institutions to new voices and formerly excluded strata, is never complete. It must always be seen as open-ended and fallible. (Cohen, 2019)

Therefore, instead of offering any real way forward, the Locke–Shaftesbury model merely helps exacerbate the already existent radical reductionism in populism by channeling anger and violence into moral depositories; by means of mediating the emotive dualisms within antagonistic parties engaged in a populist feud. That is the reason that Comaroff has observed that this particular mode encourages us to

> seek nothing more in politics than our own, narcissistic reflection, for everything else (critique or struggle for more encompassing insight

> or justice) is dubbed spoiling, elitist, or a "politics of envy." This is populist energy without any social consciousness, any ethics of social responsibility. From this no truly emancipatory politics can emerge. (Comaroff, 2011)

Perhaps it would now be germane to re-read the properly *concerned* and vigilante phrase that we had begun with—'rehabilitate yourself.' It is a hailing, an interpellative gesture. Between them, the two words camouflage a whole story, nay, a method of running life, fortified by a not so veiled threat that is as brutal and relentless as its demand for polite conduct is.

Bibliography

Baltes, John. "Locke's Inverted Quarantine: Discipline, Panopticism, and the Making of the Liberal Subject". *The Review of Politics, 75* (2013): 173–192.

Chetankranti, Ramkumar. *Rehabilitation.* (private circulation).

Cohen, Jean L. "Populism and the Politics of Resentment." *Jus Cogens, 1* (1) (2019): 5–39.

Comaroff, Jean. "Populism and Late Liberalism: A Special Affinity?" *The Annals of the American Academy of Political and Social Science, 637*, Race, Religion, and Late Democracy (September 2011): 99–111.

Galston, William A. "The Populist Challenge to Liberal Democracy." *Journal of Democracy, 29* (2) (April 2018): 5–19.

Locke, John. *Two Treatises of Government.* Edited by Peter Laslett. Cambridge: Cambridge University Press, 1960.

——. *Some Thoughts Concerning Education.* Oxford: Clarendon Press, 2000.

Markley, Robert. "Sentimentality as Performance: Shaftesbury, Sterne and the Theatrics of Virtue." In *The New Eighteenth Century: Theory, Politics, English Literature*, edited by Felicity Nussbaum and Laura Brown. New York: Methuen, 1987.

Schneewind, J.B. *The Invention of Autonomy.* Cambridge: Cambridge University Press, 1998.

Sewell, Jr., William H. *Work and Revolution in France: The Language of Labor from the Old Regime to 1848.* Cambridge: Cambridge University Press, 1980.

Strauss, Leo. *Natural Right and History.* Chicago: University of Chicago Press, 1953.

Tarcov, Nathan. "Locke's 'Second Treatise' and the 'Best Fence against Rebellion,'" *The Review of Politics, 43* (2) (April 1981): 198–217.

Third Earl of Shaftesbury, Anthony Ashley Cooper. *Characteristicks of Men, Manners, Opinions, Times, 3 Volumes.* Indianapolis: Liberty Fund, 2001.

Tully, James. "Governing Conduct." In *Conscience and Casuistry in Early Modern Europe*, edited by Edmund Leites, 12–71. Cambridge: Cambridge University Press, 1988.

Yousef, Nancy. "Feeling for Philosophy: Shaftesbury and the Limits of Sentimental Certainty," *ELH*, *78* (3) (FALL 2011): 609–632.

——. *Isolated Cases: The Anxieties of Autonomy in Enlightenment Philosophy and Romantic Literature*. Ithaca: Cornell University Press, 2004.

EXPOSITIONS

8

THE BORROWED GEOGRAPHIES OF NEOLIBERAL NEIGHBOURHOODS POPULIST GOVERNANCE IN INDIA

Rajarshi Dasgupta*

The study of populist politics when simplified can be seen to take any one of the two major trajectories. One of these explores the making of what Laclau calls the chain of equivalence between the differential claims and demands of disparate groups, followed by the delivery of targeted benefits among population accordingly after taking over power.[1] Given its ideological thinness, pointed out by the likes of Cas Mudde,[2] the other trajectory leads us to the framing of an individual as the supreme leader who can cut through the bureaucracy, middlemen and anonymous institutions and directly reach the masses, who are in turn staged as authentic people and pitted against a section seen as the elite and enemy. Such is the structure of the narrative necessary for the leader's staking claim to power. However, what receives less attention in this otherwise useful schema is where and how these two different trajectories overlap and intersect in practice—how does the leader's delivery of targeted benefits, for example, produce a loyal support base, and why is it different from the more familiar framework of clientelist politics. Again, many recent analyses of populism correctly underscore a psychological dimension that becomes crucial for understanding how support for populist leaders can set aside rational deliberations and considered judgements otherwise shaping peoples' decisions and take on the nature of a blind devotion akin to religious cults.[3] At the same time, we find fleeting insights in other studies about the relationship of such political formations with petty businessmen and crony capitalism but these are neither sufficiently fleshed out nor linked up with aspects like that of psychological manipulation. The upshot of this lack of internal connections between the various features and aspects of populism is that more often than not it becomes difficult to distinguish populist politics from what is not populist and merely electoral or traditional patronage practices packaged with the convenient image of a leader. Most of all, we are left wondering what is really specific to populism today and how is it changing politics as we know it. Despite the emerging wealth of scholarship on populism, descriptions of it increasingly resemble what we have experienced as electoral politics since independence in this country. True, there may be historical variations of the phenomenon but surely there must be something to it that is new and eludes our familiar analytical grids. How does one capture those aspects which may be transforming political practice today in novel ways we don't always realize? This is roughly the problematic that serves as the point of departure for this chapter that takes up a specific case within the thematic of populist governance in order to provide a better handle on the questions flagged previously.

Urban development and the transformation of cityscapes is an important strategy of contemporary populist governance. It often involves beautification and the creation of new leisure spaces, apart from new housing projects, gated communities and places of recreation such as shopping malls. However, as noted earlier, it is not always clear how such a change is qualitatively different from those wrought in the past. Indeed, what makes it all of a sudden 'populist'? Does it throw up new types of space and modes of experience that are important for populist mobilizations? Can we observe new kinds of public goods and services that generate a sense of well-being among targeted population groups? How does it translate into economic logic when growth is slowing down, jobs are downsized and the budgets allocated for such projects are getting tighter by the day? Where exactly does it figure in the actual scheme of populist politics done on the ground that involves, as we know, a wide array of symbolic and affective registers and the capacity to create and manipulate social coalitions? How does it bear upon decision-making by the people and their political behaviour at large? Does it lead to a paradoxical development where the democratic inclusion of more people could converge with increasing support for an authoritarian regime? It is important for us to ask these questions today even if we cannot arrive at definite answers within the scope of this chapter.

What follows is a modest attempt to address these questions, drawing upon two case studies chosen from the localities emerging as minor recreational hubs on the eastern fringe of Kolkata in the state of West Bengal. These sites are Lake Town, located near the north of the Eastern Metropolitan Bypass, and Patuli, in the south of the same highway, which is taking the urban spread further south to localities like Kamalgazi that used to be farmlands even a few years back. The larger idea is to look at these neighbourhoods as illustrations of a key strategy of populist governance—the creation of neoliberal neighbourhoods in India. Their peculiarity and distinctiveness lies in the fact that these are not just newly built neighbourhoods, showcasing highways and arterial roads, housing projects, shopping malls and gated communities that are replacing older grids of lanes and alleyways, smaller building clusters and community parks with familiar pockets of population. They are at the same time neighbourhoods that are being designed to perform and display a synthetic and fabricated hyper-reality that is perennially festive and cheery, sometimes creating the illusion of an upmarket or older posh locality of the city. At other times they take on a theme park look crowded with musical soirees and frequent fairs, prettified pavements and pastiche statuary. They showcase fibreglass replicas of famous landmarks along with cartoon figures, logos, tableaux and mini spectacles dotting the landscape for public consumption. A wide variety of people frequent these new neighbourhoods, including many who travel from other localities to enjoy the 'feel' of these sites, strolling and taking selfies in front of the lit-up showpieces, sitting by the water, shooting short videos to share on social media, eating snacks and taking part in the petty consumption on the offer. Apart from families, a good number of them are young people from the middle and lower-middle classes, cutting across religion, gender and caste who seem happy to be in such spaces that make them feel included in the modern urban experience at a cost they are able to afford. Significantly, the local neighbourhood clubs have been made into active partners in this transformation by the regime, fashioning these spaces in a manner that has led to a much more open and different mode of socialization in the area from what these clubs used to periodically organize in the past in temporary and smaller scales. Unlike on those occasions, the number of local inhabitants may not be very high among the people gathered outdoors, say, on a weekend evening, and the clubs do not necessarily control the activities in such publics that are encouraged and patronized by the local councillor with the endorsement of the Chief Minister.

These are neighbourhoods that literally showcase urban development in the regime of Mamata Banerjee, a prominent example of regional populist leaders in India that includes the likes of the late Jayalalitha in Tamil Nadu, Mayawati in UP, Modi in Gujarat before he became the Prime Minister and Kejriwal currently in Delhi. I believe these neoliberal neighbourhoods are not unique to Mamata's style of populist governance. They resonate with and do speak more widely to recent models of urban development, with telling parallels in cities like Ahmedabad and elsewhere in the global south including countries in Latin America and they provide a valuable basis to the respective regime's political legitimacy. Broadly speaking, making these neoliberal neighbourhoods involves developing certain focal points along the urban periphery, preferably located next to an infrastructure corridor or highway. The land-use patterns are likely to be volatile and changing in such areas, with existing water bodies getting filled up or repurposed and farmlands undergoing rapid assetization. The demographic profile soon changes with the influx of migrant labour and young professionals who take up residences on rent in the area and enter the informal sector and gig economies commuting across the inner city.[4] At these focal points on the city border, where the state wants to attract investment, it looks to mainly facilitate and organize retail consumption by organizing formerly decentralized and petty private players as the trigger for urbanization, instead of extending municipal infrastructure and delivery of public goods to the local population in the way cities used to expand in the past. It is crucial to note in this process how the idea of governance as the state's delivery of targeted services to population groups is undergoing a tactical switchover. What we are looking at is a stealthy shift to a smart model where the responsibility for much of what one perceives as development is passed on to private players and retail consumption and the political leadership is thereby finding ways to diversify both the risk and the cost to the exchequer involved in delivering governance. This is how the process appears to fit in with the slowing growth rate and budget cuts, where the regime is devising a way around the financial and infrastructural constraints to deliver urbanization.

However, the making of these neoliberal neighbourhoods is not merely a matter of administrative and economic convenience for populist regimes in power. Rather than the economic cost and financial risk management involved in such transformation, this chapter tries to draw attention to the dimension of beautification and aesthetic fashioning of these neighbourhoods that are deliberately designed to provide a major platform for political messaging of the ruling party. As we shall see in the discussion of the cases studies to follow, this messaging can be seen to take place in three different ways leading to a strategic outcome. The first manner of this messaging concerns the very nature and function of beautification which is very different from earlier drives of facelift of Indian cities that saw the poor masses as a nuisance and source of ugliness in the cityscape. The logic behind these earlier drives was captured best by scholars like D. Asher Ghertner in his study of Delhi.[5] Such drives were accompanied with clearing up squatter settlements and gentrification of localities, making them somewhat exclusive and expensive spaces for the underclass public. The new kind of beautification stands in sharp contrast to this earlier mode. It mobilizes a very different idea of beauty that the cultivated and well-heeled may find kitschy and tacky, making up an aesthetic experience that directly caters to the masses who may not care too much for a sense of distinction in their choice of consumption. At the same time, such aesthetic fashioning deliberately plays with a sense of simulation and culture of copies and replicas in the statuary and showpieces mounted across the site. They reference the authentic in such a manner that makes it readily accessible to low-cost circuits of circulation and consumption. The pleasure of this access spans from statuary and landmarks to 'classy' colonial neighbourhoods, like recreating the festive mood of Park Street on a Christmas night with Santa Claus cut-outs, fairy lights and buntings decorating stretches of Lake Town throughout the entire winter season. The exclusive experience of an inner-city hotspot on a special night thus becomes a retail commodity, to be accessed by masses and people of modest means at their leisure and free time. That is the unique gift of the regime that effectively works as a message for the masses who can now enjoy a good that was strictly limited to elites for long. The second manner of messaging is more direct. It involves the endless repetition and amplification of the leader's face, along with the images of local leaders and related ideological symbols and iconography mounted across these neighbourhoods and leisure spaces. Along with the decorative statuary and replicas these visages of the leader advertising her successful projects and vision for a global branding of the state mesh with the iconography of the region's cultural and nationalist heritage, erasing the signs of any alternative or older (leftist) political discourse and rewriting the landscape as it were in the process. The result is an unavoidable sense of saturation of only one political idiom, that of the ruling party and only one genuine leader available and deserving to lead the people. This is further underscored in the sartorial styling of the leader, who is displayed as someone shorn of all signs of luxury and excess, embodying a severe ascetic simplicity in her starched white cotton saree and rubber slippers, a 'didi' or the familial sister who enjoys living like one of the masses despite being their elected leader, for now, close to a decade. This leads us to the third way in which the political messaging works that combines the first two modes. It involves what I would like to describe as a kind of psychological priming. It constitutes the identification of two sets of elements that radically alters what behavioural economists would describe as the architecture of choice for the actor, by arranging motivating factors and disincentives in such a manner that one is driven to only one kind of (political) choice and blinded to other alternatives. Before we go on to a more detailed discussion of the case studies let me very briefly indicate how this takes place. To begin with, there is on the one hand the delivery of a new kind of public good in these synthetic neighbourhoods which alters the very manner in which we understand public good. What we are looking at in this case is something that approximates the experience of consumption and recreation which is being made available at heavily discounted rates to a population that presumably cannot afford to have this experience at the authentic source or location. Nevertheless, it carries the sense of redistributing certain elements of luxury that might be seen to constitute elements of a prosperous life among a wider section of people that used to be limited to the few who are rich and well-off in the urban society. This redistribution that does not involve concrete goods and services but the ease of access to previously excluded experiences is projected as what has solely become possible by the initiatives of a certain regime, whose leader (as 'didi') personally embodies the commitment to such redistribution and the inclusion of poor people into the privileged ambit of urban existence. Any rejection or disavowal of this leader and her regime would, therefore, imply an end to this inclusive redistribution and return of elite control over good life and the luxuries promised in the big city. In other words, it creates a situation where the people are voluntarily locked into the support of the regime.

It should not be difficult to fathom that there are a number of troubling consequences to such development. Let me flag two particularly worrisome aspects briefly. First, underneath the apparently inclusive and democratic implication of developing spaces like the neighbourhoods we are looking at, there should be no mistaking the highly cosmetic nature of the change being wrought. The perennially festive facelift of these neighbourhoods are not really backed up with corresponding development of better infrastructure, connectivity and civic facilities like the inner city localities are seen to enjoy. Neither do they seem to attract major business houses or big private players in a bid to launch public-private partnership projects in the area with the potential of generating employment and disposable income for the local population. In fact, apart from a few exceptions, the organization of retail stalls and small trade, as well as the minor projects of beautification of the leisure spaces, appear to involve a regularized chain of petty corruption involving members of the local club, the ruling party cadres and the traders they choose to favour. The benefits of increasing footfall in the neighbourhood are thus mostly appropriated by these small traders and party functionaries often accused by the opposition parties and media of flourishing on 'cut-money'. There are very few actual signs so far that would indicate the prospect of such neighbourhoods transforming from a signalling of notional prosperity to a more substantive reality of well-being. While the former is bound to give rise to a surge of aspirations among the youth in the area, the real lack of opportunities could lead before long to frustrations and bitter resentment with grave consequences. Second, let us consider the wider political implication of the psychological priming at work in these neighbourhoods. To begin with, such priming involves various kinds of identification and collapsing of categories. For instance, it confuses a certain cosmetic beautification and facilitation of petty consumption with the more substantive idea of development in popular perception. This renders any effort by the political executive at extending actual provisions of municipal facilities and public goods understood in a substantive sense ironically unrewarding given the political cost besides the drain on the exchequer. However, what is more problematic is the identification of a certain leader with the perceived redistribution of certain elements of good life and luxury among previously excluded masses. Such a leader and her regime will not only appear as the best choice for those who are convinced about the redistributive commitment and capacity of this leader. Any political competitor who contests the claims to such redistribution as hollow is bound to be seen as cynic and part of the elite clique who are unsettled by the leader's efforts at redistribution. Given the coveted and fragile nature of benefits such as the experience of fabricated leisure spaces at low cost, it is not difficult to visualize how one could imagine they will be gone the moment a certain leader and regime is removed from power, especially when that regime has precisely erased the signs of the earlier dispensation from the landscape. Unlike a system of patronage where the client can seek benefits to some extent from several competing patrons in return of electoral support, this is a far more insidious arrangement where the person who regards himself as the beneficiary becomes politically locked into a relationship of loyal and grateful support for the leader, by and large, unable to think of alternatives. Once such a political locking in takes place the committed supporter is willing to go along with excesses committed by the regime and regards centralization and consolidation of power by the authority as welcome. It is not unlikely that any opposition and criticism of authority will begin to appear at this point as unnecessary impediments to a radical transformation the leader should no longer wait to usher in and the prospect of such a change is worthy of doing away with opposition and suspending the norms of democracy. In short, the upshot of such psychological priming is the consolidation of a support base for authoritarian regimes. Paradoxically, this move towards authoritarianism is a possibility that comes riding on the back of democratic principles of inclusion and redistribution and this is where populism poses its biggest threat. It can make a shrewd and cynic use of democracy from within to subvert its core and foundation. However, what looks uncertain is whether the turn to authoritarianism can actually deliver the promised prosperity that neoliberalism has helped to stoke among the masses. The reality of poverty is never too far from the borrowed geographies under review in this chapter.

How did these geographies begin to take shape in the first place? It is a narrative waiting to be fully fleshed out but its outlines nevertheless reveal the fascinating manner in which the transformation of urban space overlaps with political history and successive electoral regimes in a state. What is common to both Lake Town and Patuli is that these localities are intimately linked to the history of the partition and refugee influx in the city. Topographically they were marshlands and water bodies lying on the eastern fringe of the old city that were primarily used for farming and fishing before they underwent landfill and were gradually turned into tenements and settlements for the people who came in from what has now become Bangladesh. These localities thus house the history of a postcolonial Kolkata, one which used to fall outside the city proper and struggled to be integrated with its urban geography until the late years of the twentieth century. Patuli developed in the 1990s as the extension of Baishnabghata that stood at the periphery of south Kolkata which stretched from Jadavpur to Garia, mainly populated by refugee squatter colonies that slowly turned into middle and upper-middle class gentrified localities by the turn of the century. During the three-decade-long rule of the communist party-led Left Front, the organization of these localities were led by local clubs. These clubs were formed by underclass refugees in many cases that housed libraries, held cultural events, organized annual religious festivals and functioned as hubs of socialization and focus of political mobilization in the area. The phenomena have been highlighted by Partha Chatterjee as an important example in his theoretical formulation of 'political society'.[6] It is these clubs that came to play an instrumental role in the process of changes that led to what we are describing today as neoliberal neighbourhoods in this chapter.

This transformation has been mapped with absorbing wealth of details in the case of Lake Town and Sreebhumi in the work of Sounita Mukherjee who underlines the significance of the recent changes in the urban landscape for thinking about populist politics in Bengal.[7] Mukherjee has described at length how a number of lakes and marshy lowlands of the Patipukur area, formerly owned by local landlords, were gradually converted into what became the Lake Town neighbourhood in the 1960s, with a new VIP road coming to be constructed next to the locality connecting the city with the airport in Dumdum. Significantly, her narrative highlights the vital role of an older association, the 'Gandhi Seva Sangha' in 'giving the locality and its residents its social cohesiveness' and the sense of a 'moral community'. One could easily find parallels of the 'Gandhi Seva Sangha' in similar south Kolkata neighbourhoods, for instance, in the 'Baisakhi' club in Ganguly bagan or the 'Jatra Shuru Sangha' in Baisnabghata which functioned precisely to create this sense of a collective 'moral community' among the refugee settlers of a newly occupied area around the middle of twentieth century. Thus, the 'Jatra Shuru Sangha' began to organize the annual Durga puja, introducing a special five idol feature of 'Panchadurga' that quickly became a crowd-puller and gave the locality a new respectability in the early 1980s. It also staged plays and musical programmes, craft fairs and cultural festivals, periodic athletic events and blood donation camps, along with trainers supervising the daily activities of games and physical exercises for children and teenagers, besides housing a modest public library. The activities of such clubs reflected a sober mix of Gandhian ethics of self-organization and progressive values at times inflected with socialist sentiments as the club functionaries began to overlap with the local cadres of communist parties that led the regime from the 1980s. However, such club activities corresponded to the creation of a different nature of neighbourhoods in those times that placed a premium on sobriety, cultivated taste and distance from ostentatious displays of wealth. In sharp contrast, a different set of activities usually ushered in by younger clubs appeared to take over these neighbourhoods as they began to undergo the latest round of transformation around the turn of the century. As the Eastern Metropolitan Bypass began to take shape from the 1990s, it led to taking over of the marshlands and water bodies lying between the new highway and Baisnabghata, and the landfill began to give rise to the new neighbourhood of Patuli. Initially developed as clusters of low-income housing projects by the municipality, most of them were resold and redeveloped as middle-class residential housing societies, extending into new localities, and giving rise to new clubs in the area, like the Patuli Central Club that plays a crucial role in the current set of transformations. This includes taking an active part in the beautification drive of the area, including the embellishment of the embankment with decorative tableaus, replicas and statuary of cartoon figures along with film stars, famous artists, cultural and nationalist icons on the one hand. On the other hand, it involves facilitating the organization of a series of craft and food fairs throughout the year in the neighbourhood, including the holding of a relatively grand scale annual 'Patuli Utsav'. Clearly, the role of Patuli Central Club, and the patronage of the powerful local councillor of the area, Bappaditya Dasgupta, has become far more instrumental in moulding the neighbourhood today than the 'Jatra Shuru Sangha'. Dasgupta has been the key person in getting the municipality to develop a 'floating market' on the Patuli lake, where people from far and near come to buy daily groceries travelling on a wooden walkway meandering through retailers selling their wares on tethered boats. Dasgupta has also made clever use of recycled scrap iron fabricated in a local factory for a local Puja decoration under his patronage in order to create a mini replica model of the Howrah Bridge that is installed across another stretch of the lake illuminated at night.

In a somewhat similar way, the role of the 'Sreebhumi Sporting Club' has come to overshadow the 'Gandhi Seva Sangha' in Mukherjee's narrative of Lake Town which found a new leader and patron in Sujit Bose, a trusted deputy of Mamata Banerjee, who has catapulted the locality into the limelight as a site of perennial festivities. The new Lake Town now boasts of recreational sites like a children's park, a leisure park, prettified pedestrians' walk-ways and decorative street lights, with kiosks and food stalls lined up along the canal, all of them 'embellished with a blaze of blue and white illumination', the colours associated with the ruling party, as pointed out by Mukherjee. Instead of the older set of welfare activities, Lake Town has now begun to host events like 'Rakhi Utsav', 'Ganesh Utsav' and 'Freedom at Midnight', when the celebration of independence becomes what Mukherjee describes as a 'staged display of public charity'. A large number of people regularly flock to visit the Big Ben prototype installed on the VIP road, taking selfies in front of the *Biswa Bangla* logo and marvelling at the latest Durga Puja pavilion that resembles a spectacular palace from the latest blockbuster film. In a nutshell, the neighbourhoods like Lake Town on the VIP road and Patuli on the Eastern Bypass look very much like indigenous fragments of Disneyland tailored for masses who want to consume the experience of citizenship in ways that are pleasing and fleeting at the same time.

Mukherjee's narrative of the transformation of Lake Town is meant to illustrate what she describes as a new populist politics that is centred on spectacles and festivals, spawning a culture of leisure and entertainment, geared to an affective management of the masses with aesthetic renovation of the civic sphere. It is an insight that builds upon the important argument of the historian Tapati Guha-Thakurta who makes a larger case through what she describes as the 'festival mode' of Mamata Banerjee's governance and the visual thrust of populism in Bengal which uses the Durga Puja as a template for an aesthetic overhaul of the entire city. However, Guha-Thakurta points out that despite the city-wide drive for beautification,

> there are certain key zones on the outer ring of the city—like Baishnabghata Patuli on the south-eastern fringe, and Lake Town, Salt Lake, and New Town Rajarhat, on the northern eastern flank of the city—that have been subjected to the intense and cost-intensive projects of the creations of popular 'art'.[8]

These zones present us a new kind of site for thinking about the relationship between populism, urbanization and neoliberal strategies of governance. It is precisely where one finds an important analytical possibility that this chapter has tried to explore. This possibility involves pushing in a direction, as suggested by Guha-Thakurta, that avoids juxtaposing development with beautification or making governance and festivities as mutually exclusive or implicitly antagonistic phenomena. The point is to investigate how the two poles modify each other: What does the new aesthetic makeover do to the process of political mobilization? How does the content of governance change when politics seeks to deliver consumption? In a sense, it takes us back to the problem of pulling together the two different strands of the schematic of populism that Partha Chatterjee has posed in his latest work.[9] Where does the ideological strand of populism intersect with that of governance today? I believe that in a limited and provisional manner we could begin to seek the answers in the site described as neoliberal neighbourhoods in India.

Notes

* The author warmly acknowledges the generous assistance of the DSA program at the Centre for Political Studies, JNU, for making the ethnography possible for writing this essay.

1 E. Laclau, *On Populist Reason* (London: Verso Books, 2005).

2 C. Mudde, "The Populist Zeitgeist", *Government and Opposition* 39, no. 4(2004): 541–563.

3 Ajay Gudavarthy, *India after Modi: Populism and the Right* (New Delhi: Bloomsbury, 2019).

4 For a detailed discussion on the political economy and social dynamics of such geographies, see Shubhra Gururani and Rajarshi Dasgupta, "Frontier Urbanism: Urbanisation beyond Cities in South Asia," *Economic & Political Weekly* 53, no. 12(2018): 41–45.

5 D. Asher Ghertner, *Rule by Aesthetics: World-Class City making in Delhi* (New York: Oxford University Press, 2015).

6 For the argument of 'political society' see Partha Chatterjee, *The Politics of the Governed: Reflections on Popular Politics in Most of the World* (New Delhi: Permanent Black, 2004) and *Lineages of Political Society: Studies in Postcolonial Democracy* (New Delhi: Permanent Black, 2011).

7 Sounita Mukherjee, "The City As Political Exhibitionary Space: Kolkata 2011-2018", Thesis submitted in partial fulfilment of the requirements for the degree of Master of Philosophy in Social Sciences at Jadavpur University, Kolkata. Also, see Sounita Mukherjee, "Transforming City Spaces and the Politics of Spectacle in Contemporary Kolkata: A Case Study of the Neighbourhoods of Sreebhumi and Lake Town", *Journal of Humanities and Social Sciences*, no.16 (December 2019): 178–196.

8 Tapati Guha-Thakurta, "A Goddess, a Chief Minister and a City: Reflections on a Festival Mode of Populist Politics," in *The State of Democracy*, ed. Manas Ray (forthcoming).

9 Partha Chatterjee, *I am the People, Reflections on Popular Sovereignty Today* (New Delhi: Permanent Black, 2020).

9

INDIVIDUATION AND THE AUTHORITARIAN PUBLIC: RAJELAKSHMY'S *A PATH AND MANY SHADOWS*

Urmila G. and Nikhil Govind

In their influential book *Cultural Backlash: Trump, Brexit and Authoritarian Populism* (2019), scholars Pippa Norris and Ronald Inglehart stress that the most consistent and statistically robust protection against authoritarian populism is the evolution of gender roles.

> A wealth of research in sociology, public opinion, and gender studies has documented birth-cohort linked change in sex role attitudes, in the US and Europe. These studies report that a gender gap can be observed among the more egalitarian younger generations, with women's views shifting further and faster than men's, due in part to women's experience of rising educational levels, growing labour force participation, the ideological impact of the second-wave women's movement, and declining religiosity and marriage rates. (Norris and Inglehart 2019: 90)

This chapter will focus on a novel, *A Path and Many Shadows* (2016, translated by R.K. Jayasree) which was originally published in 1960 in Malayalam by Rajelakshmy (1930–1965). The novel captures the anguish and puzzlement of a protagonist's complex 'unveiling' of female selves in public. Norris and Inglehart's (2019) list of terms, such as historical period/birth cohort, egalitarian impulses toward a homogenized public sphere and the concomitant backlash, the struggle for education and livelihood, rights within relationships as they ravel and unravel, and the persistent mutations of familial ideas of conservatism and religion, find fine nuance as themes in the novel. Unlike her strained protagonist Mani, Rajelakshmy committed suicide at the age of thirty-five, partly due to a public scandal regarding her work. Even though the event of the suicide is over fifty years old, the incident is still raw in Kerala, and oft-invoked in contemporary debates regarding threats to free speech and with a view to build anti-authoritarian public spheres.

The coinciding of freedom with responsibility constitutes the I, doubled with itself, encumbered with itself (Levinas 1969: 271).

Introduction

The shadow of life and oeuvre of the Malayalam writer Rajelakshmy (1930–1965) remains long in Kerala. In 2018, the novelist S. Hareesh withdrew his novel *Meesha* (Moustache) from serialization in one of the state's most prominent media outlets *Mathrubhumi* (Motherland), as the novel allegedly offended Hindu women. The prominent online news website Scroll covered many aspects of the story. *Scroll* noted that the controversy was over a conversation between two characters, in which one imputed that women dressing well while visiting temples was due to a subconscious desire to attract men (*Scroll* 2018). The withdrawal of *Meesha* followed on the heels of the more famous withdrawal of a novel by Tamil writer Perumal Murugan in 2015, again for allegedly offending a community with regard to the norms of sexuality. Scroll contacted many sources, including poet K. Satchidanandan and novelist Anita Nair and Benyamin, for their responses. A writer who spoke at length was the novelist C.V. Balakrishnan (who himself had written a novel *Ayussinte Pustakam* [The Book of Life] in 1984 which was criticized by the Church). Balakrishnan referred to a longer history of the difficulty of free speech in Kerala, and recalled one of its most famous incidents—the suicide of the thirty-five-year-old writer Rajelakshmy in 1965, following harassment regarding her publications. Rejelakshmy's work was also being serialized in *Mathrubhumi*, and she had recalled her novel after only eight chapters had been published. Rajelakshmy's suicide note said that she had decided to kill herself so as to not have to write anymore—she also burnt the remainder of the novel (Raveendran 2016: 3). In the Scroll (2018) article, C.V. Balakrishnan, recalled the incident, "It was a brilliant work with a biographical touch… She faced lot of criticism and harassment from family and society for writing such an explosive novel. The reactions made her angry and she got the manuscript back from *Mathrubhumi* editor N.V. Krishna Warrier. Later she committed suicide." Thus, the public sphere in Kerala remains fraught with regard to literary publishing up to today, and one sees the even distribution of varied kinds of censorship across the decades, from the 1960s to the 1980s into the teens of the twenty-first century.

While there would always be unanswered questions over any suicide, one might consider some of the contexts that could provoke such a step. At the time of her death, Rajelakshmy had been a well-known and successful writer—a single working woman, and the first woman to win the Kerala Sahitya Akademi Award (in 1960) for the novel *A Path and Many Shadows*—the subject of this article. The aim here is not to correlate the events of the novel and life, or to see autobiographical residues, but to think the difficulty of the act of intertwined solitude and sharing that writing necessarily is. It would be hard to separate the arrows of hurt into clear domains of public and private, of life and work, or of educational and sexual freedoms. One may remember the pointed details of the terse suicide note: that "she would live only as a writer and that she was leaving because she did not want to appear to be continually hurting others through her fiction" (Menon 2005: 23, cited in Rajelakshmy 2016).

It is necessary to give a brief view of Rajelakshmy's life, drawn from senior literary scholar P.P. Raveendran's Introduction to *A Path and Many Shadows*. Rajelakshmy was born in 1930 in the district of Palakkad, which has produced very influential Malayalam writers such as Vallathol Narayana Menon (1878–1958), as well as Rajelakshmy's contemporaries M.T. Vasudevan Nair (1933–) and O.V. Vijayan (1930–2005). Rajelakshmy studied in Benares Hindu University, Varanasi, where she obtained a Masters in Physics. The rest of her life was spent teaching in various colleges in Kerala. Not only did she become the first woman to win the Kerala Sahitya Akademi Award but she was also published in the most prestigious and widely read literary and media forums of the time. Her uniqueness and confidence had been widely hailed. She committed suicide when her second novel was being serialized in 1965. She thus had a brief, if fertile, publishing career for about ten years from the mid-fifties to the mid-sixties, writing in the era of the dominant 'social realism' of writers like Thakazhi Sivasankara Pillai (1912–1999), P. Kesava Dev (1904–1983) and K. Saraswathi Amma (1919–1975).

Rajelakshmy's noted contemporary, the novelist M.T. Vasudevan Nair compared her to the British stylist Virginia Woolf in their supposedly shared 'spiritual isolation', and Rajelakshmy herself was deeply interested in Woolf, especially in *A Room of One's Own*—a lecture on the work has been found among her papers (2016: 5). As Raveendran remarks, this would have been unusual in the early sixties, when an organized Indian feminist movement had not quite taken off, and what Rajelakshmy saw in Woolf was less spiritual isolation and more the mundane requirement for eking out writing time and space, amidst the demands of a full-time employment (Rajelakshmy 2016: 6). Though the broader discussion of the Kerala literary milieu is beyond the scope of this chapter, one needs to flesh out some historical context to situate the question that this chapter addresses—the vexed emergence and exposure of a gendered literary subject.

The cultural historian J. Devika in her influential book *En-Gendering Individuals: The Language of Re-forming in Twentieth Century Keralam* (2006) has highlighted several aspects of the relation of gender to the public sphere in Kerala from the late nineteenth century onwards. First, well into the early twentieth century, "eating, dressing, talking—just about everything signified one's position in the social hierarchy and one's difference from others" (Devika 2006: 2). Despite this, by the 1920s, "the first generation of women educated in the modern style [literacy] was a significant presence in the Malayalee public sphere. Such women were also beginning to gain employment in schools, medical institutions and the government (Devika 2006: 5)". Gender relations had to refashion themselves substantially—for example, the dominant caste Nairs who used to practice matriliny, had to re-think the very notion of 'husband' as a type of legal and public active provider. Devika quotes the autobiography of the aforementioned well-known novelist Thakazhi Sivasankara Pillai who recalled the agitated speeches of the Nair reformers of his childhood: "There is prosperity only in those homes provided for by husbands. We need to keep our women in place by making them virtuous. For this husbands must be made to bear their expenses" (2006: 73). This theme is important, as one of the strengths of *A Path and Many Shadows* is its thematization of the stresses of not just women in entering a public sphere, but also the strains in the reconfiguration of masculinity that was required (to reveal a spoiler, the person the protagonist Mani finally chooses to marry is a low-paid, tubercular clerk in distant Bombay). Leaving aside the further difficulties of the even more disadvantaged castes, it is evident that it was a long fight to enter the competitive public sphere even for dominant castes like the Nairs (which Rajelakshmy belonged to), as also of the Brahmins like the Nambutiris, from whom some of the Nair women were socially expected to cohabit. Indeed, the most famous literature of the Nambutiris (such as, novel *Agnisakshi* [Fire, My Witness] by Lalithambika Antharjanam [2015]) often dealt directly with how women were expected to navigate the public sphere. Nambutiri women were called *Antharjanam* (literally, inner people), and were in theory not even to be exposed to sunlight—in practice, this meant they never went outside the land around the house, except to the temple, and when they did, there were strict rules of dress, and each had to possess a mandatory cadjun umbrella to rebut any unwanted gaze. Kerala had many caste practices that were extreme, even by South Asian standards. Nevertheless, there were also strong forces of resistance, and by the 1950s when Rajelakshmy began to write, Devika argues that "in practical terms it [forces of reform] justified the entry of women into the public domain, particularly into institutions such as schools, hospitals, charity organization, reform institutions or orphanages" (2006: 173). As in many parts of the world, including India, women were allowed to enter more in the service-oriented sectors—one may recall the importance of the college years in the descriptions of writers like Ismat Chughtai and Qurratulain Hyder during the 1940s and 1950s (Chughtai [1944]2006; Hyder 1959). College was a time of intense politicization and intense romance, and both politics and romance fed into each other during this period (Govind 2019). It is unsurprising that Rajelakshmy chose to become a college teacher, and that the space and time of college is integral to *A Path and Many Shadows*.

In the essay on Woolf, Rajelakshmy had written about how hard it was to sustain creativity amidst the demands of work, necessary though, work was to entitle one to a house of one's own. It would thus seem that teaching symbolized no particular liberatory power for Rajelakshmy beyond paying the rent, and many of her short stories also speak of the difficulties of workplace politics (such as in 'The Apology', in Rajelakshmy 2016). The political scientist Ajay Gudavarthy in his book on populism remarks on the number of single people who capitalized on the rhetoric of pure public *seva* (service)—after mentioning Narendra Modi, Atal Bihari Vajpayee, Mamata Banerjee, Jayalalitha, Naveen Patnaik, Mayawati, Rahul Gandhi and so on, Gudavarthy remarks that this rhetoric cuts across the political spectrum, and it is fervently believed that the "good leader is ascetic, who believes in renouncing his personal and private pursuits for the larger cause of the nation. By this logic, without a family are often, *ipso facto*, considered to be honest leaders… mass leaders and politician in India rarely ever announce retirement from public life" (Gudavarthy 2019: 17–18). In contrast to this, Rajelakshmy may be said to represent a different ethos—while the very act of being a single working woman was quite pioneering in Kerala of the 1950s, she nevertheless did not hyperbolize public service, but instead exposed the public as both puritanical and wounding of other, deeper sources of human and public creativity. Indeed, despite being a short novel, perhaps a novella (it runs into approximately 150 pages), *A Path and Many Shadows* exhibits a comprehensive gamut of all the fatiguing tribulation that a girl child undergoes within a family as she matures into a young woman—then this young woman is suspended without preparation into the even more anxiety-inducing sphere of the college. The literary scholar Udaya Kumar has mentioned a similar autobiographical journey of this time period, where a life "can no longer be told in a linear narrative of progressive self-realization. It weaves in memory and guilt, destitution and acquisition, intimacy and sacrifice, in ambivalent moves" (Kumar 2016: 256). The art of Rajelakshmy's novel is thus the constant back and forth of that unveiling of the self in public, of relapse and arrest as much as the simple accumulation of confidence or worldly power and goods. To track this evolution in its full, fervid complexity, it is now time to turn to the novel itself.

Reading A Path and Many Shadows

As many readers would not be familiar with the novel, the analysis below closely follows the plot-line. The novel is organized in a straightforward, linear fashion, but does not provide simple, progressive self-realization. The novel begins with the female protagonist called a "little girl" (though her precise age is not given), and ends after she completes her undergraduate degree (Rajelakshmy 2016: 153). The first chapter has her wandering through a beautiful rural landscape of home and school, holding her books and lunch box, idly picking yellow flowers and following dragonflies amidst fields of sesame, and groves of cashew. There is a solitude already granted to her (though at this point it is unshadowed), and her walk through the lovingly described landscape slows the movement of the time of reading. This quality of temporality is different from a more fevered adult life, which is crowded with other people. The landscape also houses kind old storytellers, including one who was by profession an oracle. He is ever willing to oblige her taste for archaic, mythic stories of goddesses and demons. It is a moment of seductive, earnest innocence that will not easily return to the novel, for as Remani (called Mani by everyone) grows older, complications accumulate.

Even as a child, part of the reason for Mani's continual wandering was that her home was not an entirely friendly space. There were aunts and grandmothers who were scolds, and an immobile, ill mother (with "lifeless eyes… bony hands… knotted tracery of veins"), whose room was full of pictures of gods and always smelt the same—an indeterminate mixture of incense, ash, sandalwood, spittoon, castor oil for the lamps, ayurvedic potions (Rajelakshmy 2016: 161).

At home she missed the storyteller, "[t]he girl who could not bond with her kin and the old man who had no kin to bond with. Though she lived surrounded by next of kin in the two-storey house by the hillside, she was essentially alone" (ibid.: 161). The mother's immobility and the daughter's aimless wanderings light the narrative with a dreamy air—there is a heightened perception of the interior of the family home and the ritualized relations within. She felt little connection with her brother: "Only a year separated the brother [Gopu] from the sister, but the difference in their nature was more than a whole world. He had no problem doing as he was told" (ibid.: 162). As to the father: "They hardly ever saw Achan [father]. He was never home half the time. And if he happened to be home, even a leaf was supposed to move only with the consciousness that he was home. She had never seen him talk or laugh loudly. She had also never seen him get angry or lose his temper. He always maintained the same facial expression and the same tone of voice. She too was afraid of Achan. Her only thought was to avoid, at all costs, running into him" (ibid.: 162). The coldness and remoteness of the father were almost worse than the naked anger—but in time, she would face that naked anger too.

The death of her dear companion—the old oracle—is something that creeps upon Mani slowly. She had gone into his house the day before his death and had seen him lying down. She did not think to ask why he lay thus—and he had given her a trinket from the bed. The next day, his eyes were closed and he was wheezing, not registering her presence or call. She left, and by the evening the crowd outside his house indicated that he was dying. Though it was only her that had a relationship with the abandoned old man, when it was the time of his death, she was brushed off as an irritant asking uncomfortable questions. She was unable to sleep, and the next day went alone to confront the starkness of his room, the empty coir cot, and his beloved dog who had also mysteriously died. The cold body of the dog made her understand death viscerally. The day was the "very first wound to the heart... she didn't know how to cry" (166), and her consciousness learned to possess within its folds this first experienced death. Mani needed to breathe and took refuge within the horizon of blue mountains that provide what little consolation there was—this was before the scolding grandmother reappeared, making her return to the petty nothingness of family routine.

Throughout the novel, nature appears as a key site of subjectivation, the true home away from home—it takes on the varied, tiered effects of consolation, privacy, of necessary respite, even of sensuality. It is the self in its state of expansion, as opposed to the constricting Other of family and obligation. But the family had its less onerous members. After the death of the oracle, she became friends with a cousin who had moved back with his family to her village. This cousin—called Appettan—was the person she eventually chose to marry. It may be remembered that certain types of cousins are sanctioned to marry in Kerala (here, it is the father's sister's son). Appettan and family began to visit her more frequently, and that was when she began to notice him. Soon, they met more frequently, and she was struck by the kindness and thoughtfulness of Appettan, but even more, of his father Kochachan. They started going to school together, ambling through the emerald rice saplings, tasting cinnamon leaves, she would prefer to stay in his house as late as possible. For this last, she was once beaten with a cane on her palms by her father. Her father disliked Kochachan as he had intended his sister to marry someone else who had more property, but his sister eloped with Kochachan. This was why it took them many years to return to her natal village. Despite this strain in the family history, Mani and Appettan's childhood togetherness continued apace, amidst a shared love of poetry, singing and gardening. He went out of his way to source books for her. But in her was already an inlaid melancholy—this, before any concrete sorrow had descended: "She wasn't so much reading books as devouring them… She would put down a book of poems only when she had learnt the contents by heart… Only the poetry of tears was good." (184).

But sorrow in the form of separation was not long in coming—Appettan said he had to leave for college one day, teary-eyed in their favourite hillside cashew grove. He said he felt obliged to explore a larger world. The initial spate of letters from him died and she was left to wander the hillsides and terraced slopes alone, with no one to tease. She learned with some disgust that her ill mother was going to have another child. The birth took place in candle-light and rain and the baby was pre-term and fragile: "It was a period when she [Mani] did not want to meet anyone. Even talking to people had become unbearable." (197). Later she was to say that "her little brother had arrived in the world unwanted. She had never even held him with affection. He was growing up, like the personification of mistakes committed by others…" (218).

The alienation from the family was so complete that Mani did not even want to meet Appettan when he came home during the college vacation. Within the next year, Kochachan died, and she threw herself into school work so that she could go to some college far from home—"salvation lay in scoring well" (199). At end of the novel she indeed flew all the way to Bombay—a city seen with no romance in and of itself (indeed she would always prefer cashew groves to city-lights), but one that did have the insuperable merits of distance and anonymity. The desire for the marriage to Appettan at the end of the novel was partly a desire for a personal annihilation and death (his tuberculosis, but also the accumulated series of deaths of the oracle and his animal companion, of Appettan's father Kochachan, of her endlessly dying mother). Death completes and fulfills, and is the relief of not having to worry about someone anymore—thus, though there is a linear, optimistic public narrative of education and marriage and citizenship, there is also a pervasive underside of decay and defeat, of what Levinas has called "an identity undone to the limit" (1991: 196).

Perhaps understanding something of Mani's nature, and in tune with his own dominating personality, Mani's father, always suspicious of her affection for Appettan and Kochachan, got her admission into a more distant residential college. Though seeing through his plans, Mani was nevertheless relieved to simply get away, and the farther the better. It was her first train ride, her first extended stay away from home, her first encounter with wardens and roommates and showers (in the village they had used water from the well). The college was located within a similar landscape to where she had grown up—about three hours by train and bus. Life in college felt surprisingly leisurely, and she had time to observe, for the first time, the young men and women from various parts of Kerala state, itself only formally amalgamated in the Indian Union in 1956.

Mani was just beginning to feel at home when she received an incoherent, anguished letter from Appettan—essentially it conveyed that he had failed his exams and could not bear to take them again. Over the next few letters, she learned that he had relocated to Bombay, that he wanted a new place that held no painful memories and was determined against all odds to find some employment, paltry though it may be. He finally did get a poorly paying clerical job. The world of college held something new for Mani, and Appettan seemed to represent (though she would not admit it) the parochialism and small ambitions of the village. She was soon immersed in the social issues of college-life—some of her friends were being married off without completing their degree, her poems were beginning to be published in magazines, she was hungrily discovering large swathes of the library, she was getting closer to her roommate Ammu and Ammu's brother Chettan who recommended still more books and publication avenues, and so on. It was a heady time, a mixture of the dense homo-sociality of room and hostel mates, of brothers and friends of these women, of incipient fame as a poet and actor in college productions—she performed once as "Mother India with sadness in her eyes and a smile on her lips" (238).

The joy of college made returning home doubly difficult—one remembers similar sentiments in Chughtai's *The Crooked Line*. The family seemed ever more out of touch, stuck in a time-warp of ayurvedic potions—she began to suffer from 'college-sickness'. She could not wait to get back from this mofussil world where they would soon begin to plot her marriage. She chose to study English literature, which had more women than men even in the 1950s. Mani was both a star-performer (the poet with admirers who gave her anonymous roses and sweets, and it did not hurt to also have "doe eyes and long tresses"), but she was also someone who continued to feel apart (241). She found the college's literary purveyors easier to yield to—fluent teachers with vivid and deep voices chanting Shakespeare, and who were also part of college life in sports and art. As in Chughtai, one of the very few sanctioned ways that young men could meet young women was through politics and electioneering. Here too, of course, lofty debates on socialism could easily also serve (sometimes) as covers or veneers for more routine romance. There were all the traditional undergraduate rites of passage with different men—feelings of romance intermixed with friendship, mentorship, "worship", feelings of more sibling ("*rakhi*") affection than attraction, of misunderstood mentorship (sometimes she was the misunderstood mentor, sometimes the misunderstood mentee) (244). She met men a few years older than her who were intensely involved in the dangerous world of real-world politics—people who had served in prison, and who had suffered violence and had perhaps inflicted violence. It was, in other words, that first utopian discovery of the full public sphere in all its diversity and largeness. This is what should have ideally made for a full citizenship for a woman—but, as should be clear by now from the narrative telos of the novel, such a utopian feeling was not bound to last, and would soon enough be undermined. The public sphere soon enough retracts to all the constraints of traditional masculinism—lovers or teachers or fathers all converge to shrink her embrace of the world.

Let us stay, however, for a few moments in that utopian moment when the public world still seems fully accessible. For Mani, the attraction of that larger world imprinted itself most on the concrete register of reading and scholarship. She began to read more world and contemporary history. There was the inevitable mixture of this larger world and the men through whom she accessed it. For a while, each new lover came with a different reading list, and it became part of her happy, exuberant growth. But in time, the cracks of that world began to show—she became linked with too many men, and at least with some it seemed that the attraction was more unconscionable: some seemed to possess no more than a stylish silhouette of eyes, fingers and cigarettes.

In the nature of such college tragedies, it was unclear why exactly Mani couldn't be with the man she was most clearly attracted to. Gratuitous advice and warnings came from all, including teachers and Chettan. Then there was the stress of poorly designed academic exams and calendars. Finally came the looming presence of her father who was attempting to marry her off as early as possible as she was accused of becoming more and more unmanageable. The objects of her attraction were small against these forces—she realized that beyond the eagerly awaited footfalls in the library, and the charged criss-crossing of gazes, there were only severally aborted futures. Poetry was easier to write than those magical utterances that would have bridged their divided silence—it required a courage that neither she nor her admirers had. The dream of that simple public—a couple openly facing an encouraging, well-wishing audience—was still too farfetched in that small, conservative college in the Kerala of the 1950s. A certain depressive silence takes over the last section of the book—a silence that traverses both the public world of the college, as well as her internal world. A letter from Appettan captured her mood—"Don't you find loneliness unbearable on this thoroughfare?" (296). Indeed, the inward loneliness of the private could only be captured against the constant din of public censure, and the novel ended with her yielding to the temptation to pick that "white fruit of sacrifice dangling before her. She had only to extend her hand." (298).

There is little point in moralizing the end of the novel, insisting that it should have had a more uplifting, agential ending. Rather, it is preferable to allow the novel to lucidly unveil all the difficulties that a woman faces for simply appearing and speaking in public (family or college), which is always ready with the sharpened end of rumour and denigration. One must listen with sympathy to a novel that is about the difficulties of solitude and growth. This *bildung* is an inchoate metabolization of the world, of the figures of the dominating father, the alienated siblings, the absent mother, the allure of death/suicide/sacrifice. Mani never quite accessed a full, public 'outside', a domain of free political ideas and experimentation, that many of the men of the novel inhabit with ease, and as if by right. She never shared the same 'public' space with them—rather, she was caught in a series of different, constraining institutional 'insides'—home, school, college. This is why her fate seemed to lead her inexorably to choosing the tubercular lover, instead of some of the more plain-speaking, vigorous men she met at college.

The hermeneuticist Paul Ricoeur observes that the "finality of the tragic spectacle infinitely exceeds every directly didactic intention" (1992: 242). The authoritarian violence of a public sphere pushes the subject into the interiority of the private, gouging more and more out of that interiority. Thus, it is not surprising that scholars such as Ann Cvetkovich in *Depression: A Public Feeling* (2012) make the case that depression, far from being a merely internal psychic illness or death wish is a public action and reaction, a way of rendering and responding to an oft-pathological, contracting public world. So many public and legal battles today in India (for example, on privacy vis a vis state and market surveillance) converge on this modified language of 'privacy', i.e., a privacy not as counterpoised to the public, but as capable of expanding the necessary meaningfulness of that vitiated and authoritarian public sphere (Bhatia 2018). This is a new language of interiority seeking protection and freedom, one that has to scramble to assemble assorted scraps of self, intimacy and legitimacy. Citizenship, the public norm par excellence, is no longer a given, and one could be turned into a refugee overnight in one's own country even if one's ancestors have never left one's village or city. Norris and Inglehart point out the costs of ignoring these subtler signs of our times, the ever-greater intrusions into bodies, psyches and consciences: "Democracy is thereby attacked, but not directly, which would raise too many red flags. No coup d'état is hatched. The military stay in the barracks. Elections are not cancelled. Opponents are not jailed. But democratic norms are gradually degraded…" (2019: 6). The hope that is held out in the novelistic imagination of *A Path and Many Shadows* is precisely this individuation that carves itself out of the increased degradation of contemporary authoritarian publics.

Note

All Malayalam translations are from R.K. Jayasree in Rajelakshmy, *A Path and Many Shadows and Twelve Stories*, Orient BlackSwan, 2016, New Delhi. The spelling of Rajelakshmy, as mentioned, has also been retained.

Bibliography

Antharjanam, Lalithambika. [1976] 2015. *Agnisakshi (Fire, My Witness)*. Translated by Vasanthi Sankaranarayanan. Delhi: Oxford University Press.

Arunima, G. 2003. *There Comes Papa: Colonialism and the Transformation of Matriliny in Kerala, Malabar, c 1850–1940*. Delhi: Orient BlackSwan.

Bhatia, Gautam. 2018. *Offend, Shock, or Disturb: Free Speech Under the Indian Constitution*. Delhi: Oxford University Press.

Chughtai, Ismat. 2006. *The Crooked Line*. Translated by Tahira Naqvi. New York: Feminist Press.

Cvetkovich, Ann. 2012. *Depression: A Public Feeling*. Durham: Duke University Press.

Devika, J. 2006. *Engendering Individuals: The Language of Reforming in Early Twentieth-Century Keralam*. New Delhi: Orient BlackSwan.

Govind, Nikhil. 2019. *Inlays of Subjectivity: Affect and Action in Modern Indian Literature*. Delhi: Oxford University Press.

Gudavarthy, Ajay. 2019. *India After Modi: Populism and the Right*. Delhi: Bloomsbury.

Hyder, Qurratulain. [1959] 2003. *River of Fire*. Delhi: Women Unlimited.

Inglehart, Ronald and Pippa Norris. 2019. *Cultural Backlash: Trump, Brexit, and Authoritarian Populism*. Cambridge: Cambridge University Press.

Jeffrey, Robin. 1992. *Politics, Women and Well-being: How Kerala became a 'Model'*. Delhi: Palgrave Macmillan.

Kumar, Udaya. 2016. *Writing The First Person: Literature, History, and Autobiography in Modern Kerala*. Delhi: Permanent Black.

Levinas, Emmanuel. [1961] 1969. *Totality and Infinity: An Essay on Exteriority*. Translated by Alphonso Lingis. Pittsburgh: Duquesne University Press.

________. [1978] 1991. *Otherwise than Being or Beyond Essence*. Translated by Alphonso Lingis. Dordrecht: Kluwer Academic Publishers.

Menon, Dilip M. 2005. *The Blindness of Insight: Essays on Caste in Modern India*. New Delhi: Navayana.

——. 2008. *Caste, Nationalism and Communism in South India: Malabar 1900–1948*. Cambridge: Cambridge University Press.

Osella, Filippo and Caroline Osella. 2000. *Social Mobility in Kerala: Modernity and Identity in Conflict*. London: Pluto Press.

P.P. Raveendran. 2016. "Introduction." In *A Path and Many Shadows*. Delhi: Orient BlackSwan.

Rajelakshmy. [1960] 2016. *A Path and Many Shadows and Twelve Stories*. Translated by R.K. Jayasree. Delhi: Orient BlackSwan.

Ricoeur, Paul. [1990] 1992. *Oneself as Another*. Translated by Kathleen Blamey. Chicago: University of Chicago Press.

Saradamoni, K. 1999. *Matriliny Transformed: Family, Law and Ideology in Twentieth Century Travancore*. Delhi: SAGE Publications.

Scroll. 23 July 2018. "Writers Decry Withdrawal of Serial Novel from Kerala Magazine after Author Receives Death Threats." Available at: https://scroll.in/article/887544/writers-decry-withdrawal-of-serial-novel-from-kerala-magazine-after-author-receives-death-threats (last accessed 26 June 2019).

10

THE POPULAR, POPULIST AND THE POLITICAL IN PRIYADARSHAN'S FILMS

Yadukrishnan P.T.

Perhaps there is no other time period in the history of Malayalam cinema that has invoked as much conversation (academic and otherwise) than the 1980s. For the most part, this time period is praised for bearing witness to the peak of the 'middlebrow' movement in Malayalam Cinema—which had appropriated the realist aesthetics of the 1970s art house productions (which were also dubbed as 'Parallel cinema') so as to target the newly formed middle-class spectators (Radhakrishnan 2010: 28). Whereas more recently, these movies have been criticized for catering exclusively to the upper caste middle-class audience whereby a great deal of hostility was shown in these movies towards the non-Hindu and lower caste communities which were also slowly attaining the status of middle-class at the time (Jayakumar 2014: 45). Rajesh M.R. discusses the cultural significance of Dalit employees joining the public sector in the 1970s and how the anxieties surrounding this event were reflected in the cinema of the years that followed (M.R. 2012: 90). This tension surrounding the middle-class status was also caused by a series of land reforms throughout the 1960s which provided rights for the tenant on land ownership and the increase in wealth of the non-Hindu non-upper caste subject because of the 'Gulf boom' (ibid.). It is to be noted that these anxieties were not limited to the middlebrow cinema of the time which towards the end of the 1980s was on its decline. The popular Malayalam cinema of that time had often gone to the extent to claim that the failures of democracy were a direct result of lower caste communities entering government and political sectors (ibid.). The political thrillers of this time period were especially invested in this manufactured paranoia. Hence, one of the most significant products of this time period was the 'upper caste victim'—a new kind of protagonist in the political films of the late 1980s and early 1990s, whose way of life and even his very own existence is threatened by the new political and economic elite of Kerala, supposedly comprising chiefly of Dalits, non-Hindus and other marginalized communities.

Priyadarshan[1] is one of the filmmakers who popularized this trend in Malayalam cinema in the late 1980s and early 1990s, primarily through his collaboration with screenwriter T. Damodaran.[2] This chapter closely looks into two of the films that came out of this collaboration, namely *Aryan* (1988) and *Adhwaytham* (Doctrine of non-duality, 1992), and argues that these films constructed a 'populist'[3] narrative revolving around the angry disenfranchised *savarna* youth who were claimed to be the victims of the corruption and hostility of the new political and economic elites in Kerala. This new class of elites purportedly constituted of Dalits, non-Hindus and other backward communities who are portrayed in these films to have benefitted immensely from the social programmes of the Communist party in Kerala. Political theorist Margaret Canovan, while looking into the specificities of anti-elitist rhetoric in populist ideology, discusses the significance of populist imagery in fiction, with "the rhetoric of the underdog, the pathos of the "little man", his struggles, and his virtues" (Canovan 1981: 297). She subsequently claims that "such images have the great advantage that since fictional figures are simultaneously concrete individuals and symbolic representations of Everyman–they can evade the real-life difficulties of establishing *who* 'the common man' is, and just what are the interests of the people" (ibid.). This chapter will delve into the characteristics of the carefully constructed populist narrative in *Aryan* and *Adhwaytham*, its 'common man' protagonist, the corrupt economic and political elites that he is struggling against, and the communities that this narrative poses as 'the other'. I will also try to argue that this particular populist narrative can be seen evolving from *Aryan* to *Adhwaytham*, that is, from 1988 to 1992 where it can be seen moving and aligning itself to the Hindu nationalistic rhetoric that was becoming highly popular and mainstream towards the early 1990s.

What is important to keep in mind about the populist imagery constructed in these films is that they were grounded in the specific caste dynamics of Kerala. Therefore before proceeding, a brief summary of the distinctiveness of caste practise in Kerala is in order.

Caste System in Kerala

Caste, as it was practised in Kerala, was significantly different from the way it was practised elsewhere in India. "The highest in the caste hierarchy were the Namboothiri Brahmins who, together with the

Nairs, made up the landed class. The intermediary castes were the Ezhavas, who were followed by the lower castes and tribes who were predominantly landless labourers" (Pillai 2013: 103). This particular system of caste had developed and expanded greatly, whereby towards the twentieth century there were over 500 divisions and subdivisions. Not to mention how the concept of 'pollution' in caste had been extended from 'untouchability' to 'unapproachability' (Mohan 2015: xii). Historian Sanal Mohan in his book *Modernity of Slavery*, discusses the prevalence of comparative studies in the nineteenth century on the conditions of the 'caste slavery' in Kerala with that of 'Atlantic slavery'. Mohan denotes on how the missionary scholar Samuel Mateer had commented that "the Pulayan [one of the Dalit castes in Kerala] was in an infinitely worse condition than ever the American slave was" (ibid.). In the latter half of the nineteenth century and in the first half of twentieth century there were a series of reform movements in Kerala that tried to fight the caste hierarchy and the general social structure of the region in the spirit of modernity (Pillai 2013: 104).

Cultural Historian Dilip Menon in his work discusses the ways in which the culture of the upper caste Hindus were dubbed as Kerala's culture in its entirety in the years leading to the formation of the Kerala state in 1956 (Menon 2011: 62). He also states the ways in which literature and cinema have always attempted to pose the stories of the upper caste landed elites as the story of Kerala in its entirety, sidelining the narratives and histories of the marginalized communities even after Independence and state formation (Menon 2005: 318). Scholar Jenny Rowena also discusses the same in her work, but through a very different lens, where she points towards the hegemony enjoyed by the upper caste Nairs and Brahmins in Malayalam film industry and how it has greatly influenced the placement of these communities in the forefront of most narratives in the history of Malayalam cinema (Rowena 2013). This is something one has to be mindful of, while looking into the ways in which *Aryan* and *Adhwaytham* frame the questions of caste and modernity in Kerala.

Aryan: *Posing Namboothiri Brahmins as 'the common man'*

Released in 1988, *Aryan* is the first collaboration between writer T. Damodaran and director Priyadarshan. The plot revolves around the life of a Brahmin priest Devanarayanan, referred to as Devan (played by Mohanlal) from the years 1982–1987, where he is forced to leave his village after being falsely accused of theft in the temple he used to work at.

Devan reaches Bombay and soon gets caught in the underworld turf war between rival factions where he becomes a trusted aide of an ageing Don. The story is about Devan trying to survive in Bombay and attempting to return home to prove his innocence and reclaim his family estate. *Aryan*, for more than half of its runtime, plays out as a crime thriller, but a big part of the film is invested in establishing the social conditions that have led to the downfall of the Namboothiri Brahmins in Kerala, focusing on the specific condition of Devan and his extended family.

In one of the opening shots of the film, Devan is wandering the Bombay streets, nowhere to go, no money in hand, whereby he comes across the familiar space of a temple where he finds saffron-clothed priests. He tries to communicate with one of them by showing his Brahmin thread, implying he is one of them and that he is starving. The temple bells are ringing in the background and Devan finds himself at ease in this space, even as it looks starkly different from the sites of worship he is familiar with in the south. The priest directs him inside the temple and here he finds a group of women, similarly dressed in saffron, singing a religious prayer. The camera zooms into Devan's face as the sound of the temple bells become disorienting and loud—he is contemplating on his current predicament, and the film cuts to a flashback, to his memories of growing up in and around a similar temple. A song starts playing.

It is important to note that Devan's memory of growing up is not just posed as his subjective experience in a particular household or a particular region, but also as representing the decline of Namboothiri Brahmins in Kerala, and this song segment very quickly ventures into problematic terrain. One of the first shots is that of a Namboothiri *Illam* (traditional aristocratic household) where Devan as a child is sitting on the lap of a family member. His parents are near him, mother (played by Sukumari) holding a traditional cadjan umbrella, his father (played by Thikkurissy Sukumaran Nair) near her—all of them are sitting in front of the *Illam* wearing traditional attire with golden embroidery (kasavu) conveying wealth and prosperity. They are all enjoying a traditional song performance by a Dalit couple who are sitting on the floor in front of the *Illam*. Standing respectfully beside the Namboothiri family is another man who is also enjoying the performance. His mundu (dhoti) does not have kasavu on it, he is Govindan Nair the caretaker (played by Innocent). What is significant about this scene is the way it conveys a sense of contentment everyone is supposedly feeling within this state of rigid caste hierarchy. The Namboothiri family is seated in front of their *Illam* happily enjoying the performance as the non-Brahmin Nair caretaker, who is visibly not allowed to sit among the family, being inferior to them, is shown content and happy to serve the family. Similarly, the Dalit singers are happy sitting on the floor entertaining the Namboothiri family. This, admittedly, is not uncommon in historical films where the relationship between the ruling class (may it be a king or a feudal lord) and the common citizen is often portrayed as harmonious—sometimes quite irresponsibly connoting (consciously or unconsciously) that democracy undermines such harmony that can only be brought forth when people remain in their pre-ordained positions. However, *Aryan* is not a historical film and neither does its story span multiple generations, for the characters in this scene are the chief characters of the film. In the next scene, a group of lower-caste landless labourers are standing in a line in front of the Namboothiri family. The labourers have brought the yield from the family's land they were working on. Arumughan (played by Soman), one of the labourers, hands over a bunch of plantains to Govindan Nair and bows down with respect while receiving his reward from Devan's father. We will meet Arumughan again, but now as the song continues, a couple of years have passed and it is Devan's Upanayana function (a Brahmin ritual where a young boy is accepted by a Guru and receives the sacred thread to be worn there on) happening inside the *Illam*. The entire village is shown to have crowded around the house but nobody (being non-Brahmins) is entering the premises of the *Illam,* the caretaker Govindan Nair and his family are trying to see the function from within the premises but outside the house through the window. This sequence attempts to establish two things. First, that the rigid caste hierarchy practiced in this time period was supposedly fair and more importantly a necessary aspect of the region's harmony, where the Namboothiri Brahmins are posed as benevolent rulers who are kind to their subjects even while practicing untouchability, unapproachability and even unseeability;[4] and second and, more importantly, this scene portrays that the *Illam* is the epicenter of the village economy and that it also provides the 'cultural cement' that unifies the region. It is significant to note that this unnamed village alongside Nila river is posed as a representation of Kerala in its entirety.

Dilip Menon in his essay "Being a Brahmin the Marxist Way" writes about how even a communist political theorist such as E.M.S. Namboothiripad (Kerala's first chief minister) had purposefully interpreted the history of Kerala in a similar way that undermined the drastic conditions that were prevalent in an era of Brahmanism (Menon 2011). Menon discusses how Namboothiripad had done a "creative misreading" of Marxist theory to argue for the Aryan invasion of the south as a historical event that had led to the progression of the region on multiple fronts such as mode of production, social organization, cultural advancements, etc. (ibid.). Namboothiripad goes even one step further by claiming the Brahminical hegemonic highbrow art (which was denied to non-Brahmins) to be Kerala's classical arts and Brahminical culture as Kerala's culture (ibid.). We see a similar strain of thought in *Aryan* during the same song sequence where we find Devan's family spectating a Kathakali performance seated, as non-Brahmins are standing aside enjoying the performance; memory of cultural prosperity that Devan later laments, not just as a loss for his family but also as a loss of the culture of Kerala. This sense of loss is a significant characteristic that defines Devan's victimhood that plays a key role in the populist narrative that the film is beginning to develop at this point.

The song ends in the flashback sequence and a couple more years have passed. Devan is now a young man who works as a junior priest in the temple. He is wearing a plain *mundu* without any *kasavu* on it and a worn-out shirt is hanging on his shoulders. The head priest is telling him how the temple is severely underfunded and how the Devaswom Board[5] has cut all the amenities for the temple and has established systems in place which are working against the temple. He asks Devan,

> Head Priest: Amidst all of this, why are you still working here? Why cannot you look for some other job?
> Devan: You do not understand. It is not that I am not trying. If I could get a job, I would not be stuck here. (Priyadarshan 1988)[6]

It is important to note here that Devan's inability to get a job is not a commentary on the lack of jobs in Kerala at the time, instead it is a commentary on the caste-based reservation system which is supposedly making it impossible for Namboothiri Brahmins to get even a menial job. Devan and the head priest are now walking on an untended path which used to be part of Devan's property and they are having a conversation about how Devan lost all his wealth and property—both due to land reform bills by the communist government[7] and through other court cases filed by former tenants. The head priest looks at Devan's *Illam* which Devan and his family are not allowed to presently occupy because of ongoing court cases, and laments about Devan's current predicament. In the next scene, Devan walks into an impoverished house where his family is currently residing, where he meets his mother, father and sisters. He hands them over the food he has brought back for them which they realize is lesser than required. Devan tells them that he already ate and his mother asks him not to lie and that they will all make do with what they have.

This is how the film poses Devan as the victim of the various social programmes in Kerala. He is unable to get a job because of the caste-based reservation system that is favouring the backward castes. He is unable to reap the benefits of the wealth he would have inherited because of the series of land reforms enacted by the communist government and the multiple court cases that have been filed by the tenants. Devan, hailing from the most elite background imaginable in Kerala, being the descendant of Namboothiri Brahmin landlords, is now being primed to represent the common man wronged by a supposedly corrupt system. But who exactly are the current elites hoarding power and wealth in this carefully constructed narrative?

While Devan is preparing to have his meal, one of his sisters tells him that Arumughan (who was shown initially as a labouring tenant of his *Illam*) is planning to cease his land and property. This is where the film reveals the details of the populist narrative it is intending to put forth with Devan as the common man struggling against the political and economic elite. Arumughan, a lower caste former tenant of Devan's *Illam* is now a rich businessman who has reaped all the benefits from the communist social programmes and is now attempting to cease Devan's old *Illam* through a court case. It is important to note the centrality of caste animosity in this narrative. Arumughan is posed as undeserving of his wealth and stature, as he belongs to a lower caste. A suspicion of corruption is assigned to his character even before the story reveals it. Soon after, Arumughan using his wealth and influence bribes the police in the region to falsely accuse and convict Devan of stealing the sacred ornaments from the temple. The police officer is also shown from a lower caste and he displays hostility towards Devan's family and is happy to arrest Devan for crimes he did not commit. Devan's father also soon turns against him believing that he has indeed stolen from the temple. Devan is forced to leave his village for Bombay.

This is how the political landscape of Kerala is constructed in the film. Lower caste communities have supposedly been enriched by the social reform policies and currently possess economic and political capital, effectively making them the new elites in Kerala. Historian J. Devika discards the myth of vanishing caste disparity due to the abolition of the landlord system. In fact, she states how it is the Dalit community in Kerala who has been left out of the benefits of the land reforms, and how caste disparity is still very much prevalent in Kerala (Devika 2010: 802). Nevertheless, *Aryan* is a desperate attempt to create an alternate populist narrative and portray the condition of the Namboothiri Brahmins as somehow worse than that of the Dalit communities at the time. There is a scene in the film where Karunan (played by Sreenivasan), a Dalit communist labourer, is directing a play based on the poem 'Vazhakkula' (a bunch of plantains) by Changambuzha Krishna Pillai (1911–1948). The poem is about the hardships of a Pulaya family who are exploited by the wealthy upper-caste *Jenmis* (roughly translated as 'feudal landlord'). Devan is annoyed by the poem and claims that it is not relevant to the times since according to him it is the Namboothiri Brahmins who are the downtrodden now. The poem famously ends with the landlord ordering the tenant to carry the plantain bunch that the tenant laboured for, which his poor family was desperate to eat, to the landlord's house. In a later scene we see Devan stealing a bunch of plantains for his family, since they have nothing to eat. His ageing father, upon discovering this, gets infuriated and decides to carry it back to the farm Devan stole it from. As the old Namboothiri man is carrying the plantain bunch on his shoulders at the middle of the night, we hear the rehearsal of the play, where the final lines of 'Vazhakkula' are being recited, an attempt to portray that the Namboothiri Brahmins are supposedly the new downtrodden caste in Kerala.

What is perhaps most interesting about Devan's time in Bombay is his encounter and interactions with the hyper-exoticized Muslim characters. The first person Devan meets in Bombay is a benevolent Keralite Muslim tea-shop owner Kunjalikka (played by Balan K. Nair), who is bearded, dons a skullcap and has a thick Malabar accent. Kunjalikka takes Devan home and gives him a job. Later in the film, Devan becomes the right-hand man of an ageing Muslim gangster, Kareem (referred to as Kareem Saab). Kareem Saab's son is shown to be a Hindustani classical singer and the film is invested in establishing the cultural difference between Devan and Kareem Saab. It is to be noted that in this film, Muslims are conspicuously absent in Kerala even though the state has a significantly large Muslim population.[8] Muslim characters are only made visible in the city space of Bombay as gangsters and other characters with close proximity to crime. Through this, *Aryan* clearly positions the Muslim community as 'the other'.

When Devan returns back home, the year is shown to be 1987 and the communist party has come to power in Kerala. Karunan is a big figure in the communist party now and he is shown to be corrupt. It is important to note that the problem for *Aryan* is not with communist ideology per se, for it is not interested in engaging with it seriously. The film perceives the supposedly bad policies and corruption in the party as a result of the ingress of the lower-caste communities into the party. Devan makes use of Karunan's political power and bribes him to successfully reclaim his *Illam* and also makes him pressure the police department to reopen the case which had falsely convicted Devan of theft. He proves his innocence in front of his family and thrashes the elites who had wronged him. But soon after, his former life in Bombay comes back to haunt him, as a rival gangster follows him back to Kerala to kill him and take his money and, during this conflict, his fiancé is murdered. In the final shot of the film, where Devan is in trial in front of the court for murder, he gives an infuriated speech about how the system has made an 'innocent Brahmin' like him a thief and a murderer and then in English he screams out: "How can you punish me more?" (Priyadarshan 1988).

Devan here fails to reclaim power from the political and economic elites and is subjected to the legal system that has already failed him once, which he claims to be rigged against people like him. Perhaps, the populist imagery of *Aryan* falls short in putting forth a sense of immediacy to the dangers of such a socio-political scenario, fictitious as it may be. Paul Taggart discusses the significance of posing a crisis, breakdown or a threat in a populist narrative in politics (Taggart 2000: 5). This is something that *Adhwaytham* attempts to set up very early in the film, wasting no time to present the viewers with a larger crisis to communal peace and harmony that has emerged in the region because of the very same social conditions that animated *Aryan*.

Adhwaytham: *Influence of Hindutva politics on the populist narrative*

In his essay "The Return of the Thampurans", A. Soman discusses how the saffronization of national politics in the early 1990s had impacted popular Malayalam cinema, where many of the Hindu upper-caste writers and directors were engaging with the rhetoric of right-wing nationalism (Soman 2012: 237). Released in 1992, at the peak of the Babri Masjid conflict, *Adhwaytham* tells the story of Swami Amritananda (played by Mohanlal), a spiritual guru, who has come to Kerala amidst a series of communal riots with a mission of restoring peace.[9] The plot revolves around Amritananda looking back at his life where he was once Shivaprasad (referred to as Shivan). He reminiscences about his past after meeting with district collector Lakshmi (played by Revathi) who was once his lover.

Shivan was born into a family of Nair landlords and his father was a Namboothiri Brahmin, who disowned him and his mother when he was a young boy.[10] Shivan develops an anger towards religion (more accurately Brahmanism) because of this experience. Shivan and his mother also lose all their property rights to their *taravad* (traditional matrilineal household) after Shivan's uncle Krishnankutty Menon (played by Janardhanan) tricks them into signing over their rights to the property. They are later forced out of the *taravad* by Menon. Very much like Devan in *Aryan* who dreams of gaining back rights to his *Illam*, Shivan too intends to win back his *taravad* one day. What is significant to note here is that Menon who forces Shivan and his mother out the *taravad* is portrayed as someone who became rich by working abroad. It is because of Menon's affiliation to a foreign land and the wealth that he has earned from that space that the film portrays him as someone who respects neither the sanctity of the household nor the values that it upholds. Malayalam cinema since the 1960s has made use of this trope where family members in a Nair joint family who are returning from a foreign land are shown to be corrupted by the supposedly illegitimate wealth that they have earned (Menon 2005: 322–323). Therefore, Krishnankutti Menon in *Adhwaytham* is thereafter revealed as someone who engages in illegal activities with this 'illegitimate wealth'. Menon does not respect the sanctity of the *taravad* because of this and he is in many ways posed as a traitor figure of the Nair community and to the larger Brahminical culture.

Shivan, later in his youth, is recruited into the communist party and is politically exploited by Shekharan (played by Soman), a corrupt communist politician, who is portrayed belonging to a lower caste community. It is to be noted that the socio-political realm constructed in *Adhwaytham* is identical to that of *Aryan*, where the corrupt lower-caste politician represents the political and economic elite. In *Adhwaytham* also, the victims of the elites are poor Namboothiri Brahmins who are defending an old temple against corruption. Shivan, for the longest time, is complicit in this corruption until he realizes his mistakes. The positioning of Shivan in this space and his evolution as a political figure is important to observe, for he begins his career as a labour union member, then later when the party comes into power, he is appointed as the secretary of a *Devaswom* board by Shekharan where he mismanages funds and engages in corruption on behalf of Shekharan. Later when his best friend from childhood, Vasu (played by Jayaram), is murdered by Shekharan, Shivan speaks against him whereby he is beaten up by the Communist party and is taken into police custody. His mother dies amidst all of this, believing it was Devan who killed Vasu for the party. Shivan, heartbroken and disillusioned by all of this, leaves Kerala and travels to North India where he finds spirituality. From there he becomes a revered swami figure and changes his name to Amritananda. He now has long hair and a thick beard with tripundra (the Saivite tilaka with three horizontal ash lines and a dot) on his forehead.

What is significant about Amritananda is that he represents an ideology and a certain perception of political discourse that is not indigenous to the region of Kerala. Amritananda represents and espouses a pan North Indian Hindu nationalism. In one of the scenes in which he is arguing with a politician, he claims that there is no one to represent the will of the majority and that for the longest time the government has been overly considerate towards minorities at the expense of the majority. Amritananda, therefore, claims to be representing the collective will of the Hindu majority. It is also to be noted that he does not dress like the guru figures in South India, instead his attire has visible resemblances to the North Indian religious leaders of the time.

Amritananda, in order to spread peace in a state torn with communalism, decides to conduct a *Shanthi Yatra* (pilgrimage for peace) in Kerala, mirroring both the *Rath Yatra* (Chariot Festival) organized by the Bharatiya Janata Party in 1990 led by then party leader L.K. Advani to support the agitation to build a Ram temple on the place of the Babri Masjid in Ayodhya, and the *Ekta Yatra* (Unity Pilgrimage) from Kanyakumari to Srinagar (passing through Kerala) organized by Murli Manohar Joshi in 1991 that had attempted to 'cash in on the success of the *Rath Yatra* to make *yatra* politics a permanent feature of its [BJP's] strategy' (Jaffrelot 2009: 13). Incidentally, the communal tension in Kerala in the early 1990s that the film alludes to, which Amritananda is supposedly attempting to solve, were the direct results of the political atmosphere generated by these *yatras* themselves (Menon 1990; Wilkinson 2004: 186). *Adhwaytham* attempts to alter and sanitize this history by putting forth the peaceful figure of Amritananda conducting *Shanthi Yatra* for communal peace. In the film, it is Shekharan and his corrupt accomplices who are said to be the perpetrators behind the communal riots in Kerala trying to distract the masses from cases of corruption filed against them. They even try to kill Amritananda by bombing the *Shanthi Yatra*. Amritananda's former lover and then district collector, Lakshmi, intercepts this attempt and is killed in the process.

As Amritananda holds Lakshmi's bloody corpse close to him, a thick bloodstain is formed on his white clothes. This is a tipping point for him and it is time for his final transformation, the inevitable endpoint to this teleological narrative. Director Priyadarshan uses a strong dissolve shot to affirm this transformation. Amritananda is wearing white clothes signifying his mission and his temperament—one that of peace. The bloodstain from Lakshmi's corpse is shown to have formed on his chest, near his heart. The dramatic background score intensifies as the camera zooms into this bloodstain on his chest and the scene dissolves and transitions to an image of a shining sword cutting through the darkness. The momentary overlap of the bloodstain and the sword on his chest indicate a change of heart. Shivan has decided to leave behind the peaceful swami persona of Amritananda. Now he is out for the blood of his enemies. Shekharan and his accomplices are in an abandoned factory celebrating the disruption of the *Shanthi Yatra*. They are planning their next move against Amritananda, as they come to notice Shivan emerging from the darkness wielding the sword. He does not have the long hair or his thick beard anymore and he is dressed like he once used to when he was a factory worker and a political goon for the communist party—with a shirt, a thin turban and dhoti. There is only one difference, the color of his dhoti is now saffron, signifying his renewed Hindu consciousness.[11]

Shivan goes onto murder Shekharan and his accomplices, returning back with a bloodied sword to a hall filled with people expecting Swami Amritananda to address them in an event mourning the death of district collector Lakshmi. Shivan walks to the empty stage with a puzzled audience struggling to understand who he is. He keeps the bloodied sword in front of Lakshmi's photo and addresses the crowd.

> Shivan: The Panchajanya Conch echoes again in Kurukshetra land for the obliteration of the enemy that sows the seeds of destruction. Nobody that you are expecting here is going to show up. Upon realizing that the enemy cannot be defeated through self-denying asceticism and penance, I had to kill them. Before you label me as a murderer or a criminal, let me ask something first. Even after being promised a secular country, we were made to fight with each other in the name of religion as Hindu, Muslim and Christians by certain political leaders. I killed them. Is that a sin? I killed those anti-national traitors who, for personal gains, being enslaved to foreign powers, tried to destroy one's own country's culture and heritage. Is that a crime? I punished those who wanted to divide us up into North India and South India as Tamilian, Telugu and Malayali, for the lust of power. Think for once, setting aside the Gods, aren't we all one? Is it not better to gain standing together than to lose staying divided? If it was wrong to punish these people who were trying antagonize even friends and family, I am willing to accept any punishment you chose for it. Punish me. (Priyadarshan 1992.)

The last line of this speech, that is, 'punish me' echoes as the frame freezes and the credits appear on the screen. This final shot with the echoing sound and the freeze-frame is identical to that of *Aryan*, but there is a key difference. The 'common man' protagonist is now claiming to be representing the collective will of the supposedly underrepresented majority and he has moved past court rulings and is now addressing the masses directly.

It is to be noted that in his speech, Shivan, unlike Devan, with his final court statement in *Aryan*, is not lamenting about a purported cultural degradation of Kerala or any other specific regional space. Instead he is assigning the economic and political elites of Kerala the label of being traitors to the entire country and to its supposedly singular culture. The rhetoric has completely morphed into that of the mainstream Hindu right-wing populism. In *Aryan*, even after returning from a northern state, like Shivan did, Devan is not concerned with nationalist politics or its applicability in his region. His time in Bombay does not alter his diagnosis of what is wrong in Kerala's socio-political realm. The autochthonous populist narrative revolving around the decline of Namboothiri Brahmin dominance in Kerala that *Aryan* constructs in its initial segments is intact even by the very end. This can be easily discerned by the fact that the two court statements Devan gives in the film, one before leaving for Bombay and another one after coming back after five years in the final scene of the film, are identical with respect to the rhetoric it employs. However, by the time of *Adhwaytham*, this autochthonous populist narrative can be seen merging with the mainstream nationalist right-wing populism that was being popularized nationwide at the time. This is why there is a visible shift in focus from the economic anxieties articulated in *Aryan* to much more radical cultural anxieties. It is because of this that the final monologue in *Adhwaytham* espouses a militant cultural nationalism which calls for a unity which has to agree to a singular heritage. It is this unity that Shivan blames the elites to be destroying, against which 'the people' have to come together. Duncan McDonnell and Luis Cabrera write about this tendency of right-wing populism in India to blame their own self diagnosed 'elites' for disrupting national unity by working against the purportedly singular culture and heritage of the country (McDonnel and Cabrera 2018: 6). *Adhwaytham* is a very clear move towards the narrative of Hindu right-wing populism, where the 'common man' protagonist has violently overthrown the economic and political elite and is now directly addressing the masses, representing the collective will of the Hindu majority.

Conclusion

This chapter has attempted to explore the ways in which the two political thrillers directed by Priyadarshan in the late 1980s and early 1990s, *Aryan* and *Adhwaytham,* had constructed a populist narrative by placing the angry disenfranchised upper-caste victim figure at its center, posed as the 'common man' struggling against the new political and economic elite in the state of Kerala. In this exploration, we noticed how important the concept of caste was in such a narrative where the lower caste communities were demonized and misrepresented through singular strategic connections. The political and economic elites in this narrative chiefly comprise Dalits, non-Hindus and other backward communities—a picture of politics that is far removed from reality. It is to be noted that lower caste communities are depicted as undeserving of wealth and power in *Aryan* and *Adhwaytham*, where social programmes are claimed to be elevating such communities to a stature that they supposedly do not deserve. What is also important to note in such a narrative is the strategic exclusion and othering of Muslim characters from the socio-political realm of Kerala, only to be shown operating in fringe spaces in cities like Bombay.[12] Finally, I have tried to show that one can trace a shift in the autochthonous populist narrative that *Aryan* constructs in 1988 to a more mainstream nationalistic Hindutva right-wing populism in 1992 with *Adhwaytham* where the economic insecurities initially placed at the core of this populist imaginary is replaced by certain cultural insecurities that were gaining popularity by the early 1990s nationwide in India.

Notes

1 Priyadarshan is one of the most successful film directors in Indian cinema. Starting from 1984 with his debut film *Poochakkoru Mookkuthi* (A Nose-ring for the Cat) he has directed a total of 94 films till date. Apart from Malayalam films, Priyadarshan has directed 26 Hindi films, six Tamil films and two Telugu films.

2 Having come from a theatre background, writer T. Damodaran (1935–2012) was famous for his political thrillers and historical dramas. Starting from 1975 with his first screenplay *Love Marriage* directed by I.V. Sasi, Damodaran had penned screenplays for 46 films. He was said to have been a Communist party sympathizer. He had interestingly written many screenplays about angry upper caste youth unable to get jobs because of the reservation policies and social programmes (Radhakrishnan 2009: 231).

3 Political scientist Cas Mudde defines populism as “an ideology that considers society to be ultimately separated into two homogeneous and antagonistic groups, ‘the pure people’ versus ‘the corrupt elite’, and which argues that politics should be an expression of the volontégénérale (general will) of the people” (Mudde 2004: 543).

4 Sanal Mohan in *Modernity of Slavery: Struggles against Caste Inequality in Colonial Kerala* (2015) discusses in detail the decadent history of caste system in Kerala.

5 Devaswom Boards are mostly government nominated and they manage the temples and its assets. In Kerala, there are more than 3,000 temples functioning under five Devaswoms.

6 All translations from this film (dialogues) are mine.

7 The 1969 land reform act in Kerala abolished the tenancy system along with providing former tenants a set patch of land which previously was under the landlord, and it also provides legal protection from arbitrary evictions (Radhakrishnan 1981: 130).

8 Kerala has 26.57 per cent Muslim population according to the 2011 Census and in 1981 it was 21.3 per cent (Zachariah 2016: 28).

9 The Babri Masjid conflict and the subsequent spread of Hindu fundamentalism was affecting Kerala too in the early 1990s where communal riots were being incited (Menon 1990).

10 Shivan was born to a *Sambandam* between his Nair mother and Namboothiri father. *Sambandam*, which literally means ‘alliance’, was an institutionalized practice among Malayali Namboothiri Brahmins. According to the norms that existed in the Namboothiri community, only the elder son was allowed to marry from the same community. All the younger brothers engaged in *Sambandam* with women from other caste groups like Kshatriyas, Nairs, the temple castes, etc. (Devika 2011: xx).

11 The saffron Dhoti in itself has a very interesting history in Kerala. Nisar Kannangara and Jesurathnam Devarapalli in their essay “Democracy and the Politics of Dress, Color and, Symbols: An Anthropological Study of Kerala Politics” write about the evolution of the saffron dhoti from once being a mere signifier of Hindu religious identity to later becoming an outright symbol for right-wing Hindu political parties (Kannangara and Devarappally 2019).

12 The only time a Muslim character is shown in *Adhwaytham* is when a Muslim religious leader very briefly comes to visit Amritananda along with a Christian priest, where he speaks in a stereotypically thick Malabar accent.

Bibliography

Canovan, Margaret. 1981. *Populism*. New York: Harcourt Brace Jovanovich.

Devika, J. 2010. “Egalitarian Developmentalism, Communist Mobilization, and the Question of Caste in Kerala State, India.” *The Journal of Asian Studies* 69, no. 3: 799–820.

Devika, J. 2011. "Introduction: The Namboothiris of Kerala." In *Antharjanam: Memoirs of a Namboothiri Woman*, by Devika Nilayamgode, xvii–xxxi. New Delhi: Oxford University Press.

Jaffrelot, Christophe. 2009. "The Hindu Nationalist Reinterpretation of Pilgrimage in India: The Limits of Yatra Politics". *Nations and Nationalism* 15, no. 1: 1–19.

Jayakumar, K.P. 2014. *Jathivyavasthayum Malayala Cinimayum*. Kozhikode: Olive Publications.

Kannangara, Nisar, and Jesurathnam Devarapalli. 2019. "Democracy and the Politics of Dress, Color and, Symbols: An Anthropological Study of Kerala Politics." *The Oriental Anthropologist: A Bi-Annual International Journal of the Science of Man* 19, no. 2: 257–272.

McDonnell, Duncan, and Luis Cabrera. 2018. "The Right-Wing Populism of India's Bharatiya Janata Party (And why Comparativists should care)". *Democratization* 26, no. 3: 484–501.

Menon, Dilip M. 2005. "Things Fall Apart: The Cinematic Rendition of Agrarian Landscape in South India". *Journal of Peasant Studies* 32, no. 2: 304–334.

——. 2011. "Being a Brahmin the Marxist way: EMS Namboodiripad and the pasts of Kerala". In *The Blindness of Insight: Essays on Caste in Modern India*, by Dilip M. Menon, 32–72. New Delhi: Navayana.

Menon, Ramesh. 1990. "Maulvi's Death causes Havoc in Kerala". *India Today*. Available at https://www.indiatoday.in/magazine/indiascope/story/19901115-maulvi-death-causes-havoc-in-kerala-813261-1990-11-15 (last accessed 8 October 2019).

Mohan, P. Sanal. 2015. *Modernity of Slavery: Struggles against Caste Inequality in Colonial Kerala*. New Delhi: Oxford University Press.

M.R., Rajesh. 2012. *Indian Cinemayude Varthamanam*. Thiruvananthapuram: Chintha Publishers.

Mudde, Cas. 2004. "The Populist Zeitgeist". *Government and Opposition* 39, no. 4: 541–563.

Pillai, Meena T. 2013. "Matriliny to Masculinity: Performing Modernity and Gender in Malayalam Cinema". In *Routledge Handbook of Indian Cinemas*, edited by K. Moti Gokulsing and Wimal Dissanayake, 102–114. New York: Routledge.

Priyadarshan. 1992. *Adhwaytham*. Film. Grihalakshmi Productions.

——. 1988. *Aryan*. Film. Cheers Films.

Radhakrishnan, P. 1981. "Land Reforms in Theory and Practice: The Kerala Experience". *Economic and Political Weekly* 16, no. 52: 129–137.

——. 2009. "The Gulf in the Imagination: Migration, Malayalam Cinema and Regional Identity". *Contributions to Indian Sociology* 43, no. 2: 217–245.

Radhakrishnan, Ratheesh. 2010. "What is Left of Malayalam Cinema". In *Cinemas of South India: Culture, Resistance, Ideology*, edited by Sowmya Dechamma and Elavarthi Sathya Prakash, 25–48. 1st ed. New Delhi: Oxford University Press.

Rowena, Jenny. 2013. "Locating P.K. Rosy: Can a Dalit Woman Play a Nair Role in Malayalam Cinema Today?" In *P.K. Rosy Memorial Lecture*. Available at http://www.dalitweb.org/. http://www.dalitweb.org/?p=1641 (last accessed 27 September 2019).

Soman, A. 2012. "The Return of the Thampurans". In *The Oxford India Anthology of Malayalam Dalit Writing*, edited by M. Dasan, V. Pratibha, C.S. Chandrika and Pradeepan Pampirikunnu, 236–239. New Delhi: Oxford University Press.

Taggart, Paul. 2000. *Populism*. Buckingham: Open University Press.

Wilkinson, Steven I. 2004. *Votes and Violence: Electoral Competition and Ethnic Riots in India*. Cambridge: Cambridge University Press.

Zachariah, K.C. 2016. "Religious Denominations of Kerala". CDS Working Papers Series, No. 468, Centre for Developmental Studies, India.

BRANCHINGS

11

THE NON-POPULIST POPULAR AND THE CINEMATIC APOCRYPHA

Parichay Patra

Proposition

> The history of cinema resistant to an industrial perspective remains entirely to be written.
>
> Nicole Brenez (2009)

Things in/of the cinema that have once been iconoclastic get assimilated into the various behemoths, the list of the latter ranging from academia to cinephilia and/or both. The apparently non-populist, known 'popularly' as the *arthouse*, become popularized only through its acceptance within the niche market that it creates for itself, with active support from the Euro-American film festival circuit that never hides its entrepreneurial signifiers. Cinephilia loses its gnostic and iconoclastic memories, films make their way into the university discipline as the entire framework is often determined by the festival circuit.[1] Histories of cinema, an institution whose *publicness* hardly faces any challenge, are varied and industrially monolithic at the same time, not only in the domain of the popular but also in that of the non-populist popular; the popular, canonized arthouse. The unbearable burden of such an industrial history of cinema weighs heavily on the filmmaker, with several demands made by the conventions, the tyrannies of which Glauber Rocha once addressed collectively as the 'dictatorship of the industry' (2019). More often than not, standard received, well-accepted histories of cinema rely rather heavily on self-imposed hierarchical structures, relegating marginal cinemas further into the distant horizon and are transformed into hagiographies of canonical auteurs.[2] The notion of a popular art/auteur cinema gains ground through this widespread practice that dominates the festival scene as well as the academic discipline.

Introducing a few deceptively biblical coinages at this point may not be considered as an anomaly. Something like cinematic apocrypha often erupts into the known world, with cinemas eschewing all of the above, the festival, the film society, the publicness, academia, the known cinephilia and recorded histories. Circulating surreptitiously, these gospels rely on their heretics who remained forever excluded from the mainstream narratives of cinematic exhibition. This chapter is a testament-like recollection of the unusual popular and the often-unsung apocrypha at the time of a cine-political modernism.

Prologue

In a not-so-unusually-sunny Goa November, I crept into one of the two theatres in Maquinez Palace, one of the lesser-known venues of India's International Film Festival. A special section on the Indian New Wave (or the lack of it) featured Kumar Shahani's *Tarang* (*Waves*, 1984), the screening of which inaugurated the section and, for me, the festival in 2019. Over the next three hours, the screen rarely responded to the sun-decked Goa that lay outside. Its near-violent fiery nights were pierced by the Mumbai local trains, its occasionally sunny and coastal days marred by the pale and whitish death-drive of Hansa (Kawal Gandhiok), its Ophelia-like protagonist.

Experiencing it on screen for the first time, I developed an interest in its ensemble cast that was, as one would gradually discover, put into an unusual use.[3] Those popular faces, the stardom associated with our 'art cinema' of the 1970s, have rarely connoted a profound sense of misrecognition such as this. This misrecognition emanated not only from the narrative or the textual coordinates but also from its flattened cinemascope surface, its lights, its piercing trains, its cityscape and its engagement with cinema histories. But the categorization seemed more complex than what I initially assumed. This, for me, was the misrecognition of the *popular* in 'art cinema', something that sounds extremely anomalous.

Do we even need the narrative of *Tarang* to delve deep into this misrecognition? And what is this popular in art cinema that concerns us? How can a non-populist concept such as 'art cinema' that survives on its apparent exclusivity be regarded as popular? And, more importantly, where does this misrecognition lead to? To a beyond, an alternative, an apocryphal?

Tarang does not begin or end with misrecognition though. It ends with an epiphany and begins with moments of *recognition* under the starry nights of the Bombay modern, but those moments will claim our attention much later in this chapter.

The Conceptual Apparatus

The art-popular division in cinema has an infinitely complex transnational history, with several local/regional/national variations contributing to its ambiguity. With the cinematic art prevailing over older and more exclusive forms of art primarily because of its technical reproducibility and the resultant accessibility à la Walter Benjamin, the 'mass' gathered at the cinema or any form of exhibition space signified a continuation and transformation of the nineteenth-century urban experience into modernity. Gertrud Koch recollects the aesthetic of the mass in the nineteenth-century literary documents with instances from E.T.A. Hoffmann, Edgar Allan Poe and Charles Baudelaire and shows how the 'aesthetic illusion' of the cinematic mass becomes a 'revolutionary subject' in Benjamin. Characterized by its 'openness' and 'indeterminacy', the aesthetic and political aspects of the mass converge in film and history (Koch 2014). Popular cinema and its curious engagement with the cinematic mass raise significant issues concerning democracy, political will and the formation of the public. In the case of India, the advent of popular cinema as a public institution offered immensely democratic possibilities that placed purchasing power over the caste hierarchy, one of the reasons why cinema's association with the electoral politics in South India becomes a major point of concern.[4]

The arthouse, on the other hand, has a distinctive and complex history that betrays significant instances of state intervention, especially in the Indian subcontinent. The trajectory of a global category such as 'art cinema' in India has been explored by South Asian historians like Rochona Majumdar, as the latter traces the establishment of this 'universal idiom' in the post-independence India, the role of the state and its committees, of the individuals and film society collectives, and the debates around 'modernism, left politics, radical aestheticism…' (Majumdar 2016). A workable definition of such categories might also be located.

Despite (or because of) the presence of multiple popular industries and (often mutually exclusive) cinematic cultures, art cinema is perhaps easier to define in the Indian context, primarily because of its strong journalistic associations. These terms are often uncritically used in cine-journalism; for some it appeared, along with 'middle cinema', in the 1970s in different Indian regional cinema contexts, as Bindu Menon provides instances from Kerala.[5] Regional cinema cultures and cinephilia are often strongly shaped by their association with such cinema, strengthening their politics of difference from the national popular cinema aka Bollywood.[6] The regional art cinema has continued to engage with global cinema since the 1950s.[7] Moreover, the association with global art cinema may have far-reaching implications for the region. Ratheesh Radhakrishnan has argued how coming in contact with world cinema and global auteurs within the space of the international film festival contributes to the 'politics of location' and in the 'formation of the subject of the region' (Radhakrishnan 2016).

Here our concern is not art cinema per se, but the popular in art cinema. In a transnational world order, art cinema is much more widely contested than ever before. Its association with the (European) festival space and its resultant politics manifests often through auteurs from the margins of the globe, as the awards from and championing at the (European) festivals come pouring in and the auteurs become allegedly dependent on the festival space in return, with their cinematic styles compromised and aesthetically removed from the so-called 'points of origin'.[8] This is such a common occurrence in contemporary world cinema, especially with filmmakers in exile or filmmakers surviving solely on the festival circuit for the lack of an audience at home, that the umbrella-term called art cinema faces an uphill task of convincing everyone that its connotation should ideally transcend the confining space of the festival.

Defining art cinema in terms of its origin has been a challenge situated in history. The arthouse/art house in the US relied rather heavily on the respectability of its exhibits. Barbara Wilinsky, in her history of arthouses, cites sources highlighting the demarcating walls, sources that categorize an arthouse film as something that is not 'Class C horror or murder mishmash' (Wilinsky 2001). This negative mode of referencing characterizes and validates a specific discourse on art cinema and its possible *respectable* consumer, preferably and expectedly the middle class. Beyond this existed the ever-threatening 'disreputable' popular, the B movie, especially in the provinces and in regional theatres, masquerading as the 'Class C horror'.

The respectability in and of the cinema entails a specific kind of viewership, determines the exhibition space and behavioural patterns within the theatre and assumes certain apparently global characteristics. It depends on taste and class privilege and begets a profound fear of the 'other', of the disreputable, the unruly. While there is ample theorizing on class privilege and matter of judgement in the West (Bourdieu 1984; Sconce 1995), in the Indian regional context it creates problematics that are more specific and uncanny, the 'phantom viewer' being one such (Srinivas 2009).[9] These imaginary, phantom, unruly viewer/consumer, their characteristic cinematic products and an exhibition space favourable to them, remain separated from the domain of a respectable cinema, its consumer and its privilege.

The idea of a respectable art cinema with demarcating cultural walls around it leads to the issues such as the existence of a *popular* art cinema, put into specific use by an industry and its associates. Here the term popular connotes the sense of a specific people, the respectable consumer of art cinema. Wilinsky refers to art cinema as a medium selling exclusivity, relying on specific publicity modes and, in the case of the US, offering an alternative to the dominant Hollywood. Despite its carefully constructed alternative identity, the arthouse strongly betrays symptoms of an industrial arthouse, a popular in the domain of art cinema. While commenting on the careful construction of an image of difference for reasons that are financial, Wilinsky draws our attention to the way major studios "'commercialized' art cinema and produced 'art films' that may appeal to the mass audience" (Wilinsky 2001). As the number of the arthouse theatres proliferated in the 1950s and 1960s and a steady supply of European auteur cinema created a niche market in the USA, Hollywood went on to control this potential market, producing its own auteur cinema.[10]

While some of the contemporary cinema studies researchers, mostly located in the UK, argue for a worldwide resurgence of art cinema, not unusual for a university discipline that owes immensely to European art/auteur cinema of the 1950s and 1960s, the ambiguity of art cinema is not always adequately addressed.[11] The popular within the domain of art cinema remains more markedly unexplored, except for occasional references.

What stands beyond the domain of the festival touring, popular, 'commercialized' art cinema? Does that lead to the experimental, the avant-garde? How can we distinguish between the two? Is there a common ground where these two shall (and possibly can) meet?

The Ambiguity of the Art Film

The experimental or the avant-garde has several existing traditions in different parts of the world and it is mostly defined by a complete rejection of the narrative cinema traditions (not necessarily confined to the classical narrative), the regular festival space and the industrial production-distribution-exhibition model. Moreover, experimental cinema is often marked by its affinity to contemporary visual arts and its interest in exploring the intricacies of the medium itself. These traits, along with others, have shaped the parameters of the experimental, a detailed description of which is beyond the purpose and scope of this chapter.[12]

But the experimental, in the Indian context, becomes an intriguingly ambiguous affair. A researcher familiar with the Euro-American variants of the experimental may not find Indian avant-garde cinema *adequately* experimental. Richard Suchenski, in his work on Mani Kaul and Kumar Shahani, raises issues concerning the duo not abandoning narrative cinema or the more standard-accepted production-distribution-exhibition model (2017).[13] Suchenski, who teaches at the Bard College in the US which is better known for its association with a number of American experimental filmmakers, uses a different, more universal parameter for deciding upon the experimentality of the duo. Because of a visible absence of his categories, he situated Kaul and Shahani somewhere in the middle, associating them aesthetically with more canonical works as well as more experimental ones.

The advent of art cinema in India might be traced back to the 1950s and most of the histories of art cinema, cinephilia and film society activism in India follow that trajectory. But the cinema underwent decisive changes in the late 1960s, with the appearance of several significant works in 1969 and an apparent film movement.[14] Rochona Majumdar, in her archival research on the film society movement in India, shows how history can be constructed around a cataclysmic time, namely the turbulent decade of the long 1970s. A visible transition from the 'usual' art cinema exhibition to the careful programming of more politically nuanced, agit-prop cinema within the film society space has been identified (Majumdar 2012). The film societies became increasingly more left-leaning and their 'original' intention to make modernist, canonical, presumably European art cinema accessible to a specific clientele was no longer sustainable.[15] But alternative accounts are also available where explorers of avant-garde cinematic practices accused film societies in Calcutta for ostracizing the already-marginalized avant-garde practitioners.[16] There are accounts of former film society activists insinuating the movement's implicit complicity with the state in restricting the exhibition of politically and/or sexually subversive cinema (Biswas 2019).

Where does the art film stand in this quagmire? Presumably, its coordinates become increasingly complex, with several, mutually exclusive streams running towards different directions, getting relocated into different camps. But the existence of a non-populist popular seems apparent, as the film societies, despite their unambiguous political stance in the 1970s, sided with their popular notion of the art cinema.

The Context of Tarang

Mani Kaul and Kumar Shahani could make films primarily because of the existence of state support in filmmaking, but the ever-dwindling support went into decline over time and ceased to exist with the state losing interest in film production at the onslaught of economic liberalization in the 1990s. The lack of an exhibition channel for the state-sponsored alternative cinema led to the non-release of some of their films.[17] A fierce public debate on the implications and utility of their cinema continued in the print media throughout the 1970s and 1980s.

An exploration into the debate reveals its two major points of contention, aesthetic and economical. The economic logic against this cinema was unambiguous, as Bharat Rungachary accuses Mani Kaul of being 'more expensive than Manmohan Desai' (1980). An interview with Jagdish Parikh, the controversial chairman who served Film Finance Corporation (FFC) for four years, reveals how the loan vs subsidy debate was prevalent in the domain of state-sponsorship (1980). It is perhaps to be noted that Parikh's business management background and corporatized policies were the primary reason for the controversy associated with his appointment.

But the aesthetic objection against their cinema was way more complex and emanated from an earlier generation of art cinema proponents, especially from Satyajit Ray.[18] Ray's attack on Kaul and Shahani's films were near-vitriolic with occasional, mostly insignificant praises for Shahani's 'sophisticated response to colour' (1976). A debate on their cinema was raged in the pages of *Filmfare*, mostly between Ray and Bikram Singh with the latter addressing Ray's 'words of belittlement' as identical with that of the traditional French critics and audiences targeting the French New Wave and *Cahiers du cinema* (1972).

The points that Ray raised, in retrospect, sound extremely problematic and occasionally ambiguous. The apparently self-indulgent and formally experimental cinema of the duo, for Ray, was removed from the Indian tradition as 'narrative is at the core of' the latter (1972). Ray held Kaul and Shahani responsible for their 'lack of concern for social issues' (1976). For Ray, a filmmaker might indulge in the experimental devices of contemporary European cinema but not at the expense of the narrative.[19] The unbridgeable chasm between the 1950s and the 1970s Indian 'arthouse' seems unusually clear and evident in the opinions of Ray, but what is more apparent is the aesthetic differences between these different art cinemas as manifested in the heated debate on terms such as 'narrative' and 'Indian tradition'.

It was becoming increasingly clear in the 1980s that the state-support will not be easily available for the making of a cinema that cannot generate or guarantee profits/returns, the reason why Kaul was being branded as more expensive than someone like Manmohan Desai, better known for his big-budget commercial potboilers with some of the biggest stars of the industry. Moreover, this cinema did not have a strong presence in the festival circuit either. The much-needed support of the (Euro-American) festival space that was essential for an Asian cinema to be part of a global art cinema was more or less absent here.

For Kaul and Shahani, exhibition within the university space was more prevalent, especially in the West, and there has been a number of instances where the politics of programming seemed evident in the choices made by the organizers. Once Kaul refused to allow the screening of his *Dhrupad* (1983) at the Los Angeles Film School as the latter was more interested in raising money for the screening from the Indian diaspora in Los Angeles. Kaul resisted the idea of being considered as a member of an 'ethnic group' and 'not a proper filmmaker' (Bose 1983). Kaul's *Siddheshwari* (1989) was rejected at the International Film Festival of India (IFFI) 1990, he strongly objected to the process of selection and explicitly stated how the selectors would have welcomed a more widely accepted and conformist documentary on the life of Siddheshwari Devi, not something as abstract as he made (Mohamed 1989).

In his interview with Khaled Mohamed on the non-selection of his film in IFFI 1990, Kaul made a few references to the middle cinema proponents and their rejection of his cinema, 'I would rather place my trust in the makers of popular cinema…they are far more involved in the discipline of cinema than those who acquire crores of rupees from the government to make something that's neither here nor there' (1989).[20]

Tarang, made in 1984, more than a decade after Kumar Shahani's debut *Maya Darpan* (*Mirror of Illusion*, 1972), betrays several instances of these complex negotiations between an experimental work and the popular arthouse and middle cinema. These negotiations manifest not only in its narrative that is marked by a deceptively realist framework but also in its aesthetic choices.

A Journey through Tarang

Shahani spent several years on the making of *Tarang* because of severe funding problems for which critics pointed at the indirect impact of Satyajit Ray's condemnation of their cinema (Jayamanne 2015). This information refers specifically to the undercurrent of tension between the two camps that existed in different politico-aesthetic histories. Revisiting Kaul and/or Shahani's unreleased/scarcely released, much-maligned, harshly critiqued cinema is perhaps rewriting of what Nicole Brenez termed as the 'history of the defeated whose tombs we must rediscover' (2009). One such tomb will be my chance encounter with *Tarang* within the festival space of IFFI that was denied to *Siddheswari* back in 1990.

Tarang, like a few other films from the long 1970s, is concerned with the fragmentation of left politics (Rajadhyaksha 2009). In Shahani's debut *Maya Darpan* the politically turbulent time, in the garb of the news of a workers' strike and police brutality, reaches the protagonist and her feudal haveli in surreptitious ways. That was the only explicit reference to politics. *Tarang*, on the contrary, despite being much more politically active in an unequivocal way, is deceptively realistic.

Shahani, during a personal telephone conversation back in 2013, once mentioned his politics as Kosambian. Coined after the Marxist anthropologist D.D. Kosambi who used to be Shahani's mentor and one of the pioneers in shaping an anthropologically nuanced reading of Indian mythologies, the term seems to be more valid in the context of *Tarang*, in terms of its narrative, its ruptures and its politics. This will not be my primary concern here, especially since it has been relatively well-explored, but the references need to be made to his Kosambian politics, something which comes as a rupture in the arthouse narrative.

The narrative, in its usual recollection, should not occupy much space here. In a nutshell, *Tarang* is about a bitter, often-violent skirmish between some old and new capitalists in an industrialist family in the 1970s Bombay reeling under the National Emergency and industrial unrest. Here the old patriarch Sethji (Shreeram Lagoo), determined to run his business in an 'outdated' mode, is confronted by his unscrupulous son-in-law, Rahul (Amol Palekar), who is hell-bent on thwarting foreign investment in their apparently 'nationalist' venture.[21] Amidst the battle of different capitalisms and nationalisms, the other world appears with the struggling factory workers, divided as it is between unions and men with varying ideologies played by the likes of M.K. Raina and Om Puri. Then there remains Janki (Smita Patil), the mysterious widow of a murdered worker who finds employment and subsequent sexual exploitation at the Seth household as 'compensation' but gradually starts wielding power and becomes an accomplice to Rahul through seduction, as the latter is estranged from his frail and perpetually alienated wife Hansa (Kawal Gandhiok).

Tarang decidedly borders on multiple worlds that collide violently but these worlds are not always literal. The world of Rahul and Sethji, occasionally interrupted by ruthless henchmen and global conspirators such as Dinesh (Girish Karnad), the NRI nephew whose machinations were in vain because of the availability of information concerning his shady business interests abroad, is marked by the sunlit Bombay high-rise and an abundance of things in the cinema. These *things* pervade the screen; they range from the corporate furniture and telephone-sets to the glass windows and curtains, the bed and the saris. Rapes, seductions and a final intimacy before a watery death take place on such beds, with the draping and removal of clothes/saris mingled with the physicality of the sexual encounters. That home is often contrasted with the world where these henchmen live, where riots are orchestrated, murders happen, violent conflicts between trade unions lead to a blast, resulting in a ruthless bonfire that lights the skies over Bombay slums.

In the Seth household, Hansa, the Ophelia in an otherwise non-Hamlet world whose purpose is apparently limited to the bearing of a male heir for the family, remains *problematic*.[22] The unsettlingly whitish and flattened image endorses the mise-en-scène she finds herself in, with her beds, flowers, her unusual movements, behavioural obsessions that reject intimacy except for the one before her death and her passive encouragement for the seduction of Rahul by Janki.[23] Hansa, the unwanted, moves through the fading space of an unkind home and the swamp that surrounds the latter in an unusual pace reminiscent of her predecessor in *Maya Darpan*, and her anaemic demeanour is complemented by the paleness of a suffocating white. Flowers engulf everything, the home, the bed, the death and Bombay streets in summer nights. Then *eros* is coupled only with *thanatos*, a brief moment of intimacy precedes Hansa's immersion into a flower-decked watery grave.

By contrast, Janki's world is decidedly blackish grey, as she encounters the warring factions in her slum, consoles the survivors of riots, takes part in a murder, becomes complicit in the conspiracies of Rahul, is raped but seduces the ravisher in return and moves through her shanty habitation with the camera slowly panning around as her nights are pierced by marauding trains, something which Shahani inherits from various sources in the history of cinema, especially from Ritwik Ghatak, his mentor at FTII.[24]

Between these two worlds we tend to overlook many other worlds that are lost. For me, most importantly, *Tarang* inhabits, shapes and dexterously conceals the boundaries between the world of a popular art cinema and that of the avant-garde.

It starts from the moments of recognition. A little more than half an hour into the film, Janki, while silhouetted against the half-lit Bombay streets and roadside vendors in an unusual evening, is recognized as Smita Patil. Moments later, Rahul is recognized as Amol Palekar in a characteristically sunlit and whitish restaurant setting. These moments of recognition are not unusual to the Indian New Wave, the most memorable instance of which can be traced to Mrinal Sen's *Interview* (1971) where the protagonist, played by a young Ranjit Mallick, breaks the fourth wall and addresses the camera frontally in the most recognizably Brechtian manner possible, identifying himself during a tram-ride and revealing the process of filmmaking that realist cinema self-effaces.[25] Laleen Jayamanne places the recognition in *Tarang* in the same league with the international avant-garde cinema of the 1970s in terms of the latter's characteristic reflexivity (2015). But, for me, Shahani's moments of recognition arrive for a very different reason; the direct links with the fourth wall-breaking avant-garde might not be traced in his cinema. These moments are placed at the intersection of the two worlds; they reveal the two worlds and the fissures within.

Smita Patil is perhaps the most iconic figure of the Indian art cinema of the 1970s, mythologized especially after her untimely death at childbirth in 1986. Patil worked with some of the most prominent filmmakers associated with art and middle cinema including Satyajit Ray, Shyam Benegal, Ketan Mehta, Govind Nihalani et al. Om Puri, one of her co-stars in *Tarang*, has also been idolized for his roles from the decade. Amol Palekar, a middle cinema star turned filmmaker, had his rise to prominence with *Rajnigandha* (Basu Chatterjee 1974), one of the most representative middle cinema works of the time. In *Tarang*, Rahul's sexual advances towards Janki resulting in her rape and the subsequent seduction of the perpetrator successfully subvert the middle cinema aesthetic, as the 1970s middle cinema is characterized by endogamy and the idea of the urban middle class being an 'endogamous unit', *Rajnigandha* being an oft-cited instance with Amol Palekar as its hero (Prasad 1998). Smita Patil and Om Puri starred in a Govind Nihalani film that preceded *Tarang*, namely *Ardh Satya* (1983) that deals with an increasingly violent Mumbai plagued by a stagnant administration, political corruption and a near-mythical mafiosi and gangsterism. A year later, they are cast in a film that strongly recalls all such elements of the Bombay modern but departs violently from an oppressive and confining social realism.

The moments of recognition in *Tarang* arrive at this particular juncture and are spread beyond what we see on screen, these moments become more intense with the stars showing unwillingness to comply with the demands of the audience/fans. And this leads to the misrecognition that characterizes *Tarang*, a film that puts almost an entire cohort of art and middle cinema stars to a different use. Their characters may resemble their counterparts in other contemporary films but as the film progresses, the submerged subversion becomes explicit. The audience (mis)recognizes the known stars not as characters, but as figures that merely people Shahani's frames.[26] They move, confide in, conspire, drape clothes around, indulge in violence, sloganeer, frustrate, lie, fornicate and kill themselves and others.

This misrecognition helps with the epiphanic climax where Janki and Rahul trace their origins back to the myths. Janki remembers, Rahul expectedly, doesn't. Janki goes back to her celestial self despite, and because of, her sexual exploitation; Rahul momentarily loses himself in a confused state that hardly befits him. Here Shahani deploys the Urvashi-Pururavas myth from the Indian epics and classical drama that has been explored in greater detail by D.D. Kosambi who traced its circulation through the ages in the literary histories of India.[27] It should be noted that Shahani explored the epic form in Europe and India on a fellowship before the making of *Tarang*.

In Shahani's film, the sexual politics of the myth where the celestial being/nymph Urvashi allows the mere mortal king known as Pururavas to marry her is all the more apparent. In the myth, Urvashi, while leaving Pururavas due to the latter's breach of trust, refers to their frequent sexual encounters that used to happen even without her consent (Rajadhyaksha 2015). In *Tarang*, the process of seduction follows the rape of Janki.

In the climax, Shahani decidedly presents Janki in the most stylized manner possible, as the nymph appears at the daybreak and dissolves into the horizon, with a brief and final encounter with Rahul that remains ambiguous to the latter. Rahul remains the nationalist industrialist, making promises that suited the Indira Gandhi administration during the National Emergency and is unable to engage with the two women in his life as they 'reverse into the eternity of myth' (Jayamanne 2015), one as Ophelia, the other as Urvashi.[28] Shahani's cinema, departing from the respectably realist format that the Indian state was interested in, reverses into the eternity of epic forms.

More often than not, every New Wave becomes mainstream, the popular arthouse, carefully removed from the avant-garde that lies outside the industrial structure. As Annette Michelson commented on the French Nouvelle Vague figures contributing to the globalization of this nomenclature, the iconic auteurs gradually become 'the senior statesmen of a newly threatened industrial production in Europe' (Michelson 2017). A similar fate may await any of its counterparts in other parts of the world but here it is not the case, perhaps because of the misrecognition. It hinders *Tarang* from becoming another 1970s social realist document, as Shahani invests immensely in his resistance to the oppression of a social realism that pervaded his contemporary.

Epilogue

Shahani's Kosambian art and politics and his transnational perusal of the epic in its various forms make his aesthetic-political clearly distinguishable from the social realist political, the latter being the dominant discourse in Indian cinemas of his time. This distinction, as this chapter has shown, can be infinitely problematized into something more complex. And Shahani's subversion removes him from the *movement* of an industrial cinema that appropriates almost everything in its way, including the festival-touring arthouse and the agitprop.

In an introduction to their edited volume *B is for Bad Cinema*, a substantial collection of writings on cinema-hierarchy and the B movies, its aesthetics and politics, Claire Perkins and Con Verevis, apart from referring to the class privilege and cultural taste, quote Deleuze that seems significant (2014). In his *Cinema 2: The Time-Image*, Deleuze addresses bad cinema not in the sense of something comprising of disreputable genres. For him, bad cinema is something where the figurative violence of the represented carries the shock, instead of 'achieving that other violence of a movement-image developing its vibrations in a moving sequence which embeds itself within us' (Perkins and Verevis 2014).

Unlike many of its contemporary social realist arthouse films, *Tarang* does not end with the violence represented. Apart from the mysterious blast that destroys the shelter of the anarchist worker and the attack on the Seth henchman, violence is mostly off-screen. The rape of Janki differs significantly from its counterparts in South Asian popular melodramas (Jayamanne 2015). The violence embedded in Shahani's images manifests in various other ways, especially in his mode of separation from the industry and from art and middle cinema popularized by the industry. The unexpected insertion of the Kosambian into the climactic frame and the resultant transformation of Janki might perhaps be considered as Shahani's most pronounced acts of violence of the movement-image. Because of such violence and rejection, his works remain as they are, widely misunderstood either as a cinema for a niche audience or as a cinema that is not adequately experimental. It has hardly been addressed as a cinema-as-critique, as an *apocryphal* cinema, something that challenges the existing models of an Indian art cinema fundamentally and profoundly.

Silhouetted against the darkness of a Bombay night, cinema itself becomes a larger component of our modernity in the 1960s where the 'nebulous space' is marked by an impulse for exclusion, often provoked by the sheer discomfort for being into a canon.[29] *Tarang*, as our site of inquiry, responds to that discomfort through its departure from the non-populist popular as the latter, through its production and selling of exclusivity, becomes canonical.

Notes

1 The terms gnosis and iconoclasm have been borrowed from the works of Annette Michelson (2017), more of which will be referred to later in this chapter.

2 Rolando Caputo, in an article on Mario Bava, shows how some of the most standardized histories of Italian cinema by Peter Bondanella, Mira Liehm and Pierre Sorlin exclude Mario Bava for the latter's association with B movies and less reputable genres (1997). This politics of exclusion, as this chapter will show, pervades film-history in many ways across many locations.

3 *Tarang* features Shreeram Lagoo, Girish Karnad, M.K. Raina, Rohini Hattangadi and, most importantly, Smita Patil, Om Puri and Amol Palekar. Patil and Om Puri were some of the most iconic faces of the Indian New Wave of the 1970s, and Amol Palekar a near-mandatory presence in the then middle cinema.

4 For the caste issues in south India and the liberal-democratic-capitalist form of cinema posing threat to the former, see Sivathamby (1981) and Srinivas (1999).

5 Bindu Menon refers to some specific Malayalam coinages of the time, *Kala* cinema/art, *Kachavada* cinema/commercial/popular and *Madhyavarthi*/ middle cinema (2010). For more nuanced and nationally relevant theorizing on the 1970s, the film industry-Indian state negotiations and the advent of middle cinema, see Madhava Prasad (1998). For more on the Indian National Emergency and film policy in the long 1970s, see Rajadhyaksha (2009).

6 Here the term national popular is not used in a Gramscian sense, it's more generic in its reference to a specific film industry that negotiates/engages with the nation-state in many ways.

7 For Indian cinema's first association with the transnational in the form of Italian Neorealism in the 1950s, see Moinak Biswas (2007) and Neepa Majumdar (2011).

8 Iranian filmmakers in exile have often been accused of this, their marked dislocation from a cinematic legacy being arguably unable to withstand the onslaught of the European festival politics.

9 By the term 'phantom viewer' S.V. Srinivas meant those phantom figures that emerge between the spectator and the viewer, they are 'created by audiences but are thought to be produced by the cinema' (2009).

10 The list of auteurs that Wilinsky has cited betrays a historical trajectory, it starts with European (and occasionally British) auteurs such as Vittorio De Sica, Powell and Pressburger, Ingmar Bergman, Roger Vadim, Federico Fellini et al. and proceeds to their American counterparts like Otto Preminger, Stanley Kubrick and Stanley Kramer. The exhibition/circulation/importation of European cinema leading to the American studios inventing/locating their own auteurs for the possible consumer constructs an interesting and alternative history of film production and exhibition in the US.

11 Thomas Elsaesser mentioned unequivocally how, without the advent of European auteur cinema, film studies would never have been accepted as a university discipline in the US (1994). For the UK-based cinema studies cohort arguing for the global resurgence of art cinema, see Galt and Schoonover (2010).

12 It is to be noted that experimental cinema imbibes elements from various quarters outside the domain of an industrialized art cinema, even from the so-called B movie that includes horror and other disreputable genres.

13 Kaul and Shahani's state-funded/produced but non-exhibited (or exhibited outside cinema theatre) cinema should perhaps not be cited as an instance of the hardcore avant-garde in the Euro-American sense but they were not part of a popular art cinema either, something that this chapter intends to explore.

14 *Bhuvan Shome* (Mrinal Sen), *Uski Roti* (*Our Daily Bread*, Mani Kaul) and *Sara Akash* (Basu Chatterjee) were made/released in 1969 (*Uski Roti* was not released). The appearance of these new filmmakers and the Indian state's role in realizing a state-funded film movement contributed in the formation of the so-called Indian New Wave, an extremely heterogeneous film movement spread across various Indian industries.

15 Film society activists often recall how most of the festivals and screenings organized by the film societies were dominated by European cinema, while Latin American films featured in the programmes only in case of well-funded, big festivals. The reason for this, primarily, was the availability of European, especially Eastern European cinema, thanks to the left-leaning affiliation of the societies, pre-liberalization India's association with the socialist world and the interest of Eastern European embassies in the dissemination of cinematic culture.

16 Saumen Guha, a Maoist radical activist turned experimental filmmaker, the pioneering figure in small-gauge filmmaking in India, recounted this during a personal interaction in December 2018. Guha's family members suffered custodial torture during the 1970s and Amnesty International helped the family to receive better medical attention and treatment in Denmark. While in Denmark, Guha became acquainted with Super-8 movement, imported Super-8 cameras in India, organized filmmaking workshops, made several films and published two monographs in Bengali. According to Guha, they received no attention or support from the left-leaning cultural sector, not even from the film societies that were active. For more information on Guha's workshops and initiatives, see Biswas (2019).

17 In the post-emergency satire of *Jaane Bhi Do Yaaro* (Kundun Shah 1983), there is a sequence where posters of Kaul's debut *Uski Roti* (1969) with a release date for the film can be found on the wall, even though the film never had a theatrical release.

18 For a detailed account of the debate that Ray provoked, see Patra (2014).

19 The term that Ray used is 'post-Godardian', however ambiguous it may sound, and the devices that he mentioned include freeze, jumpcut, negative, splitscreen, most of which can be traced in his own cinema of the turbulent 1970s, especially in his Calcutta trilogy.

20 Kaul's responses were directed at the selection committee of IFFI 1990 and, perhaps, more at the chair of the committee, namely Ketan Mehta, better known as a middle cinema proponent.

21 The National Emergency of 1975–1977 has directly been referred to by Rahul in the film, as Rajadhyaksha mentions (2015).

22 The world is perhaps not entirely non-Hamlet, there is definitely something rotten in the state of Denmark, but the Prince never appears except for the few minutes when Rahul's monologues after Hansa's apparent suicide, directed at her brother Dinesh, uncannily resemble the Hamlet-Laertes encounter.

23 The flattening of the image is the result of Shahani's deliberate use of cinemascope which he did for the sake of a 'compositional freedom' gained through coming in contact with Kutiyattam, the ancient epic theatre form of Kerala (Jayamanne 2015).

24 Here I am referring to the ever-frequenting image of the moving train that enters through the left corner of the frame and exits into the right in Ritwik Ghatak's classic *Meghe Dhaka Tara* (*The Cloud-Capped Star*, 1960).

25 The sequence reveals Mrinal Sen's cinematographer K.K. Mahajan in the process. Mahajan, arguably the most prolific of the Indian cinematographers associated with the new Wave, incidentally but perhaps not coincidentally has also been the cinematographer of *Tarang*.

26 It should be noted that Shahani's mentor Robert Bresson preferred 'models' over actors, he has never been in favour of directing 'actors'.

27 The inclusion of the Urvashi-Pururavasmyth into *Tarang* and Shahani's indebtedness to Kosambi has been worked on, for more details see

Jayamanne (2015) and Rajadhyaksha (2015). Rajadhyaksha shows how Kosambi traced the journey of the myth from the *Satapatha Brahmana* and the *Rig Veda* to the Mahabharata and Kalidasa's fourth-century play *Vikramorvasiyam*.

28 There is a sequence where Rahul delivers a talk to his workers and his promises are strangely reminiscent of Indira Gandhi's 20-point programme and other propaganda during the Emergency (Rajadhyaksha 2015).

29 This is how Anjali Nerlekar introduces literary cultures in the 1960s Bombay modern where the recognition as well as the discomfort associated with the canon manifest within the 'nebulous space' of a city and its culture that was unsettled by the 'transnational whirlwind' (2017).

References

Biswas, A. 2019. "Tracing Kolkata's Cinephilic Encounters: An Analysis of Alternative Cinema in the City." *Studies in South Asian Film & Media*, 10(2): 113–128.

Biswas, M. 2007. "In the Mirror of an Alternative Globalism: the Neorealist Encounter in India." In *Italian Neorealism and Global Cinema*, edited by L. E. Ruberto and K. M. Wilson, 72–90. Detroit: Wayne State University Press.

Bose, S. 1983. "Bombay Calling". *ABP*, 24 December.

Bourdieu, Pierre. 1984. *Distinction: A Theoretical Critique of the Judgement of Taste*. Cambridge: Harvard University Press.

Brenez, N. 2009. "For an Insubordinate (or Rebellious) History of Cinema." *Framework: The Journal of Cinema and Media*, 50(1/2): 197–201.

Caputo, R. 1997. "Blood and Black Celluloid: Some Thoughts on the Cinema of Mario Bava." *Metro Magazine*, 110: 55–59.

Elsaesser, T. 1994. "Putting on a Show: The European Art Movie." *Sight and Sound*, 4(4): 22.

Galt, R. and K. Schoonover, eds. 2010. *Global Art Cinema: New Theories and Histories*. New York: Oxford University Press.

Jayamanne, Laleen. 2015. *The Epic Cinema of Kumar Shahani*. Bloomington: Indiana University Press.

Koch, G. 2014. "Benjamin's Mass at the Cinema." *Journal of the Moving Image*, 12: 13–24.

Majumdar, N. 2011. "Importing Neorealism, Exporting Cinema: Indian Cinema and Film Festivals in the 1950s." In *Global Neorealism: The Transnational History of a Film Style*, edited by S. Giovacchini and R. Sklar, 178–193. Jackson: University Press of Mississippi.

Majumdar, R. 2016. "Art Cinema: The Indian Career of a Global Category." *Critical Inquiry*, 42(3): 580–610.

——. 2012. "Debating Radical Cinema: A History of the Film Society Movement in India." *Modern Asian Studies*, 46(3): 731–767.

Menon, B. "Malayalam Middle Cinema and the Category of Woman." In *Women in Malayalam Cinema: Naturalising Gender Hierarchies*, edited by M.T. Pillai, 105–121. Hyderabad: Orient Blackswan.

Michelson, A. 2017. "Gnosis and Iconoclasm: A Case Study in Cinephilia." In *On the Eve of the Future: Selected Writings on Film*, 55–75. Cambridge, MA: MIT Press.

Mohamed, K. 1989. "No Way to Treat 'SiddeshwariDevi'." *The Times of India*, 2 November.

Nerlekar, Anjali. 2017. *Bombay Modern: Arun Kolatkar and Bilingual Literary Culture*. New Delhi: Speaking Tiger.

Parikh, J. 1980. "Loan or Subsidy?" *Cinema Vision*, 1(3): 20.

Patra, P. 2014. "Bombay Cinema's Aesthetic Other: Hindi Shastriya Cinema in Retrospect." In *Bollywood and Its Other(s): Towards New Configurations*, edited by V. Kishore, A. Sarwal and P. Patra, 24–38. Basingstoke: Palgrave Macmillan.

Perkins, C. and C. Verevis, eds. 2014. *B is for Bad Cinema: Aesthetic, Politics and Cultural Value*. New York: SUNY Press.

Prasad, M. Madhava. 1998. *Ideology of the Hindi Film: A Historical Construction*. New Delhi: Oxford University Press.

Radhakrishnan, R. 2016. "Kim Ki Duk's Promise, Zanussi's Betrayal: Film Festival, World Cinema and the Subject of the Region." *Inter-Asia Cultural Studies*, 17(2): 206–222.

Rajadhyaksha, Ashish. 2009. *Indian Cinema in the Time of Celluloid: From the Bollywood to the Emergency*. Bloomington: Indiana University Press.

———. 2015. "Kumar Shahani Now". In *The Shock of Desire and Other Essays*, edited by A. Rajadhyaksha, 10–98. New Delhi: Tulika.

Ray, S. 1976. "Four and a Quarter." In *Our Films, Their Films*, 100–107. New Delhi: Orient Blackswan.

———. 1972. "Satyajit Ray Writes." *Filmfare*, 25 February.

Rocha, G. 2019. "New Cinema in the World." In *On Cinema*, edited by I. Xavier, 241–252. London: I.B. Tauris.

Rungachary, B. 1980. "Mani Kaul is More Expensive than Manmohan Desai." *Filmfare*, 16 November.

Sconce, J. 1995. "'Trashing' the Academy: Taste, Excess, and an Emerging Politics of Cinematic Style." *Screen*, 36(4): 371–393.

Singh, B. 1972. "More about the Indian 'New Wave'." *Filmfare*, 24 January.

Sivathamby, Karthigesu. 1981. *The Tamil Film as a Medium of Political Communication*. Madras: New Century Book House.

Srinivas, S.V. 1999. "Gandhian Nationalism and Melodrama in the 30's Telugu Cinema." *Journal of the Moving Image*, 1: 14–36.

———. 2009. *Megastar: Chiranjeevi and Telugu Cinema after N. T. Rama Rao*. New Delhi: Oxford University Press.

Suchenski, R. 2017. "Mythic and Modern: The Aesthetics of Space in the Films of Mani Kaul and Kumar Shahani." *Positions*, 25(1): 29–50.

Wilinsky, Barbara. 2001. *Sure Seaters: The Emergence of Art House Cinema*. Minneapolis: University of Minnesota Press.

12

THE FUTURE OF NON-POPULISM

Debraj Dasgupta

Why do we need to talk about populism? Let us start with a very general example: a few days ago I came across a video clip that depicts a person trying to run a car over a few bottles of cold drinks. This particular clip received more than five million views on the internet. I think the basic necessity to talk about populism starts from here. After watching the clip and the reactions, the leading question that comes to one's mind is about the very precondition of such an exercise. What is the point of such an exercise? Is this entertainment? Some form of mass art? Is this happiness or human salvation? Where lies the purpose or the value in this cycle of performance and consumption? What kind of normalization is such a form of pleasure? On the face of it, such normalization would seem to directly contradict what one would like to demarcate as audio-visual art, even with all kinds of oddities and variations involved in such a form.

The basic problem is very simple: things which are becoming massified in this manner signal to a very deep crisis of value or in designating the measures of judgemental criteria *per se* as far as their operation in human society is concerned. A fundamental question arises: *What is the underlying point* in such exercises? Is it that all populist ways must essentially take us to meaningless expressions of relentless enjoyment? In such a case, there must be some idea of value at the opposite end of it—that is to say, in non-popular art practices. In fact, that kind of value may not be about meaning-mongering at all, as we shall see. So, on one hand, we can say that we already have a given perception of populism, and its obverse, non-populism, in terms of art practice. In this sense populism is simply a blind force that tries to gain popularity at any cost. Motives could range from pecuniary to viewership augmentation and market dynamics to our tendency to give in to immediate gratification. The motives could also lie in the ominous recesses of human nature, a coming together of a large number of people owing to narcissism, extracting vengeance or scapegoating. As its inverse, non-populism is something grainy, esoteric and recondite, Delphic almost. Its nature is not easy to understand—not so impressible and therefore often ignored by large sections of the society. In this chapter, I wish to reconfigure the two terms—populism and non-populism. I wish to particularly understand the operational aspects of these two terms. As I go on, I would also like to tentatively venture over a particular idea of value that I would characterize to be at the heart of the 'non-populist'.

In order to focus on these questions, I want to look at the difference between popular and non-popular in the history of Bengali literary criticism as a case study. So, if art practice is relativized to such an extent that there are no judgemental yardsticks any more, what ways do we have in order to make distinctions in art and life? One way is to trace a history of a certain literary criticism, on which I shall venture soon. The other is to scaffold a conceptual notion of populism right here at the outset. I would like to look at a particular aspect of Ernesto Laclau's celebrated formulations on populism, an aspect that is not so commonsensical in nature. In his well-known essay Ernesto Laclau has divided populism into two different parts. One concentrates on ideology and the other part concerns a practice. But for Laclau there is no temporal journey from populist ideology to populist practice. Laclau posits populism as a later and a constructed phenomenon that operates at the level of practice: "There is, however a second possibility—namely that the political practices do not *express* the nature of social agents but, instead constitute later."[1]

According to Laclau this journey cannot be understood in terms of the commonsensical idea of representation. On the question of representation he shares a very familiar ground of thought with Gilles Deleuze and Jacques Derrida and by doing so he tries to come up with a refracted notion of representation. Such a manner of looking into representation has a crucial link to the question of the non-popular as we shall see soon.

> One is the increasing certainty that that I have given, in my recent work, on the logic of representation. As I said before, a dislocation can only be shown through distortion of particular ontic contents. This means that such contents will represent something different from themselves; so that 'representation' is a primary and constitutive ontological terrain, because there is no full 'presentation' vis-à-vis which that representation would be a simple copy (in Platonic sense). I think that, in different ways, the writings of Derrida and Deleuze have moved in a comparable direction.[2]

Practices have a certain ontological priority over the practitioners who supposedly and actively decide 'choices' of those practices. If we follow this logic further—we shall see that it is not people who are constructed before certain populist strains emerge but it is the practice from where the 'people' emerge. People begin to morph with the change in certain circumstances and operations in society. But what might be the nature of such people? Do they arise out of rank individualism? About this matter, Laclau intervenes thus: "Individuals are not coherent totalities but merely referential identities which have to be split up into a series of localized subject positions"[3]

Therefore, localized or not, people operating within the framework of populism is not something that has been already defined. Rather, people constitute the excess of it. Is it, as it were, that people is the name of that principle which cannot be reduced into the given format of populist practice? So, apparently if we arrive from our discomfort about the aforementioned video clip to Laclau's articulation of populism we may suffer disappointment. Did Laclau want to impress upon us that a random popular thing is merely and actually potent at the level of excess? I do not think so. The fundamental claim which we take from Laclau is not the promise of a meaningless populist practice as the bedrock basis of an ideal future but rather a logical possibility of a better future from a particular kind of practice.

This logical movement is quite similar to the Derridian idea of the 'invention of the other' or 'a future to come'. In this chapter I shall try to delineate the relationship between the excess that we are referring to, this coming of the future so to say—through the debate of populist and non-populist writing in Bengali literary criticism. My focus is not to dabble too much in historical empiricism. At the level of historical information my focus would be on the nature of what can be called non-populism in two neglected Bengali authors: Kamal Kumar Majumdar and Amiya Bhushan Majumdar.

The Essay Form and Populist Purposiveness

But to begin with, let me try to understand the contributions of the aforementioned authors in the history of Bengali literature with the help of a debate that had been undertaken by Raghab Bandyopadhyay on the question of populism in literature. Bandyopadhyay's own writings can be situated within the same history of the essay form. In this case, we shall treat him as a critic though; as a mediator through whom we can delve into the core nature of the populist and the non-populist in literature. Finally, using him as a conduit, we can perhaps get into the particular mode of non-populism inaugurated by the two Majumdars.

In his essay "Barjita Manusher Akhyan" (The Narrative of the Disowned People) Raghab Bandyopadhyay writes:

> তবু, লেখার উপযোগিতা আদৌ আছে কি না, বা উপযোগিতার সীমা পেরিয়েই লেখার ভুবনের শুরু কি না, তা ভেবে দেখা যেতেই পারে।
>
> আমার এবং আরও অনেকের মতে লেখার পারপাস বা উদ্দেশ্য লেখার কাজটিই; যদিও কাজটি টেবিলের চৌহদ্দিতে আটকে থাকে না তা পড়া পর্যন্ত গড়াবেই, সবটা মিলে ভাষা-ভুবনের হৃৎস্পন্দন হয়ে উঠতে পারলেই একটা সার্থকতা অর্জন সম্ভব। ধরে নিলে ভুল হবে না যে এর মধ্যে একটি লীলার ব্যাপার আছে।.[4]
>
> [Still, it could be assessed whether there is at all any utility for writing or is it that the world of writing begins beyond the limits of utility. According to me and many others, the purpose of writing is writing itself, though the written work cannot be confined within the four corners of the table. It is inclined to reach the realm of reading. All in all, writing can achieve some success if it is able to turn itself into the heartbeat of the linguistic universe. It will not be erroneous to consider that there is an element of miracle in writing.]

It is important to mark an interesting conundrum here. We started by questioning the ephemeral and distractive nature of the video clip. And here Bandyopadhyay is arguing for a 'divine' purposelessness in art. Must the most populist of art, since it is also purposeless and distractive, find itself outside the pail of utility and therefore be considered genuine and honest in its nature? This is a productive confusion. One way to address this confusion is perhaps to read the very nature of distraction and play in art. The romantic reverie, the idealistic notion of play, the modernist distraction of the *flaneur* or forms like montage, pastiche or kitsch and the memes and videos cobbled together in order to heighten our sense of sensationalism are not one and the same thing. For that we have to have a clearer sense of what exactly is the function of play, irony and distraction in art.

The second way to address this conundrum is to take the purpose of art seriously and to assert that indeed art does have a purpose to it. But such a purpose cannot be confused with utility. The video clip did not serve any purpose other than idly taking us to distraction by using certain props and cheap thrills. The superficiality of the entertaining aspect of the clip is less a deciding factor than its not having a purpose. The crucial question is rather the following: *How to bring the idea of traces and play in art and impart that with a sense of purpose. Conversely put, what could purpose in art-practice mean if it has to keep aside the populist idea of didactic responsibility and other forms of empty and voided distraction?* To crack this code is at the heart of all non-populist art practice. In a way, as we try to unfold our argument on non-populism we also begin to open ourselves up to the question of the immeasurable and the fathomless. To do so is to actually anticipate and hope for an unknown relationship leading towards a deeper generality; indeed, a certain non-conceptuality. As methods of non-populism try to crack the code they also always express a sense of futurity. Non-populist art begins to mould a certain futurity itself in the process of its own formation. In fact, this dimension is in accord with Deleuze's conceptualization of the relation between creation and resistance. One would recall how in his essay "What is the Creative Act?" Deleuze talks about Andre Malraux's philosophical concept of the work of art as the only resistance to death. "Malraux developed an admirable philosophical concept. He said something very simple about art. He said it was the only thing that resists death."[5]

Deleuze would extend this very line of thought and try to work out a specific relationship between the work of art and the act of resistance. But obviously the point of my writing is not to cultivate these strange similarities. It is rather to show how the act of cracking the code inevitably leads non-populist works of art to seek expressions of the future. By raising the question of futurity I am actually trying to argue that non-populism is never equitable to the radical non-responsible or irresponsible but rather the opposite: it is always highly charged with a different kind of responsibility in which the relationship between futurity and non-populism turns out to be an inevitable one.

So, if we now go back to the Bandyopadhyay citation, we shall observe that there is a similarity between his claim and the Derridian idea of writing, where writing is not confined within a restricted economy. Derrida overturns the idealistic idea of play in continental thought. All writing overflows beyond the writer, reader and book that takes us to the larger idea of textuality. Consider the following comment so that we can have a basic sense of Derridian 'inscription':

> Now we tend to say 'writing' for all that and more: to designate not only the physical gestures of literal pictographic or ideographic inscription, but also the totality of what makes it possible; and also, beyond the signifying face, the signified face itself. And thus we say 'writing' for all that gives rise to an inscription in general, whether it is literal or not and even if what it distributes in space is alien to the order of the voice: cinematography, choreography, of course, but also pictorial, musical, sculptural 'writing'.[6]

This pivotal idea of Derridian writing is quite well known: Writing based on the origin and imbued with a 'dangerous supplement'; and his insistence on traces. Writing moves from a restricted secondariness towards a general original economy.

Consider now this very interesting personal remark by Derrida made in one of his interviews with Derek Attridge:

> What is interesting here is thus the invention of the addressee capable of countersigning and saying 'Yes' in a committed and lucid way. But this "yes" is also an inaugural performance, and we recover the structure of inerrability which would prevent us, at this point, from distinguishing rigorously between performance and competence, as between producer and receiver. As much as that between the addressee and the signatory or the writer and the reader. This is the space in which *The Post Card* is involved. It did so in a certain fashion. At the same time general and singular. Other ways are certainly possible—and yes, I would also like to involve myself in them.[7]

Here Derrida is very precise about a certain kind of writing which can push its limit towards the general economy of writing. He says that in *The Post Card* he could create that space and he hopes to explore the space in his other writings too. It is, as it were, he waits for that writing to come. We shall arrive to the question of this conception of 'to come'. At this point the focal questions for my purpose could be posed thus: can we at all make a difference between a populist and a non-populist writing in terms of the division that Derrida makes between *The Post Card* and his other writings? And does this difference lead us to the question of the value of non-populism?

In Raghab Bandyopadhyay, this causeless, 'excessive' concept of writing is not exactly so general so as to operate at the level of practice. Rather it is very much restricted into specific types of writing which he would always claim as non-populist. In his case, the recognition of non-populist literature often astonishes us at the level of content or comes across as experimental at the level of form. In his book *Marginer Lekha ar Lekhar Margine* as Bandyopadhyay deals with the major trends of Bengali non-populist writing he shows us how such a claim can be made beginning right from nineteenth-century non-elite literature till the writings of his contemporaries like Sandipan Chattopadhyay, Nabarun Bhattacharya and others. But what does he wish to tell us when Bandyopadhyay makes such a claim? Does he wish to point towards a certain value in writing? Whenever he picks up a writer whom he would like to consider as non-popular in terms of experimentation and rigour, Bandyopadhyay would always bind them in a thread of a certain value; as if these writers had something to protect, something to differentiate. In fact, in many cases Bandyopadhyay would not agree with the individual writers' idea of literature. For instance, at some points he has called Sandipan Chattopadhyay a writer who loves being a cult, thereby running the risk of getting reduced to a certain image. For Raghab Bandyopadhyay, such a reduction should always be resisted. Cultism is always a damaging exercise: a product of inverse snobbery. In writing, Bandyopadhyay tries to indicate a certain form of honesty instead. This is the domain of non-populism: where writing means the direct, powerful and honest voice of the artist. Such a voice consistently takes us towards the vocation of a writer as a ground for uncompromising honesty; a ground which works steadfastly against the market-value of massified products. This is one axis of the idea of value that lies within the heart of non-populist ventures.

The mode of criticism he nurtures against populist writings shall become clearer if we see the manner in which he traces the philosophy of writing within the history of Bengali literary criticism. Among the most valuable voices of literary criticism, Bandyopadhyay always cultivated a distinct 'non-populist' voice. He repeatedly reminds us about the helplessness of a non-populist writer and his endless suffering for recognition. At the same time he keeps on highlighting ceaselessly the impelling of excess which a non-populist holds in his womb like a mother.

To arrive at Bandyopadhyay's position of non-populism we will try to see the history of Bengali critical essay form from an ambiguous gaze of responsibility. I shall begin with a general idea of responsibility and then later try to complicate it for the purpose of our discussion. At the end of our essay these apparent fragmented signifiers which we have been constantly using so far—'excess', 'value', 'responsibility' or even 'non-populism'—will perhaps come to a point of convergence. Adhir Dey, in his not so well-known book of the history of Bengali Modern essay, *Adhunik Bangla Prabandha Sahityer Dhara*,[8] provides us with a history of Bengali essay form. Dey tells us that in seventeenth century there were two important essays written in Bengali by Dom Antonioni and Monoel da Assumpcam. Thereafter, a series of writers enters into the scene like William Carey and Thomas Marshman, Fort William College—Ram Ram Basu, Mrityunjay Vidyalankar, Goloknath Sharma and others. The major essayist of this era was Rammohan Roy. His essays on society and reforms are well known. These kinds of essays were primarily written in the form of critiques. These essays placed upon themselves a huge burden: that of social responsibility. Next to Rammohan was Krishanamohan Bandyopadhyay—who penned an encyclopedia, called *Bidyakalpadru* which again is fired with a huge social responsibility. After the generation of Rammohan, Akshay Kumar Dutta, Iswar Chandra Vidyasagar, Debendranath Thakur and Bhudeb Mukhopadhyay arrived. All of them also wrote primarily about society, education and so on. Akshay Kumar Dutta was the first man who wrote thoroughly about science and scientific philosophy. He also wrote about the tradition of saints in India. Rangalal Bandyapadhay was the first literary critic of Bengal in technical term. Iswar Gupta, Nandakumar Nyayachanchu, Pyarichand Mitra, Dijendranath Thakur and then Bankim Chandra Chatterjee followed. The era of Bankim Chandra Chatterjee starts from 1872 with his justly famous magazine *Bangadarshan*. Again we notice a huge amount of responsibility in him too. Everywhere, didactic exhortations are rife. The fundamental project of Bankimchandra's *Bangadarshan* was to define and distinguish good literature from bad ones and urging us to keep away the latter. This tradition of criticism Bankim Chandra received from his teacher Iswar Gupta who edited a work titled *Kabi Jibani* (*Life of the Poets*). There have been many more important essayists in nineteenth-century Bengal such as Ram Das Sen, Rajani Kanta Gupta, Akshay Chandra Sarkar, Sanjib Chandra Chatterjee, Sibnath Shastri, Keshab Chandra Sen and others. But the ground-breaking essays materialized when Rabindranath Tagore took to the essay form. Tagore started composing essays from the perspective of an artist. In fact, it is better to say that his fundamental contribution to the form was to inscribe the perspective of a poet within the figure of the essayist. The critic and scholar Buddhadeb Basu has to say this about such a turn:

> He (Rabindranath) puts metaphor instead of argument, Imagery in the place of information; where his actual intention is to attract the reader towards his own opinion, there he makes all the senses sharper; where the need is to prove something intellectually, there he illegally provokes us emotionally… we have to admit, the way Aristotle, Anandavardhana or Mallinath are critics is not the way how Rabindranath is a critic of literature.[9]

Though Tagore changed the fundamental way of writing we still notice a deep sense of aesthetic, formal and other responsibilities in his exhortations. Pramatha Chaudhuri, another important literary critic who appeared after Tagore, rebelled against the orthodox style of Bengali language and started publishing a literary journal in colloquial Bengali. My point is possibly plain by now: almost all the essayists did pick up their pen having a great sense of responsibility. And this went unabated even when the nationalist movement took different shapes and contours in the first half of twentieth century; in fact, essays turned even more purposive and didactic. Almost all writing had a purpose to serve. Till the first half of twentieth century Bengali essays more or less dealt with this exactitude and pure purposiveness.

In that tradition of responsibility, Raghab Bandyopadhyay arrives as the absolute voice for the non-popular in his essays. But it was a very different idea of responsibility. And by doing so he antagonizes two different groups at the same time: first, the popular literary writers who received attention for their scurrilous raillery and pornographic excesses. The other group comprised the 'academics' who were more inclined to deal with the Continental thought after the 1970s. In conscious opposition to both these trends, Bandyopadhyay tried to chart a unique way of seeing, arguing and thinking the history of Bengali critical essay form, as if it was a search for some authentic Bengali thought process. This gets specifically highlighted when he deals with the essays of Bhudeb Mukhopadhyay in *Marginer Lekha ar Lekhar Margine*. He seeks values outside of the consumptive. This is something which he continued to do till his last breath. Undoubtedly, one of the reasons for his deep affection for Kamal Kumar Majumdar's writing is precisely this penchant. His essays not only fought for the recognition of non-populist writers but also began to shoulder a different responsibility, drawing our attention to an exclusively Bengali way of critical thinking. It was a vertical journey in search for a certain depth in our collective consciousness. Chauvinism is not my point here. I wish to emphasize the non-populist aspects of such a venture. This is the attitude through which a non-populist always tries to protect and propel certain base values and a sense of non-compromising uniqueness. Apropos of a certain structure of populist attitude in and around Kolkata, Bandyopadhyay has often made remarks such as the following:

"এখানকার ফুকো টুকো পড়া লোকজন হেসে উড়িয়ে দেবেন। আমাদের যৌবনে একে ভাববাদের গাড্ডা বলে পাত্তাই দেওয়া হত না।"

> [The Foucault-reading generation shall laugh it off but during our youth as such things would be ridiculed as slipping into the borehole of idealism.][10]

পেশাদার তাত্ত্বিকদের (এক্ষেত্রে অধ্যাপককুলকেই ধরতে হবে, কারণ তার বাইরে তত্ত্ব আলোচকের সংখ্যা নগণ্য। সেই স্বল্প সংখ্যক তাত্ত্বিকেরাও আবার অ্যাকাডেমিক তাত্ত্বিকদের দ্বারা যথেষ্ট প্রভাবিত।) বাইরে বাংলা সমালোচনা সাহিত্যের চর্চা-কারীদের মধ্যে কবিদেরই প্রাধান্য...আবার খেদটা দু তরফেই বর্তমান। দু-তরফই বলবেন – বাংলা সমালোচনা সাহিত্য খুব দুর্বল।

> [Beyond the professional intellectuals (one has to consider the professorial class in this instance since few people would dabble in abstract theories outside of this genus. Even those who are independent are often influenced by the academic intellectuals). Beyond this section, literary criticism in Bengali is mostly carried out by the poets. And both the cohorts would cavil and carp to pronounce that the domain of criticism in Bengali is rather weak.][11]

বাংলায় লেখালিখির দুনিয়ায় তা কখনো কখনো ডেকে আনছে একপেশেমি। যেমন, উত্তুরে (আধুনিক) বাতাসই এখন প্রবল। তবু, ন্যারেটিভের একমাত্রিক জনমোহিনীরিতিই আঁকড়ে আছেন অতিশয় প্রতিষ্ঠিত লেখকেরা।

> [We often notice a certain one-dimensionality in the world of Bengali writing. For example, the prevailing trend is the postmodern. But most established authors still latch on to one-dimensional populist ways when it comes to tackling the narrative.][12]

In this context, here is another clarificatory example: in a very subtle editing of a title of an essay Bandyopadhyay has shown an explicit mark of apathy against the populist exercise of the practice of abstruse theory in writings. To that end, he altered the title from "Ek Arbachiner Dakghar Path" to "Mrityunjoy Amal". Readers would recall the familiar character from Tagore's *Dakghar*—Amal—who was a symbol of odd resistance against the grains of elitist knowledge. At the same time, Bandyopadhyay defends his own non-populist position as a writer in a very suppressed elitist manner:

.সময় নিয়ে টানাটানি নেই। লেখার লাইনের লোক বলতে সচরাচর যা বোঝানো হয়, সেই গোত্রের মধ্যেই পড়ি। সুতরাং লেখার কাজটি আটকায় কে? 'সাহিত্য' অভিধা-ভুক্ত আমার সামান্য লেখালিখি নিয়ে কেউই তেমন উৎসাহিত নন, অর্থাৎ যাকে বলে পাঠক আনুকূল্য আমি তা বিশেষ পাইনি।

> [There is no dearth of time. I fall under the rubric of someone who is associated with the *business of writing*. So, there is none to interfere in my effort to write. Though, no one is much interested in the little writing that I do under the heading of literature; that is to say, I have never enjoyed the confidence and support of the readers.][13]

Even when he discusses his compatriot Sandipan Chattopadhyay (perhaps more popular than Bandyopadhyay in public perception), Bandyopadhyay emphasizes on a space where a writer can talk about his fellow beings: other writers. What exactly did he mean in seeking a separate space—if not an elitist discursive zone? (As I have mentioned earlier, Bandyopadhyay's literature is not my concern here. I just try to use his perspective of non-populism as a way of looking at non-populism in general). For his publishing house *Charcha* he actually claimed a ground for something secluded and esoteric. In his two essays: 'Bajar Chalti Sabek Akhyan' and 'Ekti Khasra', he draws a straight line from Bankimchandra to the current nature of populist writing. He discards massified writings by invoking the old fashioned high art and popular art division. There is an important dilemma taking place here: at one level Bandyopadhyay turns into a layman when the question of argumentative and philosophical debate takes place but on the other hand he turns into an inverted elite when the question of literary practice becomes the issue. I always found this very dilemma also present in Kamal Kumar Majumdar and Amiya Bhushan Majumdar: between recognition and rejection, between argumentative knowledge and autonomous experience, between submitting one to the excesses and holding oneself back from the masses. At the root of this dilemma is the self-transcendental nature of non-populism, where a non-populist self always tries to find an authenticity of his own and precisely begins to turn alienated from the social world by that same move. But the story does not end here. Rather, this is the precise point of departure for non-populism.

Excess and Relationality

Kamal Kumar Majumdar started publishing his writings from the early days of the third decade of twentieth century. He became a cult figure much later and started to get celebrated after almost two decades of his death. Majumdar was surely one idol for Raghab Bandyopadhyay. The latter wrote a whole book on him called *Kamalkumar Kolkata, Pichutaner Itihas*. For him Kamal Kumar used to be the very symbol and insignia of non-populism—someone who denied any kind of recognition and took the task of writing as an expression of the unsayable and immeasurable—as if our worldly transactions are something very sacred to be shored through writing. But how can we understand this idea of the expression of the interior? I think this move is very much modernist in nature although it is a serious response to our modern condition too. Majumdar did some unusual experimentation with Bengali prose in order to tap the irrational and sensual expressions of the unsayable and the immeasurable. He was obsessed with non-modernity, especially with the idea of community. He always tried to locate the signs of the immeasurable within the zone of non-modern and pre-modern nuances of community life. This he tried to locate at the more formal level too. Perhaps he believed that a particular experimental prose can open us up to the immeasurable? Consequently, his prose is salvific. But such a rhetorical flourish could not have happened without a painful investment in reading, including going through modernist prose. The pain was personal though. And he knew that none will be interested to invest themselves into that pain. It was the inverse responsibility to care for and value the immeasurable. To compare this particular drive to Kantian disinterestedness or as an investment in aesthetic purity (art for art's sake) will be reductionist. In Majumdar's case the urgings of the immeasurable were much more associated with the cultural politics of Bengali non-modern language itself. There works a curious dialectic in his case too: not much between recognition and rejection but between a highly sophisticated formal experiment and an absolutely grounded, sometimes tribal non-modern content of literature. This is a dilemma between elitist taste of the civil society and the marginal way of everyday life. Consumptive and massified art would never pass through this productive tension. As I have said earlier, Majumdar's writing always presupposes an excess, a leap from the possible domain of already practiced communicability (measurability) to the unknown and the cosmological—be it in *Antarjali Yatra* or *Suhashinir Pometom*. This immeasurability cannot be reduced to mere *ontic* elements. There is a very important essay by Majumdar titled 'Pariprekkhit' (The Perspective). At one point he says this:

> "I don't count the stream of events as the means of writing; therefore many incidents stayed with me after it has been refined."[14]

So, an apparent series of events that we usually designate by the name of plot is not something that interests him. Instead, he tries to find excess in a same event by repeatedly *writing the same event*. Things are denotative rather than connotative in their repeatability. Even in his manuscripts, I found a series of paragraphs that are repetitions. A writer can write the same event through diverse storylines. Time and again we approach the immeasurable in the already measured series of events. The point is not exactly what Bandyopadhyay or Majumdar was describing in the storylines but how they were describing those events and to what end. It is, as it were, the whole act of writing produces the event itself (in Majumdar's vocabulary: 'purifies'). This is much as Laclau describes that the social agent is not someone who actually conducts the political movement but get produced through the movement. This happens because the foundation of his writing is not the content that writing represents but to fathom certain vertical abyss of immeasurability. The telling of tales or succession of events was a very purposeful exercise: of creating something that has not been measured before. This was not just communicable through a simple way of telling things. Rather, such a mode of engagement demands life-long penance and devotion of a different order. The practitioner of such an art form denies any simple way of communication and tries to open up a field which may allow the excess to bloom gradually. We mark an act of impossibility to represent the event. All non-populist writing shall forever open itself up to such impossibility. Again and again. This very act of pushing the boundary of mere representation and communication opens up the possibility of traversing towards a general economy of writing. Therefore, 'writing' itself is always foregrounded in such forms in contrast to 'communication': as if the interior of a writer is suffused with immeasurability and he must disclose that in order to be open up to the *other*. The writer actually *reveals the relationality* in living in this manner. We will come back to this question later in the chapter. This act of opening up to play off the excess for Majumdar was inevitable for writing. It was also inevitable to Amiya Bhushan Majumdar. In one of his essays '*Why Write?*' Amiya Bhushan Majumdar says:

> There is some excess in the interior and that is the reason literature is written. Of course it is difficult to figure out the essence of this excess.[15]

Amiya Bhushan always claimed himself to be a private writer who kept on writing all through his life. He too was staunchly against saleability. He had an inclination to recognize and understand pre-modern literary traditions and wrote a book on the process of writing titled *Likhane ki Ghate*. In some of his writings he tried to tap the excess as something psychological though a rudimentary reading of Lacanian psychoanalysis. He tried to explain the process of writing through two Lacanican psychoanalytical exercises—escape and trauma. But let us reserve a discussion of that aspect for another occasion. These two writers were highly familiar with the ongoing movements in twentieth century French thought. Though, as I have pointed out earlier, none of them were fond of abstraction for its own sake. So, when we try to understand such a notion of non-populism through a philosophical framework, we experience a very interesting moment of fitting togetherness at the level of thought.

Immersion and Unlearning

What binds these three authors is their faith in creative writing as journeys in excess; writing itself as transcendental work to be painstakingly carried on in a private manner. Writing is a secluded act. This is the very basis of immersing oneself in whatever is non-popular, so that one can try to fathom the immeasurable. It is a silent and life-long penance. As I have mentioned, Kamal Kumar Majumdar's literary output was enormous. His landmark novel *Antarjali Jatra* deals with the theme of the journey towards God. In the case of Amiya Bhushan Majumdar, apart from his early novels like *Gar Srikhand* and *Rajnagar* it would be germane to delve deeper into his other masterpieces: *Madhu Sadhu Kha* and *Chand Bene.*

Consciously and deliberately, both of these writers reject any possibility of becoming popular. But let me repeat the fundamental question with which I began this chapter: What is the underlying point of indulging in populist ventures? What takes us towards such social responsibility? What is the purpose of such visibility? What is the point of indulging in art and literature that is consumed and then dumped to oblivion? I am trying to deliberately draw the equivalence between a social media meme or a video and a highly engaged art practice: pray, what is the point in such indulgence?

The easiest way will be to make a straight and naïve distinction: to enjoy viewership means to indulge in the pleasure of immediate gratification. This is the justification of the sensuous and sensory though that is refracted in such cases of consumption. Consumption of this kind is actually the obverse of genuine hedonism and natural decadence. But the point could be seeking pleasure in distraction. For the other side, the point is immersion in the immeasurable—a value which cannot be fathomed though the exchanges of the market or through such kinds of non-relationality.

But the larger question is this: How can one be so sure that the work of the immeasurable or the excessive is present only in the non-populist art and not in a random video which accrues a million viewers? This brings me to the controversial matter of value and judgement. I shall claim that indeed non-populist art forms do contain a specific set of values that populist art cannot claim to have. Let me try and justify my claim and gradually get into the question of relationality and into another strange but important conception of forgetting in order to achieve the previously declared goal of our chapter.

But prior to that let us get back to the point of Raghab Bandyopadhyay's existential framework that operates behind his position of his backing non-populism. Here are some lines from Bandyopadhyay:

লেখাপড়াটা আমার হল না। কত তত্ত্বকথা শুনি, না শুনে উপায় নেই বলে। অজ্ঞতার আশীর্বাদ আমার মাথায় পর্যাপ্ত পরিমাণে বর্ষিত হয়েছে। যাঁরা নিষ্ঠার সঙ্গে বিদ্যাচর্চা করেন, সেমিনার হল কিংবা ছাপা-বই, পত্রিকা অথবা সাইবার স্পেসে যাঁদের জ্ঞান-দ্যুতি বিচ্ছুরিত হয়—তাঁদের সকলের দিকে অপার শ্রদ্ধায়, প্রায় এক শিশুর মত নিষ্পলক তাকিয়ে থাকি। অথচ আমি হারিয়ে ফেলেছি অজ্ঞানতার কৌমার্য।

> [Reading and writing eludes me. One gets to hear much abstract theories since there is not much of a choice. I have been adequately blessed by inanity. With great respect I look up to those who are sincerely engaged in practicing knowledge, those who spread the fruits of their learning in seminar halls and printed books, in magazines and on the cyber space. I look up to them with almost a child-like exuberance. And yet I have lost the innocence of the ignorant.][16]

সন্দীপন বিষয়ে রাঘব বন্দ্যোপাধ্যায়ের বক্তব্য – "...কিন্তু কি লিখছি এই প্রশ্নটা তো তিনি স্থগিত রাখেন, সন্দীপনের এক চিন্তা, কিভাবে লিখি, কার ভাষায়।"

> [Commenting on Sandipan Chattopadhyay, Bandyopadhyay would say this – "but he holds at abeyance the issue of the content; the only thing that took up his mind was—how to write and in whose language?]"[17]

...আজকের তরুণ লেখককেও সন্দীপন থেকে অনেকটাই সরে আসতে হবে। তাঁকে ভুলতে শিখতে হবে। সাহিত্যকে মহিমা-চ্যুত করা তাঁর আশু কর্তব্য।

> [The young, contemporary writer must remove himself quite a bit from Sandipan. He must learn to forget. His main and immediate obligation is in obliterating the grandeur of literature.][18]

এইখানে স্পষ্ট বলে নেওয়া যাক – শিল্পের বিনোদন আর বিশুদ্ধ আনন্দের মধ্যে আমরা নিশ্চিত তফাৎ করি।

> [It must be clearly mentioned here that we make a distinct differentiation between the entertainment value of art and pure pleasure.][19]

Forgetting and Futurability

I wish to highlight an important phrase here, a very theme in fact: the act of forgetting. A young writer should forget. What shall he forget? He must forget the inheritance of writing itself and the ways of certain expressions. Why will he forget certain ways of conducting business? Because the line between actually conducting a formal experiment in art (which is also rhetorical as it is rich in its mnemonic sensibility) and the instant artifice of showing off has really blurred. *Here we can define populism precisely as that part of non-populism which always tries to slip out of the penance of a non-populist and immersed writer.* But again why such a form of penance is at all necessary? The act of penance is necessary for another kind of forgetting. It is not just a simple forgetting of the popular or the exorcising of mere intellectual information about creative art practice. Let us build up a chain of signifiers that I have already used in this chapter—a chain that can hold all the similar concepts which can be signified as transcendental: the signifiers are excess, impossible, immeasurable, people and a futurity to come. Have we already understood the signs that Raghab Bandyopadhyay collectively gives the name of forgetting?

> সে কি চাট্টিখানি কথা। একের পর এক আবরণ উন্মোচনের সেই প্রক্রিয়া থেকে যায় আমাদের অলক্ষ্যে। সেই প্রক্রিয়ার অনিবার্য সহযোগী পাঠভোলার চেতনা, ইংরেজিতে বললে সহজ হয় -

process of unlearning

> [This is not an easy affair. The process of gradual unveiling of layers and layers of sheathings remain outside of our view. The inexorable companion to such an operation is another undertaking: the process of unlearning.][20]

What actually does a young writer need to unlearn? What is this consciousness of unlearning?

> প্রণাম নৈঃশবদ্যকে, কেননা এবার ক্ষান্ত হওয়া একান্ত কাম্য। আমার আর কতটুকু সাধ্য। শিল্পের জিয়ঙ্কাঠিই পারে স্মৃতি-ঐশ্বর্যকে নবজীবন দান করতে। অহল্যার মতো বারবার বেঁচে ওঠা অনন্ত সেই জীবনকে প্রণাম।

> [I supplicate to stillness, because it is absolutely imperative to give things a rest. I have little power myself. It is only art's magic-wand which gives fresh lease of life to the treasures of memory. Hail to this infinite life which, like Ahalya, resurrects itself again and yet again.][21]

How exactly does a writing open up a way towards the impossible? What does it mean for a writing to form a deep relationality? In the Derridian world what does it mean to go from a restricted to a general economy of writing?

Let us glean two important insights from Derrida at this juncture. The first is from an essay on Time—"The Time of the King". Here is how poetically the essay begins:

> The king takes all my time; I give the rest to Saint-Cyr, to whom I would like to give all.[22]

By a subtle movement, as is his wont, Derrida picks up the word *rest* from this line. Two important questions arise: What does he mean by *giving the rest*? How can one give the rest when everything is already given? The question of play becomes crucial. When everything is given by the economy of exchange (exchange value in Marxian sense) how can there be a rest? If there is a rest or as if there is no rest (nothing)—it must be immeasurable. For Derrida it is the gift that cannot be measured within the economy of give and take, within the measurable. And it cannot be given in terms of giving and taking. Derrida extends this logic and argues that in contrast to certain methods of psychoanalysis only if there is radical forgetting through play the idea of the gift becomes possible. One cannot give a gift and the other cannot keep the memory of it intact and secure. This forgetting is something beyond the psychoanalytical remembering and forgetting.

> For there to be a gift, not only must the donor or donee not perceive the gift as such, have no consciousness of it, no memory, no recognition; he or she must also forget it right away...and moreover this forgetting must be so radical that it exceeds even the psychoanalytical category of forgetting.[23]

Here is my claim as to where exactly the value resides in non-populist forms of art and literature: *Such works always open themselves up to the coming of the gift without knowing the possibility of its arrival.* Is such an act only possible because of the time that has been given to its being formed? It is only the measurable amount of time that is actually given to its unfolding. But the rest—the immeasurable, is not given; which cannot be given, which is a gift by definition, an impossible act of giving—beyond the transactional economy of giving and taking. Hence, *yet to be given*. That is an impossible, radical future to come. This is the idea of the people in Laclau too, in congruence with the idea of the excess in Kamal Kumar Majumdar and Amiya Bhushan Majumdar. The only value for the non-populist artist is the *labour of penance*. An impossible labour. Not even measurable in the economy of memory—a radical forgetting. It is, as it were, positing silently a value of the writing to come; the value of the general economy of writing to come.

But again, *pace* Laclau, perhaps as a discursive formation we can read from the creative practice that there is a *value to come* in the labour of those writers. But from the perspective of a writer how can one say that he writes in order to exceed the restricted economy of writing? Why cannot we say that all artists try to exceed the restricted economy of writing? Here I want to cite a line from another essay by Derrida called "Psyche: the Invention of the Other":

> To say this is the only future is not to advocate amnesia. The coming of invention cannot make itself foreign to repetition and memory. For the other is not the new. But its coming extends beyond this past present that once able to construct …"[24]

According to Derrida, the invention of the other is also the invention of the self or rather "it is another we that is offered to this inventiveness."[25] There is always a 'we to come' in the act of invention. Derrida would call it the novelty. One can rename it as a kind of radical newness. Any art form must aspire to be open to this newness. If it becomes open—it can invent the other and it shall prise open an impossible future, an immeasurable and unexpected people to emerge.

If such is the basic premise of all writing (in general), why does populist writing fail to achieve such a goal? Why a random YouTube video clip cannot hold the value which an actual non-populist penance of writing can? The answer is quite simple: it has to do with addressing the question of relationality. One may say it is an impossible relation between things (here I put the word things in a very Heideggerian sense, Heidegger called it *The Ding*.) The future to come means a relation to come. And for a writer it is necessary to not get enclosed within the cycle of the gratification of the count, of the measurable. The moment such a thing happens art is bound to fall into the trap of a restricted economy. But the labour of non-populism must always actually open up to the possibility to a people to emerge—an impossible future to come. That is the reason Raghab Bandyopadhyay says a young writer must forget. I think he actually wanted to say a young writer must radically forget the populist pull of the 'measurable'.

There is a very beautiful reading of Derridian futurity that was made by Drucilla Cornell, gathered in a book which was written by many significant thinkers after the death of Derrida as homage to him. At one point in her essay Cornell says

> The imminence here is that death may arrive at any moment. Heidegger discusses this brilliantly in *Being and Time* and the fact that death may arrive at any moment gives justice to the character of an immediate injunction. To be faithful to the future, then, is to open ourselves to the address, "What are you doing today?"[26]

Perhaps, finally, all the apparently disconnected flotsam shall find a point of convergence here? My central argument is the following: in comparison to populisms which are always already enclosed within their own measures, the underlying basis of non-populism is radical openness. The non-popular should always forget the tug and seduction of the measurable in order to become that value which is to come: the value that joyfully embraces the openness and immeasurability of our relationalities. One can always call this value as an ongoing thrust and movement towards a new and unknown measure of an impossible future. It is for this reason that to embrace and turn into the non-popular is not just a mere passive waiting for a specific call of the future but also a determined and active 'writing', a constant and dogged response to silence.

Notes

1 David Howarth, ed. *Ernesto Laclau: Post-Marxism, Populism and Critique* (London: Routledge, 2015), 152.
2 Ibid., 258–259.
3 Ibid., 154.
4 Raghab Bandyopadhyay, "Marginer Lekha Lekhar Margine," *Saptarshi* (January 2012), 33.
5 Gilles Deleuze, *Two Regimes of Madness: Texts and Interviews 1975–1995* ed. David Lapoujade, trans. Ames odges and Mike Taormina (Semiotext(e) Foreign Agents distributed by Cambridge: MIT Press, 2006), 323.
6 Jacques Derrida, *Of Grammatology*, ed. and trans. Gayatri Spivak (Maryland, USA: The Johns Hopkins University Press, 1976).
7 Derek Attridge, ed. *Acts of Literature* (London: Routledge, 1992), 75.
8 Adhir Dey, *Adhunik Bangla Prabandha Sahityer Dhara* (Kolkata: Sristi Publication, 1930).
9 Buddhadeb Basu, *Prabandha Sankalan*, April, 1966, 21.
10 Bandyopadhyay, "Marginer Lekha", 3.
11 Ibid., 95–96.
12 Ibid., 69.
13 Ibid., 10.
14 Kamalkumar Majumdar, *Kabitirtha (Janmashatabarsha Sankhya)*, 2014, 42.

15 Amiya Bhushan Majumdar, *Prabhandhasangraha*, October 2017, 19.
16 Ibid., 180.
17 Ibid., 74.
18 Ibid., 80.
19 Ibid., 172.
20 Raghab Bandyopadhyay, "Marginer Lekha", 131.
21 Ibid., 18.
22 Jacques Derrida, "Given Time: The Time of the King," trans. Peggy Kamuf, *Critical Inquiry* 18, no. 2(1992): 161–187.
23 Ibid., 174.
24 Jacques Derrida, "From Psyche: The Invention of the Other." In *Acts of Literature*, ed. Derek Attridge (London: Routledge, 1992), 343
25 Ibid., 342.
26 Costas Douzinas, ed. *Adieu Derrida* (Basingstoke: Palgrave Macmillan, 2007), 107.

ABOUT THE EDITOR AND CONTRIBUTORS

Editor

Prasanta Chakravarty teaches English at the University of Delhi. His works include *Time, Doubt and Wonder in the Humanities* (Bloomsbury, 2019), *The Opulence of Existence* (Three Essays Collective, 2018) and *Like Parchment in the Fire: Literature and Radicalism in the English Civil War* (Routledge, 2006). He is the editor of the anthology *Shrapnel Minima: Essays from Humanities Underground* (Seagull Books and University of Chicago Press, 2016).

Contributors

Debraj Dasgupta wrote his MPhil thesis on Kamal Kumar Majumdar and is engaged in his doctoral work on aspects of the concept of 'writing' at Centre for Studies in Social Sciences, Calcutta. His interest areas include literature, continental philosophy and vernacular histories.

Gautam Basu Thakur is Associate Professor of English at Boise State University, USA. He is the author of *Postcolonial Theory and Avatar* (2015) and *Postcolonial Lack: Identity, Culture, Surplus* (2020) and co-editor of *Lacan and the Nonhuman* (2018) and *Reading Lacan's Seminar VIII: Transference* (2020).

Meghant Sudan teaches philosophy at Boise State University, USA, after having completed doctoral studies on *Matter and Motion in Kant's Philosophy of Science* from State University of New York (USA) and after having held visiting positions and student and faculty fellowships at Concordia University (Montreal, Canada), Bergische Universität (Wuppertal, Germany) and Colby College (Waterville, USA). His research covers German Idealism, Phenomenology, and Critical Theory and his recent work includes articles on how the conceptions of imagination in Kant and Hegel show a shared model of the mind as integrated subjectivity and on how ancient scepticism acquires a general philosophical form through the encounter with Kantian and post-Kantian idealism.

Milind Wakankar teaches philosophy and literature at the Indian Institute of Technology, Delhi. He is the author of *Subalternity and Religion: The Prehistory of Dalit Empowerment in South Asia* (Routledge, 2010).

Nikhil Govind is Head of the Manipal Centre of Humanities, Manipal Academy of Higher Education (MAHE), Karnataka. His publications include two books: *Between Love and Freedom: The Revolutionary in the Hindi Novel* (Routledge, 2014) and *Inlays of Subjectivity: Affect and Action in Modern Indian Literature* (Oxford University Press, 2019).

Parichay Patra is an Assistant Professor at the Department of Humanities and Social Sciences, IIT Jodhpur. His primary interest lies in transnationalism and the global cine-waves of the 1970s. He is co-editing a volume on the Filipino auteur Lav Diaz (forthcoming in 2020).

Raghu Menon Jayakumar is a doctoral research student at the Manipal Centre for Humanities, Manipal Academy of Higher Education (MAHE). His dissertation examines the concepts of time, process and ontology in the works of Gilles Deleuze and the *Sarvāstivāda* school of Indian Buddhist philosophy.

Rajarshi Dasgupta teaches at the Centre for Political Studies, JNU. Formerly a Fellow at the Centre for Studies in Social Sciences, Calcutta, he did his BA from Presidency, Calcutta, MA and MPhil from JNU and DPhil from Oxford University. Dasgupta mainly teaches courses on Biopolitics and Political Theory. His research and publications address the history of Indian radicalism, the relations of politics with culture and ethics and urbanization in South Asia. Some of his publications have been included in *Indian Political Thought* edited by P.K. Datta and S. Palshikar, *Critical Studies in Politics* edited by Nivedita Menon, Aditya Nigam and Sanjay Palshikar and in *Studies in History*. His latest publications have appeared in *Economic & Political Weekly* and in *Capital in the East: Reflections on Marx* edited by Chakrabarty et al.

Samir Gandesha is an Associate Professor in the Department of Humanities and the Director of the Institute for the Humanities at Simon Fraser University. He specializes in modern European thought and culture, with a particular emphasis on the nineteenth and twentieth centuries. His work has appeared in *Political Theory*, *New German Critique*, *Constellations*, *Logos*, *Kant Studien*, *Philosophy and Social Criticism*, *Topia*, the *European Legacy*, the *European Journal of Social Theory*, *Art Papers*, *Radical Philosophy*, the *Cambridge Companion to Adorno* and *Herbert Marcuse: A Critical Reader* as well as in several other edited books. He is the co-editor *Arendt and Adorno: Political and Philosophical Investigations* with Lars Rensmann (Stanford, 2012). He has co-edited (with Johan Hartle) *Spell of Capital: Reification and Spectacle* (University of Amsterdam Press, 2017) and *Aesthetic Marx* (Bloomsbury Press, 2017) also with Johan Hartle. He is currently editing a book entitled *Spectres of Fascism* (Pluto Press) and preparing a manuscript on the concept of the "Neoliberal Personality."

Sanil V. is Professor of philosophy at the Department of Humanities and Social Sciences, Indian Institute of Technology, New Delhi, India. He obtained his bachelor degree in Mechanical Engineering and worked as a scientist in the Defense Research and Development Organisation. In 1995, he obtained his PhD in Philosophy from IIT Kanpur. His recent publications include: *Public Sphere from Outside the West*, *Vastu Purusha Mandala: Myth, Meaning and Measurement in Ancient Indian Architecture*, *Time Passing: Kant Goes to Movies*, *On Hating One's Own Children*, *Thought and Context: Philosophy on the Eve of Colonialism*. He was the Watumall Distinguished Professor at Department of Philosophy, University of Hawaii, USA, Charles Wallace Fellow at the Department of Philosophy, University of Liverpool, UK and Directeur d'études Associés at Maison des sciences de l'homme Paris, Research Excellence Fellow, CEU Budapest. He writes and publishes in Malayalam language.

Shaj Mohan is a philosopher based in the subcontinent. With Divya Dwivedi, he has coauthored *Gandhi and Philosophy: On Theological Antipolitics* (Bloomsbury, 2019).

Urmila G. is a PhD scholar in the Manipal Centre of Humanities, Manipal Academy of Higher Education (MAHE), Karnataka. Her doctoral dissertation is a study of three canonical women writers of the latter half of the twentieth century in Kerala—Lalithambika Antharjanam (1909–1987), K. Saraswati Amma (1919–1975) and Rajelakshmy (1930–1965).

Yadukrishnan P.T. is a PhD scholar in the Manipal Centre of Humanities, Manipal Academy of Higher Education (MAHE), Karnataka. He is the author of *The Noblest Fallen: Making and Unmaking of Bhagat Singh's Political Thought* (Manipal Universal Press, 2019). His current research focuses on the construction and articulation of dominant caste identities in Malayalam cinema in the closing decades of the twentieth century.

INDEX